Inductive Study Curriculum
Teacher's Guide

OLD TESTAMENT / *Book of*
JUDGES

© *2008 Precept Ministries International*

Judges
INDUCTIVE STUDY CURRICULUM
ISBN 13 978-1-934884-06-5

© 2008 Precept Ministries International. All rights reserved.
This material is published by and is the sole property of Precept Ministries International of Chattanooga, Tennessee. No part of this publication may be reproduced, translated, or transmitted in any form or by any means, electronic or mechanical, including photocopying, recording, or any information storage and retrieval system, without permission in writing from the publisher.

Unless otherwise noted, all Scripture quotations are from the New American Standard Bible, ©1960, 1962, 1963, 1968, 1971, 1972, 1973, 1975, 1977, 1995 by the Lockman Foundation, and are used by permission.

Enrichment word definitions are taken with permission from Merriam-Webster, Inc. Merriam-Webster's Collegiate Dictionary. 10th ed. Springfield, Mass., U.S.A.: Merriam-Webster, 1996, c1993.

Precept, Precept Ministries International, Precept Ministries International The Inductive Bible Study People, the Plumb Bob design, Precept Upon Precept, and In & Out are trademarks of Precept Ministries International.

1st edition
Printed in the United States of America

TABLE OF CONTENTS

Judges

INTRODUCTION
- *Before You Begin* — 7
- *How to Use the Teacher's Guide* — 9
- *Introduction to Course Scope and Sequence* — 13
- *Course Scope and Sequence* — 14
- *Icon Key* — 17
- *Introduction to Arsenal of Truth* — 19
- *Arsenal Verse Schedule* — 21
- *Glossary of Frequently Used Terms* — 23

Introduction to inductive Study 25-32

Unit One 33-78

From Victory to Defeat

- *Unit Objectives* — 33
- *Introduction / Prayer* — 34
- *Lesson One* — 35
- *Lesson Two* — 37
- *Lesson Three* — 39
- *Discussion Guide Lessons One, Two and Three* — 43
- *Lesson Four* — 47
- *Lesson Five* — 53
- *Discussion Guide Lessons Four and Five* — 57
- *Lesson Six* — 61
- *Lesson Seven* — 63
- *Discussion Guide Lessons Six and Seven* — 65
- *Locations in Judges 1-3 Map - Key* — 67
- *Unit One Quiz - Key* — 71
- *Unit One Test - Key* — 73

Unit Two 79-118

Dying to be Free

- *Unit Objectives* — 79
- *Introduction/Prayer* — 79
- *Lesson One* — 81
- *Lesson Two* — 83
- *Discussion Guide Lessons One and Two* — 87
- *Lesson Three* — 89
- *Lesson Four* — 93
- *Discussion Guide Lessons Three and Four* — 97
- *Lesson Five* — 99

TABLE OF CONTENTS

Judges

Unit Two cont.
- *Lesson Six* — *101*
- *Discussion Guide Lessons Five and Six* — *105*
- *Unit Two Quiz - Key* — *111*
- *Unit Two Test - Key* — *113*

Unit Three 119-160

Leaders and Volunteers

- *Unit Objectives* — *119*
- *Introduction/Prayer* — *119*
- *Lesson One* — *121*
- *Lesson Two* — *123*
- *Discussion Guide Lessons One and Two* — *125*
- *Lesson Three* — *127*
- *Lesson Four* — *129*
- *Discussion Guide Lessons Three and Four* — *131*
- *Lesson Five* — *135*
- *Discussion Guide Lesson Five* — *139*
- *Lesson Six* — *141*
- *Lesson Seven* — *143*
- *Discussion Guide Lessons Six and Seven* — *147*
- *The War of Deborah and Barak Map - Key* — *149*
- *The Main Characters of Judges 4-5 Chart - Key* — *151*
- *Unit Three Quiz - Key* — *155*
- *Unit Three Test - Key* — *157*

Unit Four 161-202

From Ordinary to Extraordinary

- *Unit Objectives* — *161*
- *Introduction/Prayer* — *162*
- *Lesson One* — *163*
- *Lesson Two* — *165*
- *Lesson Three* — *167*
- *Discussion Guide Lessons One, Two and Three* — *173*
- *Lesson Four* — *177*
- *Lesson Five* — *179*
- *Lesson Six* — *181*
- *Discussion Guide Lessons Four, Five and Six* — *183*
- *Lesson Seven* — *185*
- *Lesson Eight* — *187*
- *Discussion Guide Lessons Seven and Eight* — *191*
- *Romans 1:18-32 Chart - Key* — *193*

TABLE OF CONTENTS

Judges

Unit Four cont.
    Unit Four Quiz -Key   197
    Unit Four Test - Key   199

Unit Five 203-244

Who Rules You?

Unit Objectives	203
Lesson One	205
Lesson Two	209
Discussion Guide Lessons One and Two	213
Lesson Three	215
Lesson Four	217
Discussion Guide Lessons Three and Four	221
Lesson Five	223
Lesson Six	225
Lesson Seven	227
Discussion Guide Lessons Five, Six and Seven	231
Locations In Judges 9-12 Map - Key	237
Unit Five Quiz - Key	239
Unit Five Test - Key	241

Unit Six 245-296

Pursuit of Pleasure

Unit Objectives	245
Introduction/Prayer	245
Lesson One	247
Lesson Two	249
The Nazirite Vow Chart - Key	251
Discussion Guide Lessons One and Two	253
Lesson Three	257
Discussion Guide Lesson Three	261
Lesson Four	263
Discussion Guide Lesson Four	267
Lesson Five	269
Lesson Six	273
Discussion Guide Lesson Five and Six	277
Lesson Seven	279
Discussion Guide Lesson Seven	283
Samson's Women Chart - Key	285
Unit Six Quiz - Key	289
Unit Six Test -Key	291

TABLE OF CONTENTS

Judges

Unit Seven 297-346
Chaos and Corruption

Unit Objectives	*297*
Introduction/Prayer	*297*
Lesson One	*299*
Lesson Two	*301*
Lesson Three	*305*
Discussion Guide Lessons One, Two and Three	*307*
Lesson Four	*309*
Lesson Five	*311*
Discussion Guide Lessons Four and Five	*315*
Lesson Six	*317*
Lesson Seven	*319*
Discussion Guide Lessons Six and Seven	*323*
Lesson Eight	*325*
Discussion Guide Lessons Eight	*329*
Lesson Nine	*331*
Judges of Israel Chart - Key	*333*
Unit Seven Quiz - Key	*339*
Unit Seven Test - Key	*341*

Teacher's Guide

Judges

Before you begin...

We're excited you have chosen to use our inductive Bible study curriculum. We believe God will speak to those you teach through His Word. The Teacher's Guide is designed to help you instruct your students to study inductively. It includes the following:

- Tips on using this Guide effectively
- An introductory lesson with an overview on inductive Bible study
- Unit and Lesson Objectives
- Assignment Directions and Helps
- Discussion Guides
- Quiz and Test Keys
- "Arsenal Verses" (Supplemental Verse Memory Project)

We suggest you purchase our "Judges Teacher Helps Cd" at Precept.org which contains all the Observation Worksheets, maps, charts, copy-ready Tests and Quizzes, and the Arsenal Verses by unit.

These materials are designed to encourage students to go beyond an academic approach to God's Word by encouraging them to apply its truths to their daily living. The goal is for students to know God more intimately so that they'll live a life worthy of the Lord (Colossians 1:9-12).

We want to encourage you to remember that your students will receive the greatest benefit from this study when you lead them from the overflow of what God is doing in your own life. Our prayer is that you and your students will grow together in your relationships with the Lord as you study God's Word. We strongly recommend that you work through the students' lessons on your own before consulting the Teacher's Guide. Your students will be more motivated to do their own study when they see your response to the truths God is revealing to you.

Please remember that we have training available that will help you become proficient in inductive Bible study and in teaching your students how to do it. The training includes hands-on demonstrations of how to use these materials in the most effective manner. For more information, contact Precept Ministries at 1.800.763.8280. Feel free to call us with questions or comments you have concerning these materials.

© 2008 Precept Ministries International

Teacher's Guide

Judges

Teacher's Guide

Judges

HOW TO USE THE TEACHER'S GUIDE:

You will find a list of tools below included in each unit/lesson that will help you effectively navitgate the Teacher's Guide.

1. UNIT OBJECTIVE

The Unit Objective details the goals to be achieved at the completion of the unit.

2. LESSON OBJECTIVE

The Lesson Objective details the goals to be achieved at the completion of each lesson.

3. LIST OF MATERIALS NEEDED

 Each lesson begins with a list of the materials students need to complete the assignments. The wrench and hammer icon identifies this list.

4. ASSIGNMENT HELPS

Each page of the Teacher's Guide has a copy of the related student workbook page located in the bottom right-hand corner. The red, bolded font on the student workbook page corresponds with the instruction and helps for completing that assignment in the Teacher's Guide. Beside each assignment title an indicator specifies the component of inductive study the assignment focuses on (i.e. Observation, Interpretation, Application).

INDUCTIVE STUDY TIPS

 For some assignments, tips are given on how to reinforce the inductive study method or remind students of the purpose for the assignment. The plumbline icon identifies these tips.

ANSWERS

Text in red italics provides the general answer students should discover. Inductive study can yield several answers to each question (i.e. Answers to application questions will especially vary by student.) Remember, while there is only one true interpretation for each Scripture there may be many applications. "Listing" assignments will occasionally have answers in the Teacher's Guide when necessary to help you determine how to help your students compile a

© 2008 Precept Ministries International

Teacher's Guide

Judges

list or to help you determine the information essential to completing the assignment. Answers don't have to be exact; observation and interpretation questions should keep the integrity of the original text intact (avoid paraphrases or personal interpretation).

ASSIGNMENT DIRECTIONS

Text in black provides tips on how to best explain the assignment and complete it in a timely manner (e.g. group versus individual work).

5. PROJECT HELPS

When a YOUR WORLD VIEW project is suggested, the Teacher's Guide suggests how best to direct students to complete and present (display) it.

YOUR WORLD VIEW projects help students take what they learn from biblical texts and apply it to current events, worldly philosophies and their own lives. They teach students how to view the world biblically.

6. DISCUSSION GUIDES

Regular discussion times are essential to the learning process, helping students assimilate and verbalize information they have accumulated in the lessons/unit. The Discussion Guides included in the Teacher's Guide are designed to help you lead effective discussions at appropriate times in the unit. You never want to preempt students' self-discovery by discussing or lecturing on a topic they have not yet studied for themselves.

When leading discussion, ask open-ended questions (the 5 Ws and H). Because this is inductive Bible study, you want to encourage your students to share what they have learned from their observation, interpretation and application of God's Word. Lecture will hinder students' experience of discovering truth for themselves. Remember, you effectively "teach" by asking questions. Asking questions to cause your students to think is advisable, but don't ask too many questions which will make the time seem more like a drill than a discussion. The questions should *stimulate* discussion, not *stifle* it.

It is helpful to relate scriptures to current times. Work in this application throughout your discussion at appropriate points.

Teacher's Guide

Judges

7. Teacher's Helps

OBSERVATION WORKSHEETS

Biblical books being studied are printed out in the New American Standard Updated version, double spaced with wide margins. We call them "Observation Worksheets." They're provided for you to make transparencies, copies and multi-media presentations.

MAPS

Copies of every map from the Student Guide are provided for you to make transparencies, copies and multi-media presentations. Maps are helpful visual aids for discussions and for explaining assignments.

CHARTS

Charts used in lengthy listing assignments are provided for you to make transparencies, copies and multi-media presentations. Working through charts with your students will help them recognize how to effectively and efficiently compile lists.

TESTS

Tests are provided for reproduction.

QUIZZES

Quizzes are provided for reproduction.

WORD STUDY DEFINITIONS

Word study definitions are provided in case your classroom is not equipped with word study tools. We highly recommend acquiring classroom sets of word study materials (concordances, Hebrew and Greek dictionaries, etc.) for teaching your students how to do word studies on their own. Many on-line resources are available as well.

ARSENAL VERSES

If you decide to implement the Arsenal Verse program, verses specifically assigned to each unit are available for making copies, transparencies and multi-media presentations.

TEACHER'S GUIDE

TEACHER'S GUIDE

Judges

INTRODUCTION TO COURSE SCOPE AND SEQUENCE

The *Course Scope and Sequence* outlines the course.

LESSONS
Each lesson in the Student's Workbook is designed to be completed in 45 minutes. You may need to modify these lesson plans to comply with the time allotted for your class. Also, student familiarity with the inductive study method will affect how long it takes to complete these assignments. This *Course Scope and Sequence* was compiled based on an average time needed to complete each lesson.

DISCUSSION
We strongly encourage you to utilize discussion times which are essential to helping students verbalize what they learned and share how God's Word has been impacting them. You can find out more about using the *Discussion Guides* in the "How To Use This Guide" section of the Introduction.

UNIT QUIZZES
Student quizzes are in the Teacher's Helps packet included with this material, and a Quiz Key is found at the end of each unit in the Teacher's Guide. Quizzes are designed to test your students' understanding at pertinent points. Sometimes review questions will be included to ensure that your students are retaining the overall theme of the book. They will also help your students prepare for Unit Tests.

UNIT TESTS
Student tests are in the Teacher's Helps packet included with this material, and a Test Key at the end of each unit in the Teacher's Guide. Tests are designed to evaluate your students' understanding of each unit. They cover "Enrichment Words" and the main points of each unit. Sometimes review questions are included.

© 2008 Precept Ministries International

Teacher's Guide

Judges

COURSE SCOPE AND SEQUENCE

UNIT ONE

Lesson One
Lesson Two
Lesson Three
Discussion Lesson 1, 2 & 3
Lesson Four
Lesson Five
Discussion Lesson 4 & 5
Unit One Quiz
Lesson Six
Lesson Seven
Discussion Lesson 6 & 7
Unit One Test

UNIT TWO

Lesson One
Lesson Two
Discussion Lesson 1 & 2
Lesson Three
Lesson Four
Discussion Lesson 3 & 4
Unit Two Quiz
Lesson Five
Lesson Six
Discussion Lesson 5 & 6
Unit Two Test

UNIT THREE

Lesson One
Lesson Two
Discussion Lesson 1 & 2
Lesson Three
Lesson Four
Discussion Lesson 3 & 4
Unit Two Quiz

UNIT THREE CONT.

Lesson Five
Discussion Lesson 5
Lesson Six
Lesson Seven
Discussion Lesson 6 & 7
Unit Three Test

UNIT FOUR

Lesson One
Lesson Two
Lesson Three
Discussion Lesson 1, 2 & 3
Unit Four Quiz
Lesson Four
Lesson Five
Lesson Six
Discussion Lesson 4, 5 & 6
Lesson Seven
Lesson Eight
Discussion Lesson 7 & 8
Unit Four Test

UNIT FIVE

Lesson One
Lesson Two
Lesson Three
Discussion Lesson 1, 2 & 3
Unit Four Quiz
Lesson Four
Lesson Five
Lesson Six
Discussion Lesson 4, 5 & 6
Lesson Seven
Lesson Eight

Teacher's Guide

Judges

Unit Five cont.

Discussion 7 & 8
Unit Four Test

Unit Six

Lesson One
Lesson Two
Discussion 1 & 2
Lesson Three
Discussion Lesson 3
Lesson Four
Discussion Lesson 4
Unit Six Quiz
Lesson Five
Lesson Six
Discussion Lesson 5 & 6
Lesson Seven
Discussion Lesson 7
Unit Six Test

Unit Seven

Lesson One
Lesson Two
Lesson Three
Discussion Lesson 1, 2 & 3
Lesson Four
Lesson Five
Discussion Lesson 4 & 5
Unit Seven Quiz
Lesson Six
Discussion Lesson 6
Lesson Seven
Lesson Eight
Discussion Lesson 8
Lesson Nine
Discussion Lesson 9
Unit Seven Test

TEACHER'S GUIDE

Teacher's Guide

Judges

Icon Key

Bolded Words: Words bolded in texts are defined in the Word Enrichment section at the end of each unit.

Icons below denote:

supplemental assignment

word-study assignment

prayer or encouragement

marking assignment

assignment utilizing the "At A Glance" chart

pull-out box with historical information, Scripture or study tip

listing assignment

materials needed to complete lesson

mapping assignment

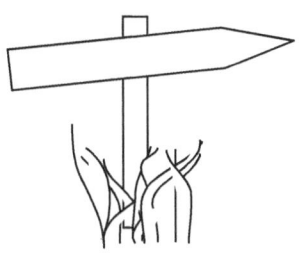
cross-referencing assignment

inductive study tip

project idea

© 2008 Precept Ministries International

Teacher's Guide

Teacher's Guide

Judges

Arsenal of truth - Details

In this course, students will study God's Word inductively and gain understanding and insight as to who God is and how they can live in light of this knowledge. In addition to the in-depth study they do each week in class, it will greatly benefit them to memorize scriptures they can use throughout their lives. They must know how to use the "Arsenal of Truth" God has given in His Word. You can add this supplemental program to your weekly schedule the following way:

Introduction:
To introduce this program, show students from God's Word why hiding His Word in the heart is essential to the spiritual life. You may want to use a format like the following:

> Read Ephesians 6:10-17 and explain the believer's role in war. Our enemy lies and deceives to steal, kill, and destroy (John 10:10). As John 8:44 says, he is a liar, the father of lies, and the truth is not in him. Explain how he questioned what God said to Adam and Eve, leading her to believe a lie over God's truth. It is the same today; the enemy attacks with lies and deceit.

> Ephesians 6 describes the armor God has given each believer to stand firm against these deceptive "schemes." Each piece of armor assists the only offensive weapon listed—the sword of the Spirit, God's Word. (Faith comes by hearing and hearing by the word of the Lord.) The belt of truth, for example, keeps the warrior from stumbling in battle and becoming more vulnerable to attack. Students must know how to stand firm using the Word of God to destroy the arsenal of lies the enemy daily throws at them.

Memorization:
In the Teacher's Materials you will find a suggested "Arsenal Verse" schedule. A copy of each verse can be found in the Teacher's Helps for making transparencies. Each unit will introduce a new "Arsenal Verse" to the class. Start each new unit by having the class discuss the details of the verse and write it on a 3x5 note card. Suggest they put this notecard in a place where they are likely to see it often (i.e. locker, mirror, etc.). Each day give the students five minutes at the beginning of class to write out the "Arsenal Verse." Also, have the class say the verse aloud together at least once each day. Tell them they'll start remembering verses if they carry this notecard with them and say the verse aloud three times in a row at least three times each day. At the end of each unit give the students an "Arsenal Verse" quiz where they must write out the verse from memory.

© 2008 Precept Ministries International

Teacher's Guide

Teacher's Guide

Judges

Arsenal Verse Schedule

Unit One	Judges 2:12
Unit Two	John 8:34-36
Unit Three	Hebrews 11:32-34
Unit Four	Judges 6:12
Unit Five	Philippians 2:3
Unit Six	2 Corinthians 12:9
Unit Seven	Judges 17:6

TEACHER'S GUIDE

Teacher's Guide

Judges

GLOSSARY OF FREQUENTLY USED TERMS

OBSERVATION WORKSHEETS
These worksheets comprise the entire book being studied, printed out in the New American Standard Updated version, double spaced with wide margins to provide room for marking words, and making lists and notations.

AT A GLANCE CHART
This chart is a helpful tool for future reference and gives a quick synopsis of the book being studied. It is designed for the student to record the main theme of each chapter beside the chapter number on the chart.

CHAPTER THEMES
A chapter theme should answer two questions: first, what is the main subject dealt with in the chapter? Second, does the theme relate to the overall book theme?

SEGMENT DIVISIONS
A segment division is a major division in a book, such as a group of verses or chapters that deal with the same subject, doctrine, person, place or event. You discover segment divisions from the text. Context determines a segment.

5WS AND H QUESTIONS
Who, What, When, Where, Why and How – These questions help students carefully observe texts and determine information that should be included in listing assignments.

OBSERVATION
The component of inductive study that answers the question: What does the text say? Careful observation is the foundation for accurate interpretation and application. This component is accomplished by reading with a purpose, marking key words, people, places, events, and making lists.

INTERPRETATION
The component of inductive study that answers the question: What is the meaning of the text? For Scripture, there is only one true interpretation: God's! This component involves cross-references, word studies, and most importantly, determining context.

© 2008 Precept Ministries International

Teacher's Guide

Judges

APPLICATION

    The component of inductive Bible study that answers the question: How does the meaning of the text apply to my life? Application is the goal of all Bible study. The goal of application is to know God and live a transformed life. This transformation includes changes in belief and behavior.

KEY WORDS

    Words vital to understanding the meaning of a text. Like a key, they "unlock" the meaning of the text. A key word or phrase is one which, if removed, leaves the passage devoid of meaning. Often key words and phrases are repeated to convey the author's point or purpose for writing.

CONTEXT

    The environment or setting in which something is living or found; the information surrounding the verse, passage or chapter being studied.

WORD STUDY

    The study of words in the original languages of the Old and New Testaments. The Bible was originally written in Hebrew, Greek, and some Aramaic, and then translated into English and other languages. As part of interpretation, going back to the original languages offers greater insight and clarification.

Introduction to Inductive Study

Judges

This lesson should be taught before students begin their work on Unit One. It will teach students unfamiliar with inductive study basic principles and tools they will use throughout this course. For those already familar with the method, this lesson will reinforce their understanding of inductive study and review what they have already learned.

If you have never studied inductively or led an inductive Bible study, this lesson will prepare you to understand its principles. It will also give you tools to effectively teach the inductive method.

Introduction to inductive study

Begin by explaining the basics of inductive Bible study. You can draw points out from students already familar with it.

1. Inductive Bible Study - using the Bible as your primary source.

Spend some time discussing what the word "primary" means. You want students to understand that the inductive method begins with and focuses on biblical texts before going to outside sources for understanding. Ask them how this method differs from how other people study the Bible. While devotionals, pastors, teachers, TV, radio, and books are good sources, the point of inductive study is what the Bible says before reading others' interpretations.

---

1. Inductive Bible Study - *Using the Bible as your primary source.*

2. There are _____ of Inductive Bible Study:

   a. _____ - _____?

   b. _____ - _____?

   c. _____ - _____?

3. Tools of Observation

   a. The _____ questions

© 2008 Precept Ministries International

25

INTRODUCTION TO INDUCTIVE STUDY

Judges

2. There are three components of Inductive Bible Study:
   a. Observation - What does the text say?
   b. Interpretation - What does the text mean?
   c. Application - How does the meaning apply to my life?

Explain that each of these components is used to answer the questions indicated (the point of Observation is to see what the text is saying). Then explain how to put each of these components into practice. To help your students remember these important components demonstrate them with body language.

Observation - Hold your hands up to your eyes like you are looking through binoculars.
Interpretation - Tap your finger to your head like you are thinking.
Application - March in place like you are walking it out.

---

1. Inductive Bible Study - *Using the Bible as your primary source.*

2. There are *Three Components* of Inductive Bible Study:
   a. *Observation* - *What does the text say?*
   b. *Interpretation* - *What does the text mean?*
   c. *Application* - *How does the meaning apply to my life?*

3. Tools of Observation

   a. The _____ questions

---

26 © 2008 Precept Ministries International

Introduction to Inductive Study

Judges

3. Tools of Observation

Begin by explaining that observation is reading the text, not scanning or skimming. Students should read with a purpose, carefully examining the text to see what it says so they can accurately interpret its meaning. They will learn to read with a purpose by training themselves to ask:

a. The 5W and H questions

Who, what, when, where, why and how; for example: Who are the main characters? What is the main event? When do these things take place? Where do they take place?

---

1. Inductive Bible Study - *Using the Bible as your primary source.*

2. There are *Three Components* of Inductive Bible Study:

   a. *Observation* - *What does the text say?* ?

   b. *Interpretation* - *What does the text mean?* ?

   c. *Application* - *How does the meaning apply to my life?* ?

3. Tools of Observation

   a. The *5 W and H* questions

© 2008 Precept Ministries International

27

Introduction to Inductive Study

Judges

Another tool that helps observation is:

b. Marking key words and people

Once you have discovered who the main characters are and identified key repeated words and phrases in a passage or chapter, you will want to mark them. Key words are words that are vital to understanding the meaning of the text. Like a key, they "unlock" the meaning of the text. If a key word or phrase is removed, the passage loses meaning. Often key words and phrases are repeated in order to emphasize the author's point or purpose for writing.

Marking is choosing a color and/or symbol to distinguish words every time they're used in the text. (You will be able to demonstrate this technique in the first unit of this course.) Explain that marking key words and people will help students slow down reading and focus attention on the important things in the text.

c. Listing

After marking, you will make a list of what you learned from key words and phrases and people present in the text. Listing will help you isolate information about a topic or person for closer examination and understanding.

b. Mark __key words__ and __people__

c. Make __lists__

4. Tools of Interpretation

   a. _____

   _____ ! It rules interpretation.

   b. _____

   c. _____

© 2008 Precept Ministries International

INTRODUCTION TO INDUCTIVE STUDY

Judges

4. Tools of Interpretation

Careful observation will lead to accurate interpretation. To accurately interpret the Bible, the most important thing to establish is:

a. Context

Context is KING! It rules interpretation. Establishing context through careful observation will ensure that you do not misinterpret a verse or passage. Context is the information surrounding the verse, passage or chapter selected. You can demonstrate this for your students with a word like TRUNK. Write the word on the board and ask students to define it. They will likely give several definitions. Explain that the definition of a word is dependent on words placed before and after it.

For example:
- The tire is in the TRUNK.
- The elephant's TRUNK is very long.
- Use the TRUNK in the attic for the old clothes.

b. Cross-References

Cross-references aid interpretation because God rarely gives all information about a topic, doctrine, person or event in one place at a time. Cross-references provide additional insights and details that add broader context (meaning) to your primary study. Interpreting Scripture with Scripture unveils deeper meaning and therefore, greater understanding.

---

b. Mark _key words_ and _people_

c. Make _lists_

4. Tools of Interpretation

　a. _Context_

　　Context is king ! It rules interpretation.

　b. _Cross-references_

　c. _____

Introduction to Inductive Study

Judges

c. Word Studies

These are the study of words in the original languages of the Old and New Testaments. The Bible was originally written in Hebrew, Greek, and some Aramaic, and then translated into English and other languages. In the process of interpretation, it often helps to go back to the original languages to gain greater insight and clarification.

---

b. Mark _key words_ and _people_

c. Make _lists_

4. Tools of Interpretation

   a. _Context_

   Context is king! It rules interpretation.

   b. _Cross-references_

   c. _Word studies_

Introduction to Inductive Study

Judges

5. Application

Application is the goal of all Bible study. If all you do is observe the text you will only know what it says. If you stop at interpreting the text, you will only add to your knowledge. Application is living out what you have clearly seen and understood from God's Word. The goal of application is:

To Know God - resulting in a changed life

When you understand who God is and what His commandments are, you choose what you will do with this information. Sometimes application is simply changing beliefs; other times it's changing behavior to match what God says is acceptable and right.

Emphasize to your students that they will understand each of these components more thoroughly with practice and use them throughout the course.

> 5. Application
>
> *To know God* - resulting in *a changed life*

© 2008 Precept Ministries International

Introduction to Inductive Study

Judges

UNIT ONE - TEACHER'S GUIDE

Judges

FROM VICTORY TO DEFEAT

UNIT OBJECTIVES:

In this unit, students will observe the book of Judges to identify its structure and division and various details covered in each section. Students will work to interpret the meaning of Judges as they identify Israel's disobedience and the consequences the tribes suffered. Students will also identify the cycle of sin outlined in Judges 2 and recognize how that cycle occurred in each judge's time. They will recognize Israel's oppression as God's judgment for their disobedience and also His mercy in raising up deliverers when they cry to Him for help. Students will identify the key repeated phrase *there was no king in Israel and every man did what was right in his own eyes*; they will recognize its significance in understanding the times of the judges. As students work through the process of observing and interpreting Judges, they will comprehend how this book applies to their lives by recognizing similarities between the judges' times and their own.

UNIT ONE

From Victory to Defeat
U-1, Chapter 1, 2, 17-21

The time of Joshua, the valiant warrior of God, was over. The Promised Land was won and the covenant God made with Abraham concerning the land was fulfilled. The book of Joshua records these final words of Joshua to the sons of Israel:

Then Joshua summoned the Reubenites and the Gadites and the half-tribe of Manasseh, and said to them, "You have kept all that Moses the servant of the Lord commanded you, and have listened to my voice in all that I commanded you. "You have not forsaken your brothers these many days to this day, but have kept the charge of the commandment of the Lord your God. "And now the Lord your God has given rest to your brothers, as He spoke to them; therefore turn now and go to your tents, to the land of your possession, which Moses the servant of the Lord gave you beyond the Jordan. "Only be very careful to observe the commandment and the law which Moses the servant of the Lord commanded you, to love the Lord your God and walk in all His ways and keep His commandments and hold fast to Him and serve Him with all your heart and with all your soul." – Joshua 22:1-5

Sadly, you will find as you begin the book of Judges that the sons of Israel did not obey Joshua's **admonishment**.

The time period of the Judges is one of the darkest recorded in the history of Israel. And although it is a book seldom studied or taught, it couldn't be more relevant for today. **Apathy** was rampant. Like a plague, it consumed the hearts of Israel. Murder, religious corruption, rape, homosexuality, war, terror, nation oppressing nation – were as common then as they are today.

As you discover the similarities between the times recorded in Judges and your own world you need to ask the following questions: What is apathy? What are the consequences to a nation, city, church or even a group of friends when no one stands up for what is right? How does God respond to an apathetic heart? What happens when there are no **absolutes**? And is there any hope for those who have given in to apathy's deadly grip?

Although the book of Judges is a dark story of a people choosing to live in sin and rebel against truth you will also discover that this book tells the story of ordinary men and women God chose to accomplish the extraordinary. You will see what can happen when one man or one woman chose to follow God and bring freedom and light to a people

Student Page 9

UNIT ONE - TEACHER'S GUIDE

Judges

Introduction/Prayer

Encourage students to pray simply and honestly that God will show them why studying Judges is important to their lives. Suggest that they also ask Him to show them something new about Himself in the chapters and passages they study. You may want to come back to this prayer at the end of the course and have them write a half-page summary on how God answered. This is a great way for them to experience firsthand how God answers prayer!

U-1, Chapter 1, 2, 17-21

crushed by the weight of their choices. These are the stories of the Judges, individuals radically impacting the world in which they lived! What can happen in your world if you choose to follow God and become one of them – the extraordinary? And will you be the one that turns the tide of this generation?

To answer these questions you need to study the book of Judges. Whenever you open God's Word, you are face to face with truth – unchanging, absolute TRUTH! The Bible is the only book that is called alive, active, and eternal. It is the only book inspired by God Himself. God desires to teach you His Word, to sit with you and reveal truth to you. Before you open His Word, you need to verbalize your need to be taught by Him! You need to express to Him your desire to not only know truth, but to handle it accurately and live it out effectively.

May your prayer for this course be like David's, one of Israel's greatest kings: "Teach me your way, oh Lord and I will walk in truth. Give me an undivided heart to fear your name!"

You can begin your study with the following prayer:

Introduction/Prayer

ONE ON ONE:

God, as I begin this study, I ask that You clearly show me both the severe consequences of disobedience and the unmerited blessing your mercy brings. I ask You to give me ears to hear and eyes to see what You want me to learn from the book of Judges. You are my teacher and I ask that You to evaluate my heart and reveal to me areas of my life that need to be transformed with truth. Show me what it means to live a life of great significance, not by the world's standards, but by Yours alone.

As I learn about the ordinary men and women You used to accomplish extraordinary tasks in the work of Your kingdom, my prayer is that You will prepare me to deliver people from the darkness that envelopes those not enlightened by Your Word.

Father, I know that the enemy does not want me to know the truths of Your Word. I ask You to give me supernatural eyes to see the things he throws my way. Father, I ask You to protect me from the ways he works. God, do whatever it takes to keep me in Your Word. Give me the grace I need to live out the truths that I will see. Though the world around me is dark, I ask You to use this study to shine the light of Christ to my generation. I surrender to Your will for me as I open Your Word. Teach me how to live. Amen.

Student Page 10

UNIT ONE - TEACHER'S GUIDE

Judges

LESSON ONE:

 Judges 1 Observation Worksheets, colored pencils, 3 x 5 index card

OBJECTIVES:

Students will observe Judges 1 by marking key words and phrases that describe time references and geographical locations. Students will also identify the repeated phrase *did not drive out* and prepare the key word bookmark to be used in the following lessons.

Lesson 1/Assignment 1 - Observation

 Remind your students that careful observation is the key to accurately handling God's Word. Without this firm foundation, accurate interpretation is impossible — before they can truly understand what the text means, they must know what it says! Observation begins with reading the text they will study, not skimming or scanning, but reading with a purpose – the purpose of identifying key words and phrases that unlock the meaning of the text.

 *Observation Worksheets* located in the Appendix of the Student Guide are the biblical text double-spaced with wide margins. The wide margins create a functional work area for marking words and making notes.

Students will begin by reading the text of Judges 1 from their Observation Worksheets and identifying the repeated phrase:
"did not drive out"

Lesson 1/Assignment 2 - Observation

 Observation tools such as marking words will help students slow down as they read the text

---

LESSON ONE

U-1, Lesson 1, Chapter 1

Indifference, unbelief, incomplete obedience – where do they lead? What do they cost? Are they worth it?

Our objective this week is to get a sense of the times of the Judges – the 340 to 360 years following the victories of Joshua. The historical and moral setting of this dark period in Israel's history, along with the cause of this darkness, is captured for us in the opening and closing chapters of the book. Therefore, this is where you'll focus your attention this week.

Lesson 1/Assignment 1
Observe Judges 1, which is printed out for you in the Appendix. Read the first chapter without pausing to figure it all out. Watch for a key phrase that is repeated several times from 1:21 to the end of the chapter.

Lesson 1/Assignment 2
Now read Judges 1 again and observe the following:

 Mark all references to time or sequence of events with a clock like this: 🕐

Double underline in green any reference to geographical locations such as cities.

When you come to any verse that gives you a clue to the historical setting of this book, put a star beside the verse number.

When you discover the key repeated phrase, write it below.

> **Observation** – Reading with a purpose. Interrogate the text as you read by asking the 5W and H questions. Once you have read it use the observation tools of marking key words and phrases and making lists to more clearly see what is said.

> **Historical Setting** – By asking the 5Ws and H, you can get clues to the historical setting of the book. These clues reveal political, social, philosophical and religious conditions of the times.

> **Key Phrase** – A key phrase is an important phrase that is repeated for emphasis either in the chapter or throughout a segment of the book or the entire book.

Student Page 11

UNIT ONE - TEACHER'S GUIDE

Judges

so they can carefully examine what it says. Help them focus on "key" information contained in a chapter or book. You may want to remind them that key words are often repeated but always essential to the meaning of the text. If removed, the text would lose meaning.

 Time phrases are important in Judges and reveal sequence of events as well as the chronology of the book. Tell your students to look for dates, but also time indicators like "then," "after," and "before."

 Establishing historic settings will help students identify contexts for understanding passages. You may need to remind them, "Context is King!"; it rules interpretation. Understanding what was happening during the times of the book will help them understand the events and people described.

Students will re-read Judges 1 and mark time phrases, geographical locations, verses that describe the historical setting (put a star beside them), and the phrase *did not drive out*, which they should have discovered in the first assignment.

You may want to do this first observation assignment together by reading it aloud and having them stop you when you reach a word or phrase they are asked to mark. This will help you be sure they understand the assignment.

Lesson 1/Assignment 3 - Observation

Students should make a bookmark with a list of how they are marking key words and phrases in Judges. This will help them mark consistently and remind them what to look for in each chapter. An example of a key word bookmark is located on the student page.

Lesson 1/Assignment 3
U-1, Lesson 1, Chapter 1

Using a 3x5 notecard make a list of key words and symbols you have used already. You will add to this card key words you discover in other chapters as we study Judges. Here's an example:

> Historical Setting ☆
> References to time 🔍
> Geographical Location

Student Page 12

UNIT ONE - TEACHER'S GUIDE

LESSON TWO:

 Judges 1 Observation Worksheets, "Locations in Judges 1-3" map from the Appendix

OBJECTIVES:

In this lesson, students will identify which tribes of Israel did not drive out inhabitants in their lands, which inhabitants remained and where.

Lesson 2/Assignment 1 - Observation

Students will need to fill in the chart with this information as they observe it from the text.

You may need to help students find the information for them to record in the appropriate column. You can use the blank copy of this chart in the Teacher's Helps to make a transparency.

LESSON TWO

Lesson 2/Assignment 1 *U-1, Lesson 2, Chapter 1*

Whoever wrote Judges 1 under the leadership of God's Spirit wanted readers of this historical account to understand two things from this chapter: first, which tribes of Israel failed to drive out enemies from the land God gave them; and secondly, the enemies or nations Israel did not destroy. To make sure that you clearly see and remember this information, fill out the chart that follows from what you learned in chapter one. The first row has been filled out for you.

JUDGES 1: THE TRIBES DID NOT DRIVE OUT THE INHABITANTS

THE TRIBE	PEOPLE GROUP THEY DID NOT DRIVE OUT	THE CITIES OR LOCATIONS OF THE PEOPLE GROUP
Judah	Canaanites (inhabitants of the valley)	In the valley

A CLOSER LOOK AT THE TRIBES OF ISRAEL:

The tribes of Israel were descendents of the sons of Jacob, who was the son of Isaac, the son of Abraham: Reuben, Simeon, Levi, Judah, Zebulun, Issachar, Dan, Gad, Asher, Naphtali, Joseph (who was given an extra portion of his father's inheritance so that each of his sons, Ephraim and Manasseh, received their own land; Genesis 48:21-22) and Benjamin. Although there were 12 tribes from 12 sons, there were 13 divisions of the land and 13 tribes referred to in Scripture once Joseph's sons were each given their own land.

THE MORE YOU KNOW...

Student Page 13

UNIT ONE - TEACHER'S GUIDE

Judges

Lesson 2/Assignment 2 - Observation
The "Locations in Judges 1-3" map at the end of this unit has the locations students should identify.

Lesson 2/Assignment 2
U-1, Lesson 2, Chapter 1

Using the map "Locations in Judges Chapters 1–3" in the Appendix, locate and circle the cities, if possible, you double underlined when you marked geographical locations. Geography is important when you study the Word of God.

When studying Scripture, seeing exactly where cities or territories are located on maps help you establish context and understand the historical setting.

For example, can you see how many inhabitants were left in the land and why the constant exposure to their idolatry and culture became a snare and stumbling block for Israel? Keep this in mind as you continue your study.

What happens when you fail to drive out the inhabitants of the land? As you look further into the times of the Judges, you will see how the inhabitants' influences led Israel into sin and captivity. What are the "inhabitants" in your land? Are there sins you participated in before coming to Christ that you have not yet put to death? Have you allowed new "inhabitants" to settle? Have you allowed trappings of the world to take up residence in your life?

"Do not love the world nor the things in the world. If anyone loves the world, the love of the Father is not in him. For all that is in the world, the lust of the flesh and the lust of the eyes and the boastful pride of life, is not from the Father, but is from the world. The world is passing away, and also its lusts; but the one who does the will of God lives forever."

—John 2:15-16

UNIT ONE - TEACHER'S GUIDE

Judges

LESSON THREE:

Judges 1 Observation Worksheets, Bible

OBJECTIVES:

Students will look at cross-references in Exodus, Deuteronomy, and Joshua to determine God's instructions and warnings to the sons of Israel about the inhabitants of the land and identify how the principles of obedience learned in Judges 1 apply to their lives.

Lesson 3/Assignment 1 - Observation/Interpretation

You may want to help your students complete this assignment to ensure they understand what information they are looking for and what to record in their workbook. Remind them to look for answers to the 5W and H questions concerning God's instructions and warnings.

Remind the student that cross-references are a part of interpretation. Not all information about a topic is contained in one passage being studied; other passages of Scripture will give further insight.

a. Exodus 23:31-33 – God told the sons of Israel that He would deliver the inhabitants of the land into their hand and drive them out from before them. They were to make no covenant with the inhabitants or their gods. The inhabitants were not to live in their land because they would make them sin against God to serve their gods – it would be a snare to them.

b. Deuteronomy 7:1-2,16, 22 – God would clear away many nations before them, the Hittites and the Girgashites and the Amorites and the Canaanites and the Perizzites and the Hivites and the Jebusites, seven nations greater and stronger than they. When He did

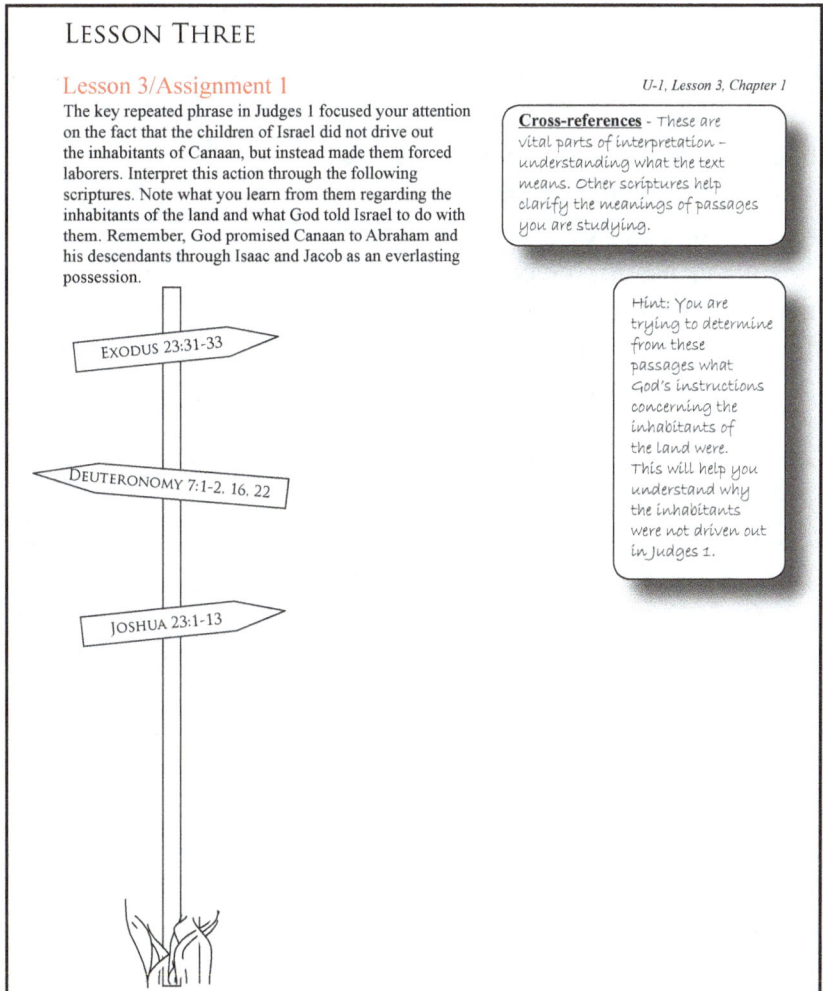

Student Page 15

UNIT ONE - TEACHER'S GUIDE

Judges

this, they were to utterly destroy them; they could not make a covenant or show favor to them. They were not to pity them or serve their gods because that would be a snare to them. God was going to clear away these nations before them little by little so the wild beasts would not grow too numerous for them.

c. Students may remember this passage of Scripture if they completed the Joshua study.
Joshua 23:1-13 – Joshua is speaking in this passage and he is old and advanced in years. He warns the sons of Israel; he reminds them of all that God had done for them in taking the land and tells them God will drive out the remaining nations. They are to be careful to obey God, not associate with the nations, and not to mention, swear, serve or bow down to their gods. They are to cling to God. God will continue to drive out the nations if they obey God; if they don't, they will be a snare and a trap – whips on their sides and thorns in their eyes until they perish from the land.

Lesson 3/Assignment 2 - Interpretation
Students should recognize that Israel's partial obedience was a step toward total disobedience. Joshua warned the people to be careful to obey God and not associate with the nations they were to drive out. Their disobedience led them to forsake God and turn to the nations' idols.

Lesson 3/Assignment 3 - Interpretation
To complete this assignment, students will consider the observations they made in Judges 1 and the information they gleaned from the cross-references. You may want to help them reason through these to conclude something close to the following:

Although the sons of Israel were obeying God by fighting against and subduing the inhabitants of the land, they were only partially obeying His commands because they did not utterly destroy them, leaving no one alive as they were instructed. Instead, they turned them into forced labor.

Lesson 3/Assignment 4 - Application

Students will think about what principles they learned in previous lessons and then determine how they can relate to

---

Lesson 3/Assignment 2   *U-1, Lesson 3, Chapter 1*
Based on your observations of Judges 1 and the cross-references, how would you describe Israel's condition in the days of the judges?

Lesson 3/Assignment 3
How would you describe the people's actions in chapter one?

Lesson 3/Assignment 4
If you already completed the Joshua study, you should remember the significance of Joshua 23. In his final words, Joshua reminds the children of Israel how God had warned them through Moses and Joshua, admonishing them to listen – to walk in obedience.

Has anyone, like your parents, grandparents, or someone close to you, ever warned you not to take a certain path – and told you what would happen if you did? Were they right? Did you listen or did you resent their counsel? Did you think you knew more than they? Did you despise their counsel? **Chafe** at their words? And what happened? Write out the situation and the result below.

> **Application** is the "So what?" part of inductive Bible study. Practice asking yourself questions like,
>
> "Joshua told the people what would happen if they did not drive out the inhabitants. They ignored him and suffered the consequences he promised... 'So what?'"
>
> You should always ask yourself how understanding what you've seen in God's Word applies to your life right now!

Student Page 16

Unit One - Teacher's Guide

Judges

them. Help your students understand that personal application may take time to think about. They need to prayerfully consider how to apply these truths to their lives.

Students may recognize times in their life when like the sons of Israel they did not listen to instruction or advice from an adult or authority.

Lesson 3/Assignment 5 - Application
Students should think about the work they completed up to this point and determine at least one or two principles that applies to their lives (e.g. obeying God completely when He gives instruction).

Lesson 3/Assignment 6 - Application
Students will think about how they have responded to God's instructions and warnings. You may want to ask them to first identify the warnings or instructions and then write out how they responded to them.

Lesson 3/Assignment 5
U-1, Lesson 3, Chapter 1

Even though you have just begun your study of the book of Judges, what lessons have you learned that you can begin to practice in your daily living?

Lesson 3/Assignment 6

If someone recorded your responses to God's instructions and warnings, what would they say? Have you been fully obedient, partially **obedient** or not obedient at all? Explain your answers.

Interesting beginning to your study on Judges, isn't it? If you already studied the book of Joshua you will remember the words of encouragement you read in today's lesson. How quickly the sons of Israel forgot God's warnings and instructions! Will you be as quick to forget what you learned from God's Word?

As you continue to study the book of Judges pay close attention to the consequences of Israel's forgetfulness and disobedience. God is the same yesterday, today, and forever. If you disobey God's warnings and instructions,, you too can expect consequences!

Student Page 17

© 2008 Precept Ministries International

UNIT ONE - TEACHER'S GUIDE

Judges

DISCUSSION GUIDE LESSONS ONE, TWO AND THREE:

Begin your discussion with the cross-references from Exodus, Deuteronomy, and Joshua.

EXODUS 23:31-33

The Lord repeats His promise of the land. The boundaries are from the Red Sea to the Mediterranean Sea, from the wilderness to the Euphrates River. He tells Israel that He will drive out the inhabitants of the land and Israel must make no covenants with them.

DEUTERONOMY

In 7:1-2, 16, and 22, the Lord repeats through Moses that when He gave the land of Canaan to Israel, they were to make no covenants with the nations in the land. He told Israel they must utterly destroy them. He reminds them that He will clear away the nations, though Israel had a part to play. They must consume idol worshipers so Israel will not be led astray from the Lord their God.

JOSHUA

In 23:1-13, Joshua, old and about to die, reminded the leaders of Israel that the Lord had been fighting for them. They had been given and conquered the main cities and nations of the land, but they still had to possess the land of their inheritance.

Verses 12-13 warn Israel that if they cling to the nations in the land and intermarry with them, the Lord will not continue to drive out their enemies. Then *Israel* will perish from the land.

JUDGES 1

Help your students relate the events of this chapter to what they discussed from the scriptures in Exodus, Deuteronomy and Joshua. Also ask your students to bring out the main points of this chapter.

These events occur after Joshua dies when Israel asks the Lord which tribe should be the first to fight the remaining Canaanites in the land.

Joshua has defeated the main cities and leaders, but each tribe needs to destroy those left within their lands.

The Lord says Judah will be the first to fight and He will be with them. The tribe of Simeon helps Judah, and the Lord gives the Canaanites into their hands.

Draw attention to the places mentioned on the map in the lesson. Especially point out Hebron, Jerusalem, and Gaza. Let your students spend a few minutes discussing what happened in those places.

© 2008 Precept Ministries International

UNIT ONE - TEACHER'S GUIDE

Judges

Discuss who is mentioned in verses 12-20 and what he was.

> Caleb was one of the 12 spies mentioned in Numbers. He and Joshua were the only two who believed the Lord would give the Promised Land to Israel and gave a good report. After Joshua died, Caleb was the only one left alive of the first generation of Israel to come out of Egypt. He is mentioned in this chapter because he was of the tribe of Judah, which took the land. Hebron was part of the inheritance given to him and his descendants.

Verse 19

> Some of Judah couldn't drive out the inhabitants of the valley because of their iron chariots. With God's help they could have. Pharaoh's chariots, for example, were in the bottom of the Red Sea.

Benjamin, verse 21

> This tribe didn't drive the Jebusites out of Jerusalem (Jebus is an old name for Jerusalem) – a direct violation of what the Lord told Israel. They were commanded to utterly destroy the inhabitants of the land. The Lord would have blessed Israel if they had only believed and acted on His promises.

> The Jebusites and others of the land were idolaters. They could lead Israel astray from the Lord their God.

The house of Joseph (Manasseh and Ephraim) is mentioned in verses 22-29.

> The Lord went up with the house of Joseph against Bethel (formerly Luz). Point out on the map that Bethel is in the area God gave Ephraim to possess. According to verse 26, the Hittites inhabited this part of the land.

> Manasseh did not take possession of Beth-shean, Taanach, Dor, Ibleam, or Megiddo although they could have done so if they had been obedient to the Lord. He would have fought for them as He had done since they entered the land years previous. Israel forced the Canaanites of these cities to labor for them.

> If Manasseh was strong enough to make them forced labor, then they were strong enough to have utterly destroyed them according to the command of the Lord.

Ephraim didn't drive out the Canaanites in Gezer.

Zebulun, verse 30

UNIT ONE - TEACHER'S GUIDE

Judges

The phrase "did not drive out" becomes more frequent in going through this list of the tribes. Zebulun enslaved the inhabitants of Kitron or Nahalol in their land.

The Canaanites lived among Manasseh, Ephraim, and Zebulun.

Asher, verses 31-32

They did not drive out inhabitants of Acco, Sidon, Ahlab, Achzib, Helbah, Aphik, and Rehob.

Naphtali, verse 33

Naphtali did not drive out inhabitants of Beth-shemesh and Beth-anath, who became forced labor.

Asher and Naphtali lived among the Canaanites.

Dan, verse 34

The Amorites forced Dan out of their inheritance and into the hill country.

Someone might notice a progression: Canaanites living with Israel; Canaanites living among Israel; Israel living among the Canaanites; Israel forced out by the Canaanites.

Verses 35-36

The Amorites also persisted in Mount Heres, Aijalon, and Shaalbim until the house of Joseph (probably a reference to the tribe of Ephraim) grew strong enough to make them forced labor. The text says, ". . . when the hand of the house of Joseph was heavy, they became forced labor."

The tribes did not obey the Lord's command to utterly destroy the nations of the land.

Ask your students what they learned from Judges 1 that they can apply to their lives.

Unit One - Teacher's Guide

UNIT ONE - TEACHER'S GUIDE

LESSON FOUR:

 Judges 2 Observation Worksheets, colored pencils, key word bookmark, "Locations in Judges 1-3" map located in the Appendix

OBJECTIVES:

In this lesson, students will observe Judges 2, identifying and marking key words, then personally applying by examining how thoroughly they obey God's Word.

Lesson 4/Assignment 1 - Observation

Students will observe this chapter by marking key words from their bookmark and including: *the land of Canaan*, *the sons of Israel did evil in the sight of the Lord*, *judges*, *anger*, *nation*, *die* and *death*, *test*, any reference to not listening to the Lord, and *covenant*. Instructions on how to mark these words are provided with the assignment.

LESSON FOUR

Lesson 4/Assignment 1
U-1, Lesson 4, Chapter 2

Read Judges 2 to grasp the overall content of the chapter. Add the following key words and phrases to your key word bookmark and then mark each in its own distinctive color or symbol (some examples are provided):

any specific reference to the *land of Canaan* God gave Abraham, Isaac, Jacob (Israel) and his twelve sons. If you want, color it blue and double underline it in green. (Mark specific references to this Promised Land the same way throughout your study of the Old Testament.)

the phrases *the sons of Israel did evil in the sight of the Lord* and the **synonymous** phrase, *they would turn back and act more corruptly*. References to "doing evil" is a very important phrase that you'll want to mark throughout Judges.

judges (use a brown gavel like this ⚒).

anger (color red).

nation (underline in brown and shade green).

die and *death* (with a black tombstone like this ▮).

test (underline in orange).

references to *not listening to the Lord* (with a green ear with a slash through it like this 👂).

covenant (put a yellow box around it and color it yellow). Whenever you see *covenant* in your Bible, you should mark it for two reasons: first, because everything God does is based on covenant, and second, because God is the sovereign administrator of all covenants.

all references to time and geographical locations. You can double-underline locations with a green pen or pencil.

Also put a star next to any verse in this chapter that provides the historical context of the times and people of the events in Judges 1-2.

> **Marking** significant words or phrases that are used throughout Scripture in consistent ways will help you quickly identify and compile information about those topics. You can simply scan through books you have studied and locate your distinctive marking for those words or phrases. Your diligence today will help you later.

> **Context** – The environment or setting in which something dwells or is found. Look for verses that help you understand what is going on during this time period or why people are doing the things they are doing.

UNIT ONE - TEACHER'S GUIDE

Judges

Lesson 4/Assignment 2 - Observation
Students will look at the "Locations in Judges 1-3" map in the Appendix to locate Gilgal and Bochim.

Students will learn that the people lifted up their voices and wept – so they named the place Bochim. Some Bibles will have a footnote that says Bochim means "weepers."

 Looking at maps to identify locations will help students visualize places and events described. It will also help them to recognize that the places described in the passages are real locations, some of which, exist today.

Lesson 4/Assignment 3 - Application
This question will remind students of the importance of understanding not just the meaning of the text, but also its application to their daily living. To answer these questions, students will think about how completely they obey the Word. They should conclude that knowing the full counsel of God's Word is essential to obedience. They will also prayerfully examine what they have not completely obeyed.

Encourage them to write out their thoughts so they can honestly and clearly identify disobedience. Then help them to work through letter c. by asking God to forgive them for these sins.

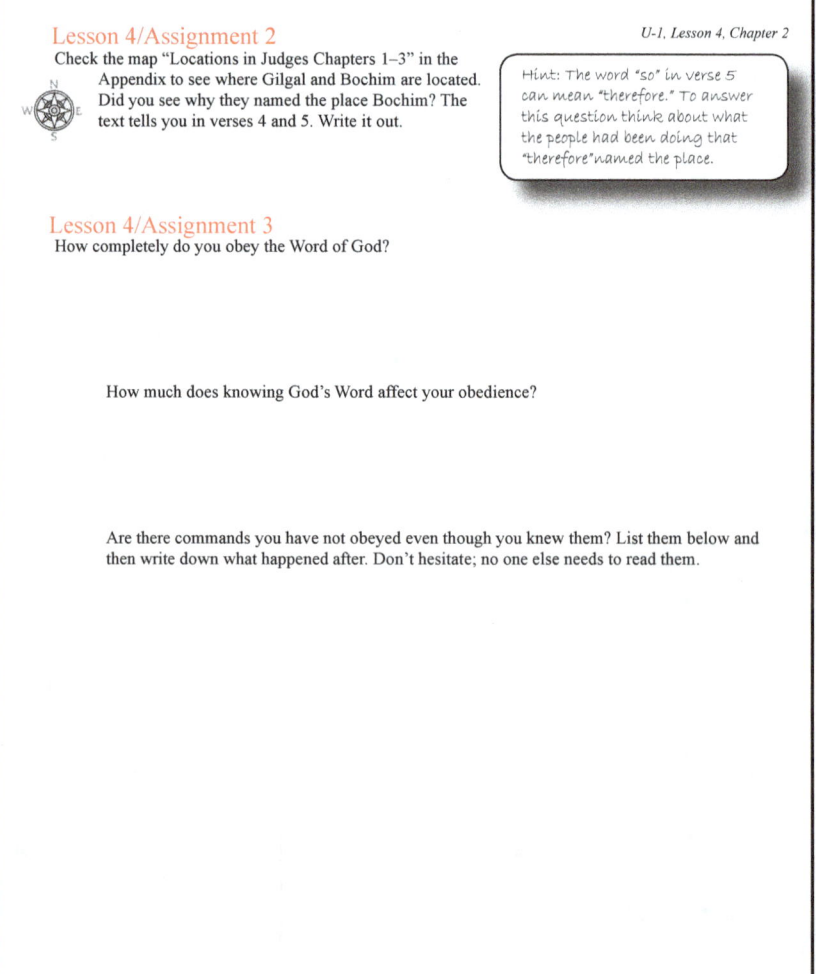

UNIT ONE - TEACHER'S GUIDE

Judges

> *U-1, Lesson 4, Chapter 2*
>
> Take your list and tell God you failed to obey, you're sorry, and you confess it as sin. Then tell Him you want Him to free you from power the enemy has in your life resulting from your disobedience. Ask Him to fill every area of your being with His Spirit and tell Him that you will resist the enemy's temptation and walk in the power of the Holy Spirit – one moment at a time. You can write out your prayer below.
>
> Do you realize that the chief source of failure in believers is their tolerance of partial obedience to the Word of God? When you fail to drive out the enemy completely, then "that sin" becomes whips in your side and thorns in your eyes. Sin becomes **tortuous**; its tenacity is unrelenting until we fall on our faces and cry out to God for deliverance, then rise to walk in obedience, vowing to give no further place of occupation to the enemy.
>
> Victory is yours for obedience just as it was for Israel because God is a merciful God and a God of grace – grace that guarantees victory.

Student Page 21

Unit One - Teacher's Guide

Judges

World View Project – What is obedience?

This project will help students identify how authorities in their lives define complete obedience. It will also help them recognize that even if authorities in their lives do not have a clear understanding of what complete obedience entails, they know from God's Word that only complete obedience is acceptable.

World View Project U-1, Lesson 4, Chapter 2

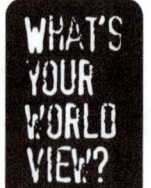

WHAT IS OBEDIENCE? - PROJECT

For this assignment, you will need the following:

The chart on the next page

Interview at least three adults in your life (parent, grandparent, aunt, uncle, teacher, pastor, etc.) and ask them to tell you what they would consider fully and partially obeying regarding the topics listed on the chart. Write their responses to each topic in the two columns.

After completing your interviews, read the verses listed for each topic and then below the chart describe full obedience concerning each topic.

Unit One - Teacher's Guide

Judges

U-1, Lesson 4, Chapter 2

Obedience to...	Full Obedience	Partial Obedience
God's Word concerning...		
Immorality *Ephesians 5:3*		
What you talk about *Ephesians 4:29, 1 Timothy 3:11*		
Idolatry *Exodus 20:3,4*		
A boss at work *Titus 2:9-10, 3:1,2*		
Government *Romans 13:1-7*		

Student Page 23

UNIT ONE - TEACHER'S GUIDE

UNIT ONE - TEACHER'S GUIDE

Judges

LESSON FIVE:

 Judges 1 and 2 Observation Worksheets, colored pencils, "The Historical Setting of Judges" and the "At A Glance" chart from the Appendix

OBJECTIVES:

Students will identify the cycle of sin outlined in Judges 2 and recognize why God left inhabitants in the land after Joshua's victories. They will also identify the characteristics of God seen in this chapter. Students will also describe the times of the judges according to the chapter and determine a theme for Judges 1 and 2.

Lesson 5/Assignment 1 - Observation
Students should identify verses that describe idolatrous practices.
Judges 2:11, 12, 13, 17, 19

Lesson 5/Assignment 2 - Observation/ Interpretation
Students should recognize from Judges 2:11-19 the following pattern or cycle of sin:
- *Sin – served other gods*
- *Captivity – sold into hands of enemies because the anger of the Lord burned against them*
- *People cry out – groan because of the oppression*
- *Judge raised up – Lord raises up a judge who delivers them from their enemies*
- *Judge dies – and people turn back, acting more corruptly than their fathers*

Lesson 5/Assignment 3 - Observation
According to Judges 2:20-23, God says He is no longer going to drive out the nations before them.

Lesson 5/Assignment 4 - Interpretation
This assignment will lead students

LESSON FIVE

Lesson 5/Assignment 1
U-1, Lesson 5, Chapter 2

After seeking God's insight and wisdom in prayer, read through Judges 2 and write *idolatry* in the margin of your Observation Worksheets next to verses that show idolatry among the Israelites. (The first one can be found in 2:11.)

Lesson 5/Assignment 2
What progression do you see in Judges 2:11-19 once the sons of Israel do evil in the sight of the Lord and serve the Baals? List it below.

> When looking for a progression of events, look at the event that takes place first then leads to other events in the text.
> Hint: The first event in this chapter is the sons of Israel doing evil in the sight of the Lord by serving other gods.

Lesson 5/Assignment 3
How do you see God responding in Judges 2:20-23, and why?

Lesson 5/Assignment 4
According to Judges 2:20-23, why were the nations not driven out by Joshua left behind?

What was the purpose of the test?

From what you learned in chapter 2, did Israel pass the test?

What do you think God would have done if they had passed the test?

Student Page 25

UNIT ONE - TEACHER'S GUIDE

through a series of questions that will teach them how to accurately interpret the passage they are studying.

According to Judges 2:20-23, the nations were left to test Israel.

a. God wanted to reveal whether they would keep the way of the Lord as their fathers did.

b. Judges 2 shows that the sons of Israel did not keep the way of the Lord; instead they served the gods of the people around them. They did not pass the test.

c. God would have driven out the inhabitants from before them as He promised. (Students should know this based on what God says He will no longer do as a result of Israel's disobedience and the cross-references in this unit.)

Lesson 5/Assignment 5 - Observation

Students will mark *God* in chapter two and then list what they learn about Him. Their lists should include most of the following:

- *Faithful to His covenant, even though the people are not.*
- *Even when reprimanding or disciplining His people, He reminds them of His Word.*
- *Idol worship and not obeying His word provokes His anger.*
- *He causes hardship in order to be known and obeyed.*
- *He's moved to pity in our distress even when we are to blame.*

Lesson 5/Assignment 6 - Observation

You may need to help your students identify the following information to list on their historical setting chart. Remind them that the historical setting is defining the time – what was going on at this time in Israel's history:

Lesson 5/Assignment 5

Go back and mark every reference to *God* in this chapter. Then list below what you learn about Him.

> The goal of Inductive Bible Study is to know God. As you observe the text, you always want to take time to think about and write out what you learned about God.

Lesson 5/Assignment 6

Now by asking the 5Ws and H, record what chapters one and two tell you with respect to the "who's" of the times, what is happening, when it is happening, where it is happening, and why. Include the spiritual and **moral** climate of the times and any indication of how it happened. You will find a page at the end of this unit entitled "The Historical Setting of Judges" to record your insights… just the facts, nothing elaborate!

Lesson 5/Assignment 7

Now record the main theme or event covered in Judges 1 and Judges 2 on the appropriate chapter lines on the "Judges At A Glance" chart in the Appendix.

> Wow! The nations which the sons of Israel didn't drive out became a test to them. Does this help you understand why Joshua didn't take all of the land God gave to the children of Israel? Joshua did his job completely! God wanted inhabitants left to see if the sons of Israel would follow Him even after Joshua was gone. Sadly, after Joshua and the elders died, the people forgot the work God had done for them – turning instead to serve other gods. What will you do when the godly influences of your parents, grandparents, pastors, and teachers are gone? When young people leave Christian schools or move away from parents, they often turn from God to serve other gods, forgetting the spiritual lessons they were taught. Will you?

UNIT ONE - TEACHER'S GUIDE

Judges

- *Joshua is dead.*
- *Israel is in the Promised Land.*
- *Inhabitants are left for the tribes to drive out, but they did not utterly destroy the inhabitants as God instructed.*
- *Joshua's generation has died.*
- *The new generation does not know the Lord or the work He has done for Israel.*
- *The sons of Israel are doing evil in the sight of the Lord by serving other gods.*
- *Anger of the Lord burned against Israel for their idolatry. He sold them into their enemies hands.*
- *God raises up judges; people are delivered from the hands of their enemies until judge dies.*
- *After the judge dies, they act more corruptly.*

Lesson 5/Assignment 7 - Observation/Interpretation

Help students determine the main point of chapters one and two and a summary statement to help them remember these chapters. Remember, everyone's summary statements do not have to be exactly the same, but all should focus on the main event or point of the chapters. Possible summary statements for these chapters are:

Judges 1 – The inhabitants not driven out
Judges 2 – The sons of Israel do evil in the sight of the Lord or The cycle of sin

Unit One - Teacher's Guide

UNIT ONE - TEACHER'S GUIDE

Judges

DISCUSSION GUIDE LESSONS FOUR AND FIVE:

JUDGES 2

Ask your students about the paragraphs of this chapter and the main event(s) or point(s) of each. This will help show that this part of Judges is not chronological.

> 1-5
> Bochim was so named because Israel wept when the Lord told them He would no longer drive out their enemies.
>
> 6-10
> Israel served the Lord all the days of Joshua.
>
> 11-15
> Israel did evil and the Lord's anger burned against them.
>
> 16-23
> The Lord raised up judges to deliver Israel.
> Nations were left to test Israel.

Verses 1-5
Discuss what happened in these verses.

> The angel of the Lord spoke to Israel when He came up from Gilgal to Bochim. Joshua camped in Gilgal when he took the land of Canaan.
>
> At Bochim, the angel of the Lord confronted Israel because they had not obeyed the Lord. He had commanded them to make no covenants with peoples in the land and tear down their altars.
>
> Because they disobeyed, the Lord said He would not drive out the inhabitants; rather they would become thorns in Israel's sides and their gods would ensnare Israel.
>
> The place was named Bochim ("weepers") because Israel wept when they heard this from the Lord.

Ask your students to discuss if they have ever been in or seen a situation like this. Many times people cry and sacrifice before the Lord because they have become aware of the consequences of their disobedience. This does not mean they're repenting – they're just sorry for the consequences of their sin. The Lord repeatedly told Israel what to do when they came into the land. Many today claim they know and love the Lord, but their actions deny it, just like Israel.

© 2008 Precept Ministries International

UNIT ONE - TEACHER'S GUIDE

Judges

Verses 6-10

These verses go back to a time before the events of Judges. They explain how Israel got into the mess they were in.

As long as Joshua was alive, Israel followed him in serving the Lord. They even followed the elders after Joshua. But when they died, no one was alive who remembered "the great work of the Lord," likely including the Exodus, the 40 years in the wilderness under the leadership of Moses, and Joshua's conquering of the land.

After Joshua died (at 110) and "all that generation" (possibly the second generation out of Egypt, which took the land) also died, another generation rose up that did not know the Lord or what He had done.

You can encourage your class to prevent a generation from arising that does not know the Lord or what He has done by teaching their children and grandchildren the Word of God and sharing what He has done in their lives.

Verses 11-23

Relate verses 11-13 to verses 1-10.

The result of Israel not obeying the Lord was just what He had said it would be. The people of the Lord went after other gods.

This provoked the Lord to anger.

Discuss the Lord's reaction to Israel's turning away.

Twice the text says the Lord's anger burned against His people (verses 14 and 20).

Help your students understand that the Lord is not only merciful and gracious but also angry toward sin.

Because they turned away from Him, the Lord gave Israel into the hands of enemies who plundered them. His mighty hand, which had been for them, turned against them. He severely distressed His people for worshiping other gods.

This happened because (as Judges 1 repeats) they did not drive out all the inhabitants of the land. They did not listen to His voice, verse 20. They transgressed His covenant.

The tribes of Israel did not consider the serious consequences of making forced laborers of the

Unit one - Teacher's Guide

Judges

Canaanites instead of utterly destroying them. Their disobedience led them to turn away from God.

Discuss with your students what they observed in verses 16-23 about Israel, the judges, and the enemies of Israel.

The Lord raised up judges to deliver Israel from their enemies.

The Lord delivered Israel during the judge's life.

Israel groaned under oppression and affliction. The Lord pitied them and raised up judges to deliver them.

When the judges died, the people turned back to more corrupt ways.

Verses 21-23 say that the Lord left some nations to test Israel because of their disobedience.

Note: Don't discuss these verses for too long because your students will study this subject more in Unit 2 on Judges 3.

UNIT ONE - TEACHER'S GUIDE

Judges

UNIT ONE - TEACHER'S GUIDE

Judges

LESSON SIX:

 Judges 17-19 Observation Worksheets, colored pencils, keyword bookmark

OBJECTIVES:

Students will observe Judges 17-19 and mark the key repeated phrase *there was no king in Israel and every man did what was right in his own eyes*. They will also identify the major sins exposed in each of the chapters. This lesson will help students recognize the segment divisions in Judges.

Lesson 6/Assignment 1 - Observation/Interpretation
The point of this lesson is to identify the main themes of chapters 17-19. Tell students they will do more thorough observations later in the unit. These assignments help them understand Judges as a whole before examining the individual chapters and segments more closely. You may assign this as group work, if you are able, and have the groups read these chapters aloud to one another.

a. Students should read Judges 17-19 and mark every reference to the repeated phrase *there was no king in Israel and every man did what was right in his own eyes*.

b. Students should identify most, if not all, of the sins exposed in these chapters. They may not use the exact wording listed below, but they should recognize the sins being committed.

Judges 17 – idolatry, anarchy, opportunism, theft, deceit, no parental discipline, Levitical law broken, priest hired for cash

Judges 18 – Danites steal priest, anarchy, more faith in a person than God, keep idols, worship idols, immorality, infidelity, lust, tolerance, syncretism, homosexuality

Judges 19 – Levite not under Levitical law—for hire to biggest bidder, rape

---

LESSON SIX

Lesson 6/Assignment 1
U-1, Lesson 6, Chapters 17-19

Your assignment today is to read Judges 17–19 straight through simply as you would read several chapters of an interesting book. As you read:

Mark in distinctive ways the phrases *no king in Israel* and *every man did what is right in his own eyes*. These are first used in Judges 17:6 and are found in no other places in Judges apart from these final chapters.

Note below the major sin(s) exposed in each chapter.

Judges 17

Judges 18

Judges 19

> Pretty gross stuff! However, does it sound at all familiar? Pick up any newspaper from around the world and you'll see much of the same thing. Ignoring God's law and choosing to do what is right in the eyes of men has led to this kind of blatant immorality for ages! Knowing God's Word for yourself will teach you what the consequences of sin are... not only in your life, but also in your society. You don't have to be unaware – you can make the right choices!

Student Page 27

© 2008 Precept Ministries International

Unit one - Teacher's Guide

UNIT ONE - TEACHER'S GUIDE

LESSON SEVEN:

 Judges 20-21 Observation Worksheets, colored pencils, key word bookmark

OBJECTIVES:

In this final lesson, students will observe Judges 20-21 and again identify and mark the key repeated phrase *there was no king in Israel and every man did what was right in his own eyes*. Students will also continue to identify the major sins exposed in each of the chapters and recognize the segment divisions and historical setting for the book of Judges. To conclude this unit, students will recognize how the times of the judges are similar to their times today.

Lesson 7/Assignment 1 - Observation
a. Students will read Judges 20-21 and mark every reference to the repeated phrase *there was no king in Israel and every man did what was right in his own eyes*.

b. Students should identify most, if not all, of the sins exposed in these chapters. They may not use the exact wording listed below, but they should recognize the sins being committed.

Judges 20 - twisting the law
Judges 21 - war, chaos

Lesson 7/Assignment 2 - Interpretation
This assignment is an opportunity for students to express in their words what the times of the judges were like. This will help them evaluate all they have learned from this unit and solidify their understanding of the historical setting of Judges.

There was no king in Israel, everyone was doing what was right in their own eyes. Israel was mixing their worship of God with the worship of the inhabitants in the land. Their sin grew from individual acts of disobedience

© 2008 Precept Ministries International

LESSON SEVEN

Lesson 7/Assignment 1
U-1, Lesson 7, Chapters 20-21

Your assignment today is to read Judges 20-21 straight through just like you did in Lesson Six.

Continue to mark in distinctive ways the phrases *no king in Israel* and *every man did what is right in his own eyes*.

Note below the major sin(s) exposed in each chapter.

Judges 20

Judges 21

Lesson 7/Assignment 2
How do these final chapters help you understand the times of the Judges?

Lesson 7/Assignment 3
Do you see any parallels today? If so, what?

Student Page 29

UNIT ONE - TEACHER'S GUIDE

Judges

to widespread sin and corruption and ultimately, civil war. Even the priesthood was tainted with sins tolerated at this time.

Lesson 7/Assignment 3 - Application

In this application question students will think about their community and society as a whole to determine how behaviors and attitudes today are similar to those observed in Judges. They should recognize that the corruption of religious leaders, rampant crimes such as rape, murder and theft, idolatry, and even nations fighting within their own boundaries, are just as prevalent today as they were during the times of the judges.

Lesson 7/Assignment 4 - Application

Encourage students to prayerfully examine their lives and to write out what they have learned from this unit that will make a difference in how they live on a day-to-day basis if they put into practice these truths.

Remind them that if all they do is gain understanding of God's Word, but never practice it, it is useless and can even be detrimental. The goal of Bible study is to know God and live transformed by the truth of who He is and His will.

Lesson 7/Assignment 4
Finally, what is the most significant thing you learned in this first week of study that spoke to you personally?

U-1, Lesson 7, Chapters 20-21

Application – Bible study isn't just another academic class you take to help you get into a good college and then land a good job. It's time spent getting to know the one, true, living God. If you know what it says, understand what it means, and live out its truths, it will impact your eternity!! So think about questions like this one. Ask God what He wants you to learn during your diligent hours of study.

Great job!! You finished your first unit of Judges! Although spending a lot of time on observation is tedious, it is vital! How can you ever truly understand God's Word and accurately interpret its meaning without first carefully seeing exactly what it says? Religions and cults base some of their beliefs on false interpretations because they don't first see what the Bible is saying. You don't want to be deceived. You want to walk in truth. Serving God can only be done one way – His! Your hard work will keep you from being deceived and you will take what you see accurately and begin to walk in truth!

Student Page 30

UNIT ONE - TEACHER'S GUIDE

Judges

DISCUSSION GUIDE LESSONS SIX AND SEVEN:

JUDGES 17–21

Ask your students how these chapters relate to Judges 1–2 and what repeated phrase appears in them. They studied these chapters at this point in the course to understand the historical setting of the book.

> Judges 17:6; 18:1; 19:1 and 21:25 repeat some part of, "In those days there was no king in Israel; every man did what was right in his own eyes."

Compared with Judges 1 and 2, we learn that Joshua and the people who had seen the work of the Lord for Israel had died, and the current generation did not follow the Lord, but their own understanding of what was right.

Judges 17-18 detail the tribe of Dan's search for an inheritance. They had been given one (Judges 1:34), but had not succeeded in possessing it. So they migrated north. The priest of these chapters did what was right in his own eyes, as did the tribe of Dan.

During their travel, the tribe of Dan named one place Mahaneh-dan (Judges 18:12), which is mentioned during the time of Samson (Judges 13:25). The events of this part of Judges took place at the beginning of the time of the judges.

Judges 19-21 are three of the most distressing chapters in the Bible. Israel almost eradicated the tribe of Benjamin in a civil war before they came up with a solution that was "right in their own eyes."

The high priest of this time was Phinehas (Judges 20:27-28), the son of Eleazar and grandson of Aaron. Phinehas was born before Israel left Egypt (Exodus 6:25). This puts the events of Judges 19-21 also at the beginning of the period of the judges.

Accordingly, your students can note on their "At A Glance" charts that these last chapters happen before Judges 3-16.

Encourage your class to study these next lessons on the judges to learn valuable lessons for their lives.

Always weave personal application into the discussion, as led by the Holy Spirit.

Unit One - Teacher's Guide

Unit One - Teacher's Guide

Locations in Judges 1-3

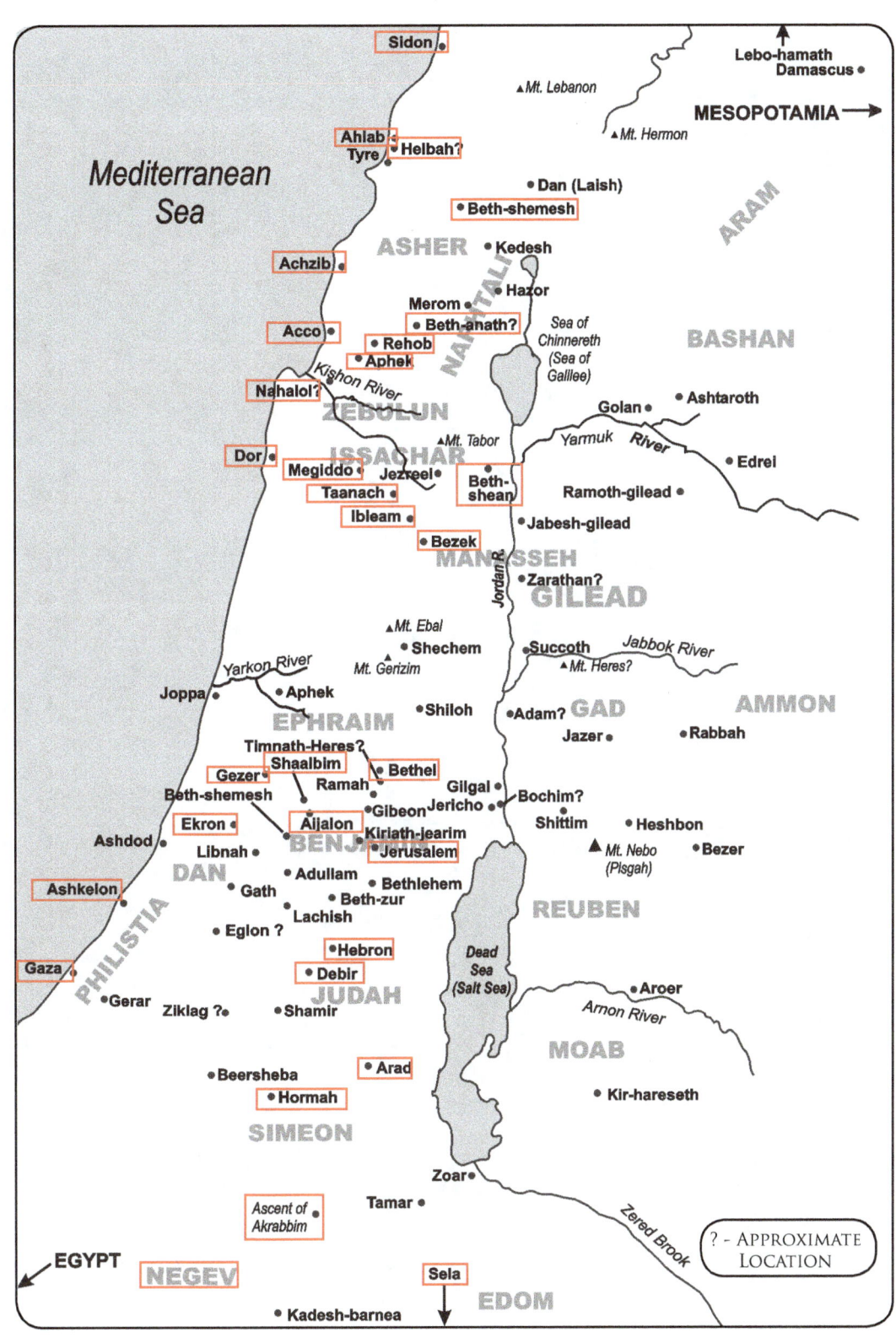

UNIT ONE - TEACHER'S GUIDE

Enrichment Words

Absolute – having no restriction, exception, or qualification.

Apathy – lack of feeling or emotion, lack of interest or concern.

Chafe – to feel irritation or discontent.

Idolatry – the worship of a physical object as a god, immoderate attachment or devotion to something.

Indifference – of no importance or value one way or the other, marked by a lack of interest, enthusiasm, or concern for something.

Moral – of or relating to principles of right and wrong in behavior.

Obedient – submissive to the restraint or command of authority, willing to obey.

Relevant – having significant and demonstrable bearing on the matter at hand.

Synonymous – alike in meaning or significance, having the same connotations, implications, or reference.

Tortuous – marked by repeated twists, bends, or turns, marked by devious or indirect tactics.

Unit one - Teacher's Guide

UNIT ONE - TEACHER'S GUIDE

Judges
Unit One Quiz

Name: _____ Date: _____

UNIT ONE - QUIZ KEY

MULTIPLE CHOICE – Circle the letter of the correct answer.

1. Which of the following is a possible chapter theme for Judges 1?
    a. Be strong and courageous to enter the land
    b. Inhabitants not driven out
    c. Joshua's final words
    d. Cycle of sin

2. Which of the following is a possible chapter theme for Judges 2?
    a. Be strong and courageous to enter the land
    b. Inhabitants not driven out
    c. Joshua's final words
    d. Cycle of sin

3. According to the cross-references in Exodus and Deuteronomy, what did God tell the sons of Israel to do with the inhabitants of the land?
    a. Leave them alone
    b. Worship their gods
    c. Make a covenant and live in peace with them
    d. Utterly destroy every living thing

4. How would God's command to destroy the inhabitants of the land protect the sons of Israel?
    a. It would allow them to set up their own government and religion without interference.
    b. It would keep them from sinning against God by serving their gods (idols).
    c. It would keep them from having disputes over the land.
    d. It would allow them to keep all of their possessions.

5. Instead of driving out the inhabitants of the land, what did most of the tribes do?
    a. Sent them to Egypt
    b. Made them forced labor
    c. Converted them to the Jewish religion
    d. Gave them back the land

© 2008 Precept Ministries International

UNIT ONE - TEACHER'S GUIDE

Judges
Unit One Quiz

6. What phrase best describes Israel's response to God's command concerning the inhabitants of the land?
    a. Complete obedience
    b. *Partial obedience*
    c. Complete ignorance
    d. Total rebellion

7. Why did God leave the nations that were not driven out by Joshua?
    a. To remind the sons of Israel that the land didn't really belong to them.
    b. *To test if Israel would keep the way of the Lord and walk in it as their fathers had.*
    c. To become laborers for the sons of Israel.
    d. Because they were too strong to be driven out.

8. According to Judges 2, what sin led the beginning of the cycle seen throughout the book of Judges?
    a. Stealing
    b. Lying to God
    c. *Serving other gods*
    d. Killing inhabitants

9. As a result of their sin in Judges 2, what did God do to the people?
    a. Made them wander in the wilderness for 40 years
    b. *Sold them into the hands of their enemies*
    c. Sent them back to Egypt
    d. Nothing

10. When the people cried out to God, how did He respond?
    a. He sent enemies to attack them.
    b. He destroyed them.
    c. He ignored them.
    d. *He raised up a judge to deliver them.*

Unit One - Teacher's Guide

Judges
Unit One Test

Name: _____ Date: _____

Unit One - Test Key

Matching - Choose one and write the letter in the blank.

__d__ Having no restriction, exception, or qualification		a. Obedient
		b. Idolatry
__b__ The worship of a physical object as a god, immoderate attachment or devotion to something		c. Apathy
		d. Absolute
		e. Moral
__a__ Submissive to the restraint or command of authority, willing to obey		
__c__ Lack of feeling or emotion, lack of interest or concern		
__e__ Of or relating to principles of right and wrong in behavior		

True or False

__F__ 6. All tribes drove out the inhabitants living in their land.

__T__ 7. Joshua admonished the sons of Israel to remember what God had done and keep His commands.

__T__ 8. Because Israel disobeyed, God would not drive out the inhabitants from their lands.

__F__ 9. The sons of Israel could mention the gods of the inhabitants of the land, but they were forbidden to serve them.

__T__ 10. After Joshua's generation died, another generation arose that did not know the Lord or the work He had done for Israel.

© 2008 Precept Ministries International

UNIT ONE - TEACHER'S GUIDE

Judges
Unit One Test

MULTIPLE CHOICE - Circle one.

11. Which of the following is a possible chapter theme for Judges 1?
    a. Be strong and courageous to enter the land
    b. Inhabitants not driven out
    c. Joshua's final words
    d. The sons of Israel do evil in the sight of the Lord – the cycle of sin

12. Which of the following is a possible chapter theme for Judges 2?
    a. Be strong and courageous to enter the land
    b. Inhabitants not driven out
    c. Joshua's final words
    d. Cycle of sin

13. According to the cross-references in Exodus and Deuteronomy, what did God tell the sons of Israel to do with the inhabitants of the land?
    a. Leave them alone
    b. Worship their gods
    c. Make a covenant and live in peace with them
    d. Utterly destroy every living thing

14. How would God's command to destroy the inhabitants of the land protect the sons of Israel?
    a. It would allow them to set up their own government and religion without interference.
    b. It would keep them from sinning against God by serving their gods (idols).
    c. It would keep them from having disputes over the land.
    d. It would allow them to keep their possessions.

15. Instead of driving out the inhabitants of the land, what did most of the tribes do with them?
    a. Sent them to Egypt
    b. Made them forced labor
    c. Converted them to the Jewish religion
    d. Gave them back the land

16. What phrase best describes Israel's response to God's command concerning the land's inhabitants?
    a. Complete obedience
    b. Partial obedience
    c. Complete ignorance
    d. Total rebellion

UNIT ONE - TEACHER'S GUIDE

Judges
Unit One Test

17. Why did God leave the nations that were not driven out by Joshua?
    a. To remind the sons of Israel that the land didn't really belong to them.
    b. *To test if Israel would keep the way of the Lord and walk in it as their fathers did.*
    c. To become laborers for the sons of Israel.
    d. Because they were too strong to be driven out.

18. According to Judges 2, what sin led to the beginning of the cycle seen throughout the book of Judges?
    a. Stealing from one another
    b. Lying to God
    c. *Serving other gods*
    d. Killing inhabitants

19. As a result of their sin in Judges 2, what did God do to the people?
    a. Made them wander in the wilderness for 40 years
    b. *Sold them into the hands of their enemies*
    c. Sent them back to Egypt
    d. Nothing

20. When the people cried out to God, how did He respond?
    a. He sent enemies to attack them.
    b. He destroyed them.
    c. He ignored them.
    d. *He raised up a judge to deliver them.*

21. What repeated phrase is used in Judges 17-21?
    a. Be strong and courageous
    b. *There was no king in Israel and every man did what was right in his own eyes*
    c. Did not drive out the inhabitants of the land
    d. Joshua's final words

22. When doing inductive Bible study, what RULES interpretation?
    a. Observation
    b. *Context*
    c. Time phrases
    d. Historical Setting

23. What is the goal of inductive Bible study?
    a. To interpret correctly
    b. To know about God
    c. To know how to study the Bible for myself
    d. *To know God and live a transformed life*

© 2008 Precept Ministries International

UNIT ONE - TEACHER'S GUIDE

Judges
Unit One Test

24. Establishing the _____ gives clues to the philosophical, social, political and religious conditions of the times.
    a. Observation
    b. Context
    c. Time phrases
    d. *Historical Setting*

25. What helps "unlock" the meaning of the text?
    a. Application words
    b. Context words
    c. *Key words*
    d. Important words

26. List at least five sins described in Judges 17-21.

Answer can be any of the following:
idolatry, anarchy, theft, deceit, Levitical law broken, priest hired for cash; Dannites steal priest, immorality, lust, syncretism, homosexuality, rape, etc.

27. List the cycle of sin described in Judges 2:11-19.

Sin
Captivity/Slavery
Crying out (not everyone may understand this as a part of the cycle at this point in the study)
Judge raised up
Judge dies
Sin

28. Explain why God left some of the land's inhabitants and what the generation after Joshua did with them.

According to Judges 2:20-23, the nations were left to test Israel to see if they would keep the way of the Lord, to walk in it as their fathers did. But the sons of Israel did not keep the way of the Lord; instead they lived among them, married their daughters, made them forced labor, and served their gods.

29. Describe the evil Israel did in the sight of the Lord.

Forgot the Lord their God and served the Baals and the Ashteroth.

Unit One - Teacher's Guide

Judges
Unit One Test

30. List at least three things you learned about God in Judges 2.

Several characteristics about God can be found in Judges 2.

ESSAY:
Choose one of the following topics, briefly summarize it, and then discuss how it applies to your life:

    1. Compare and contrast *complete* obedience and *partial* obedience
    2. The historical setting of the book of Judges
    3. Joshua's final admonishment and Israel's response

Students will identify the main points of each of these topics and then discuss how they apply to their lives.

Unit one - Teacher's Guide

Unit two - Teacher's Guide

Judges

Dying To Be Free

UNIT OBJECTIVES:

Students will observe the cycle of sin in Judges 3. They will learn God's purpose for leaving some of the land's inhabitants to test Israel. They will begin their observations by examining the judges Othniel, Ehud, and Shamgar. Students will consider how believers can get caught in cycles of sin and cry out to their Deliverer. The inductive Bible study skills incorporated in this unit will enhance students' ability to recognize and mark key words, make and analyze lists, and extract relevant applications from Scripture.

Remember it is important that you complete the assignments before reading these teacher notes. Your journey to understand God's Word will inspire and encourage your students in their journeys. Students can't follow you somewhere you've never been. Lead your students from the overflow of what God is doing in your life.

You may want students to complete some assignments in small groups when time is limited – particularly cross-reference assignments. However, we do not recommend group work for observation (reading and marking words – unless you're doing this with the whole class) or application questions, since both are individual exercises.

Introduction/Prayer

Students should begin this unit by writing a prayer in the space provided. Ask students to consider how they've experienced cycles of sin and defeat. Encourage them to confess sins and ask God for freedom. Tell them it is God's will to teach them deliverance and victory over sin from His Word.

UNIT TWO

U-2, Chapter 3

Dying to be Free

"Oh, no! I did it again! I swore I'd never fall into this sin again... but I did. Next time, next time... I'll be strong enough to say no."

Have you ever had this conversation with yourself? Did you promise God you would change if He saved you from the consequences one more time? Have you prayed, cried, and determined that this would be the last time you gave into temptation? Then a day, week, or month later you found yourself caught up in the same downward spiral of sin, more deeply **entrenched** than you were before.

Is this what life is all about – one defeat after another, never able to overcome the sin that so easily entangles you?

No! As a believer in Jesus Christ, you have a choice! When you experience this seemingly endless cycle of defeat you can choose to live according to the truth of God's Word. You have the power at work within you to walk in victory. The cycle can be broken – if you will learn war! War – God's way.

> "If you continue in My word, then you are truly disciples of Mine; and you will know the truth, and the truth will make you free...So if the Son makes you free, you will be free indeed."
> – John 8:31-32, 36

Introduction/Prayer
ONE ON ONE:

As you begin this unit, offer up your heart to the Lord by writing a prayer in the space below. Consider areas in your life in which you've experienced this cycle of sin and defeat. Express to God your desire for freedom by confessing your sin.

Then, ask God to teach you from the scriptures in these lessons how He worked in the lives of His people, how He delivered them from sin, and how He gave them strength to walk in victory despite **opposition**. Remember to ask Him to show you how to apply these truths to your life.

Student Page 35

Unit Two - Teacher's Guide

Judges

UNIT TWO - TEACHER'S GUIDE

Judges

LESSON ONE:

 Judges 3 Observation Worksheets, colored pencils, key word bookmark

OBJECTIVES:

Students will observe Judges 3 marking key words and phrases from their bookmarks. They will better comprehend Israel's sin as they examine it in this chapter.

Lesson 1/Assignment 1 - Observation
Students will observe Judges 3 by marking the key words from their bookmarks.

 Ask students which component of inductive Bible study this assignment incorporates. Periodic reminders ensure that they are understanding the method.

Lesson 1/Assignment 2 - Observation/Interpretation
Students will list what they learn from marking the key repeated phrase *the sons of Israel did what was evil in the sight of the Lord*.

 Remind students that making a list includes writing answers to the 5W and H questions concerning the word or phrase they are examining.

Students should recognize the following:
- *3:7 – forgot the Lord and served the Baals and the Asheroth*
- *3:12 – again did evil; the Lord strengthened Eglon against them*

Lesson 1/Assignment 3 - Observation/Interpretation
Students should read and mark the following verses as references to idolatry: 3:6, 7, and 19.

LESSON ONE

Lesson 1/Assignment 1
U-2, Lesson 1, Chapter 3

You studied Judges 1 and 2 and saw where disobedience leads; now you'll focus on Judges 3 and discover the Source of freedom.

1. Observe Judges 3, marking key words from the bookmark you began in Unit 1. Also watch for key phrases and write them below.

Lesson 1/Assignment 2
2. Now re-read Judges 3 and note where you marked the phrase *the sons of Israel did what was evil in the sight of the Lord*. When you see this phrase, write down what they did in the space below.

Listing – Once you identify and mark a key word or phrase, listing what the text says about them will help you remember important facts. Also, by evaluating the list (reading and thinking about it) you will understand more about the passage or book you are studying. Don't just write down facts – you will miss the excitement of interpreting the text for yourself!!

Lesson 1/Assignment 3
3. If you see any references to idolatry, write the word "idolatry" in the margin of your Observation Worksheet next to the verse that mentions it just as you did in chapters 1 and 2.

Student Page 37

© 2008 Precept Ministries International

Unit Two - Teacher's Guide

UNIT TWO - TEACHER'S GUIDE

Judges

LESSON TWO:

 Judges 2 and 3 Observation Worksheets, colored pencils, key word bookmark, Bible

OBJECTIVES:

In this lesson, students will examine Judges 3 in light of chapter two (context). They will learn more about the significance of God's testing Israel and true obedience. They will also determine if they respond to God sincerely.

Lesson 2/Assignment 1 – Observation/Interpretation
This reading assignment will help students identify the context of chapter 3 in light of the overview of the book of Judges presented in chapter 2. Students should have already marked *nations* and *test* in Unit 1 and Unit 2, Lesson 1. If not, they should do so now.

Lesson 2/Assignment 2 – Observation/Interpretation
 This is a listing assignment. Remind students to record what they learn from marking the key word *nations* by looking for answers to the 5W and H questions.

Students should recognize the following:
- *2:21 – God will no longer drive out the nations Joshua left because Israel transgressed His covenant*
- *2:23 – God allowed these nations to remain; He did not give them into Joshua's hand*
- *3:1 – Nations left to test Israel and teach war to those who hadn't experienced it*
- *3:2 – Nations left were:*
  - *five Lords of the Philistines*
  - *all the Canaanites and Sidonians and Hivites who lived in Mount Lebanon from Mount Baal-hermon as far as Lobohamath*

LESSON TWO

Lesson 2/Assignment 1
U-2, Lesson 2, Chapter 3

1. In order to fully understand any portion of Scripture, you must understand the context. Begin today by looking at Judges 2 and 3 together. Read Judges 2:8 through Judges 3.

   Be sure to mark the key words, *nations* and *test* as you did in Unit 1, Lesson 4.

   The Hebrew word nasah means, "to test"; it is translated "prove, test, try." Test is used four places in Judges: 2:22; 3:1, 4; 6:39.

Lesson 2/Assignment 2

2. Look at each place you marked *nations* and see if it answers any of the 5Ws and an H: who, what, when, where, why, and how. List below the information the text gives you with respect to the *nations*: who they are, what their purpose is, where they are, why they are there, etc.

Lesson 2/Assignment 3

3. What do you learn about the sons of Israel in these two chapters? How does the text describe them?

Student Page 39

© 2008 Precept Ministries International

UNIT TWO - TEACHER'S GUIDE

Judges

- *3:4 – They would test Israel to find out if they would obey the commandments the Lord gave through Moses*

Lesson 2/Assignment 3 – Interpretation/Application
Students will describe the sons of Israel based on what they observed in Judges 2 and 3.

Descriptions should include some of the following: disobedient, idolatrous, cried out to God when they suffered consequences, etc.

Lesson 2/Assignment 4 – Interpretation/Application
This assignment will help students interpret and understand the meaning of the text. The questions will guide them to understand God testing Israel and themselves, and their responses to those tests.

a. Students should see that God left the nations to test Israel's obedience. They may be able to identify tests like God's commands to drive out and utterly destroy inhabitants, not intermarry with them, and not serve their gods (this was seen in Joshua 23 in Unit 1 and in the Joshua study if they completed it before beginning this course).

b. Students should recognize from their observations of Judges 2 and 3 that Israel did not pass the test – they did not utterly destroy the inhabitants, they did intermarry with them, they did not know the Lord or the work He had done for Israel, and they rejected Him to serve the gods of the inhabitants.

c. Students should prayerfully consider the next four questions before attempting to answer them. Remind them that these thought-provoking questions may take time to answer as they examine their hearts and minds, sincerely searching for how these truths apply to their lives. Students should learn that God tests believers today the way He tested the sons of Israel. First Corinthians 10:6-14 will help them see this.

Lesson 2/Assignment 4
4. With respect to the testing of Israel:

   a. What was the test?

   b. How did the children of Israel respond to the test? Explain why you answer as you do.

   c. How does this relate to today? Are Christians tested? How? Read the following cross-reference to help you answer these questions.

U-2, Lesson 2, Chapter 3

Baal, which means "lord, owner, possessor or husband," was the Canaanite god of fertility. Baal was part of several compound names for locations where Canaanite deities were worshiped, such as Baal-peor.

Ashtoreth (or Ashtaroth) was the Canaanite goddess of fertility, love, and war. According to Greek **mythology**, she was the wife of Baal.

Student Page 40

84 © 2008 Precept Ministries International

UNIT TWO - TEACHER'S GUIDE

Judges

Students should recognize that believers today are tested just as Israel was. They can choose to serve God or participate in idolatry. Various temptations in the world test believers' faithfulness to God.

d. According to Judges 3 God left the nations to test Israel and teach them war. God tests believers today to see if they will obey Him and endure with a mature faith (James 1:2-4).

e. Students will examine their temptations and see if they are obeying God. You may want to help them identify areas of temptation and discuss some of God's commands to believers. Examples include: obedience to parents vs. peer pressure, words of encouragement vs. gossip, purity vs. immorality, etc.

f. Students will examine temptation in their lives to determine if they are obeying God or their fleshly desires. They will need to think about why.

Lesson 2/Assignment 5 – Observation/Interpretation
Students should recognize that the cycle of sin and deliverance in Judges 2:11-19 is clearly seen in the stories of Othniel and Ehud. They may record it like this:

Othniel – People intermarry with the inhabitants and serve their gods; do evil in the sight of the Lord; serve Baals and Asheroth; God's anger kindled; sells into the hand of Cushan-rishathaim king of Mesopotamia for eight years; Israel cries out to the Lord; the Lord raises up a deliverer, Othniel; Othniel delivers them from the king of Mesopotamia; land has rest for 40 years; Othniel dies; Israel again does evil in the sight of the Lord.

Ehud – Israel does evil in sight of the Lord; Lord strengthens Eglon the king of Moab against Israel 18 years; Israel cries out to the Lord; Lord raises up a deliverer, Ehud; Ehud kills Eglon and subdues Moab for 80 years of rest.

U-2, Lesson 2, Chapter 3

d. Based on what you studied in Judges 2 and 3, what was the purpose of these tests? Look at this cross-reference to help you answer this question.

JAMES 1:2-4

e. Are you in a place of testing? How *should* you be responding?

f. Are you? Why or why not?

Lesson 2/Assignment 5
5. As you read through Judges 3, do you see any parallels with Judges 2:11-19? If so, record them below.

UNIT TWO - TEACHER'S GUIDE

Judges

Lesson 2/Assignment 6 - Observation/Interpretation
Students will note the main points of the cycle as follows: the sons of Israel did evil in the Lord's sight; the Lord sells them into the hands of their enemies; the sons of Israel cry out to the Lord; the Lord raises up a deliverer. A circular diagram is appropriate.

Lesson 2/Assignment 7 - Interpretation/Application
a. Students should learn that knowing God's commandments alone is not enough; truly hearing God's commands is to obey them.

b. In this application question, students should examine their lives to determine if they have "heard" God's commands, but aren't obeying them.

Lesson 2/Assignment 6   U-2, Lesson 2, Chapter 3
6. In the introduction to this unit you read about the "cycle of sin." How is this cycle seen in the events of Judges 3? Write out an answer below or present it in the form of a visual diagram.

Lesson 2/Assignment 7
7. In Judges 3:4, the root meaning of the Hebrew word translated "obey" is "hear."

   a. How does this relate to the key phrase *not listening to the Lord*? What is the connection between hearing and obeying?

   b. Is there any lesson in this for you? Are you merely hearing God's commands or are you also obeying?

> God tested Israel. He left nations in the land after Joshua's death to see if His people would keep His way and walk in it as their fathers had done. If you gave them a grade on this test, what would it be? (If you're thinking an "F", you would be correct!!) All they had to do was listen and obey, but instead they chose to go their own way. Instead of driving the inhabitants out, they became just like them.
>
> What about you? Will you learn from their poor choices – engage in battle victoriously or fall into disobedience and defeat? You can pass the test by choosing to take what you have heard from God's Word and obey. You aren't the only one who needs to know God's purpose in testing believers. Share His formula for success with others!

Student Page 42
© 2008 Precept Ministries International

UNIT TWO - TEACHER'S GUIDE

Judges

DISCUSSION GUIDE LESSON ONE AND TWO:

Begin your discussion by asking students what they remember from the first lesson about the setting of Judges.

Events in Judges follow Joshua's conquering Canaan. But according to Judges 1, Israel's tribes did not continue to drive enemies out of the land. Some allowed Canaanites to remain. Israel disobeyed the Lord by not driving out all their enemies living in Canaan.

Judges 2 says Israel abandoned the Lord after Joshua and the elders died. They turned to the gods of the Canaanites, whom they had left in the land. This generation did not listen to the Lord; nor did subsequent generations.

The Lord left nations in Canaan to test Israel. According to Judges 2-3, Israel did not pass this test; they failed miserably.

During this time (before kings in Israel), every man did what was right in his own eyes. Between Joshua and the first king, Saul, no strong leaders led the nation. The Lord was to be their king, but they did not follow His clearly laid out commands, laws, statutes, and ordinances.

THE STRUCTURE OR PATTERN OF JUDGES

    Judges 1–2   Setting, Israel did evil . . . .
    Judges 3–16   The Judges
    Judges 17–21   Dan and Benjamin, every man did what was right in his own eyes
     Events in these chapters fit chronologically at the beginning of Judges.

THE CYCLE
Ask your class what they learned from Judges 2:11-19 and Judges 3.
Let them reason together about Israel's downward spiral.

　　　Israel did evil, forsook the Lord, served other gods.

　　　The anger of the Lord burned against them – He gave Israel to their enemies.

　　　When enemies distressed them, Israel cried to the Lord.

　　　He raised up a judge to deliver them.

　　　After the judge died Israel did evil and the cycle started over.

　　　Israel lived this way for more than 300 years.

UNIT TWO - TEACHER'S GUIDE

Judges

JUDGES 3

Let students discuss the nations left to test Israel. Refer to the map for their locations relative to the land the Lord gave Israel.

> Judges 2:21-3:4 says the Lord left some of the nations after Joshua to test the next generations of Israel to see if they would obey Him and to teach them war.
>
> The nations left were the:
> - five lords of the Philistines
> - Canaanites
> - Sidonians
> - Hivites who lived in Mount Lebanon.

Ask students to discuss whether the Lord tests His people today. If so, what should their response be?

Discuss results of these nations being present in the land (verses 4-6).

> Israel lived among the Canaanites, etc.
>
> Israel took Canaanite daughters as wives for their sons.
>
> Israel gave their daughters to the sons of the nations.
>
> Israel served the gods of the Canaanites.

Save discussion of specific judges from this chapter for Lessons 5 and 6.

UNIT TWO - TEACHER'S GUIDE

Judges

LESSON THREE:

 Observation Worksheets Judges 2, Bible

OBJECTIVES:

In this lesson, students will examine the cycle of sin in Judges 2 more closely. They will look at cross-references to identify the cycle of sin a believer can become entangled in and the Deliverer God sent to free them.

Note: Some of the passages may be difficult for students to understand and apply. Discuss these assignments as they complete them. Then rediscuss them as a whole in the discussion at the end of Lesson 4.

Lesson 3/Assignment 1 – Observation/Interpretation
Students should recognize that Israel should have abandoned its practices and stubborn ways to end this cycle of sin.

Lesson 3/Assignment 2 – Interpretation/Application
Students will look at other scriptures to determine how a believer can be set free from the cycle of sin.

a. According to Matthew 1:21, Jesus will save His people from their sins.

b. According to John 8:34-36, the Son sets people free from slavery to sin.

LESSON THREE

Lesson 3/Assignment 1
U-2, Lesson 3, Chapter 3

Yesterday you looked at "the cycle of sin and deliverance" described in Judges 2:11-19. Verse 19 shows you the pattern was **cyclical** – a fact the rest of the book clearly demonstrates.

1. What in verse 19 shows you the cycle could be broken – that it didn't have to continue in that pattern?

Lesson 3/Assignment 2

2. In the introduction to this unit, you were asked if you have struggled to gain victory over a **besetting** sin – a wrong and sinful action that causes continued anguish, grief, and shame without hope of victory. Must Christians, genuine children of God, live in a state of defeat? Or is there hope for victory – discovering the "enemy" and putting it to death? Are there sins you will never conquer no matter how hard you try?

Answer these questions by looking at the following scriptures and discover what God says. As you look up each verse or passage, record the truth that tells you whether or not you can overcome sin.

> *Remember, cross references aid in interpretation by providing additional context and insight on a particular subject. When you look at these passages, consider how they increase your understanding of Judges 3.*

a. What will Jesus do according to the words of this angelic messenger?

MATTHEW 1:21

Student Page 43

UNIT TWO - TEACHER'S GUIDE

Judges

c. According to Romans 6:1-7:

   1) True believers do not continue in sin

   2) Believers died to sin, body of sin is done away with, no longer slaves to sin

   3) Walk in newness of life

   4) Freed from sin because they have died to it.

U-2, Lesson 3, Chapter 3

b. According to this cross reference in John, who will be set free from slavery to sin?

JOHN 8:34-36

c. Now, read this passage in Romans and give special attention to verse 6. The "old self" (man, KJV) is all you were in Adam before you became a believer. The old self is the flesh. The "body of sin" is a reference to your body (flesh) as an instrument of sin.

ROMANS 6:1-7

   1) According to these verses, should a believer continue in sin?

   2) What have those in Christ died to?

   3) What will they now walk in?

   4) What are they free from and how?

Unit two - Teacher's Guide

Judges

d. In Romans 6:8-11, Paul tells believers to consider themselves dead to sin because Jesus died to sin once for all and they died with Him.

e. According to Romans 6:12-14, the child of God obeys the command to be dead to sin by not letting sin reign in his mortal body.

1) The believer's responsibility is not presenting his body to sin as an instrument of unrighteousness, but as an instrument of righteousness.

2) Students should recognize that they can present their body to unrighteousness by purposefully placing themselves in a position to sin – e.g., going to a party where they will be tempted to participate in activities they shouldn't, exposing themselves to media that cause them to think about things God says are unrighteous. Presenting ourselves to God means placing ourselves in situations and filling our minds with things that bring honor to God.

f. According to verse 14 sin shall not be master over you so there is no sin which a believer will not overcome through the power of the risen Christ.

U-2, Lesson 3, Chapter 3

d. According to this passage, what are you to consider yourself dead to? Why and how?

ROMANS 6:8-11

e. Now, according to this passage in Romans, how can you the child of God obey the command to be dead to sin and alive in Christ?

ROMANS 6:12-14

1) What is your responsibility?

2) How do you "present the members of your body" to sin or to God?

f. Based on your observations of these verses, is there any sin you shouldn't be able to overcome or master?

Student Page 45

UNIT TWO - TEACHER'S GUIDE

g. According to Romans 6:16-18:

1) To be free from sin that would ensnare, believers present themselves as slaves to obedience resulting in righteousness.

2) Obedience is described as "from the heart to that form of teaching to which you were committed."

Lesson 3/Assignment 3 - Application
Students should recognize that they have been freed from living in habitual sin if they have truly believed in the Son; second, the power of the risen Christ reigns in their bodies; and third, continuously offering themselves to God is obedience from the heart.

U-2, Lesson 3, Chapter 3

g. Finally, according to the passage in Romans, what is the way to be set free from sins that ensnare us? How is true obedience described in these verses?

Lesson 3/Assignment 3
3. To make sure you completely understand, write out how one can be freed from living in habitual sin. Is it simply a matter of trying harder to resist temptation?

These are revolutionary truths. Paul did not tell the church at Rome they needed to develop more willpower to overcome slavery to sin. It isn't about trying harder. Too many believers are deceived and defeated by this lie. If you are depending on yourself, then you will always fail. The answer is that you must completely die to sin, to yourself.

If you are constantly in the cycle of sin, is it possible you have never really died with Christ? If you aren't experiencing the victory over sin that both Christ and Paul talked about, could it be that you have never really been set free? Are you still **enslaved**?

Student Page 46
© 2008 Precept Ministries International

UNIT TWO - TEACHER'S GUIDE

Judges

LESSON FOUR:

 Bible

OBJECTIVES:

In this lesson, students will focus on interpreting and applying life-changing truths gained from fully understanding the cycle of sin presented in Judges 2 and in the following chapters.

Note: Some of the passages may be difficult for students to understand and apply. Discuss these assignments as they complete them. Then rediscuss them as a whole in the discussion at the end of this lesson.

Lesson 4/Assignment 1 - Interpretation
According to Exodus 34:11-16, the children of Israel were told to not make covenants with the Canaanites, Hittites, Perizzites, Hivites and Jebusites. They were told to tear down altars, smash sacred pillars and cut down Asherim because God is a jealous God. If they refused, they would play the harlot with their gods and intermarry with their daughters.

a. According to Judges 2 and 3, Israel did everything it was told not to do – the people intermarried and began to serve their gods.

b. According to these passages, God is a jealous God. His name is Jealous.

Lesson 4/Assignment 2 –
Interpretation/Application
a. Hebrews 12:1-4 commands believers to lay aside every encumbrance and the sins that so easily entangle them.

b. Believers should fix their eyes on

LESSON FOUR

Lesson 4/Assignment 1 U-2, Lesson 4, Chapter 3
1. Why were the children of Israel caught in the cycle of sin in the days of Judges? What instructions and warnings did God give the children of Israel in Exodus?

EXODUS 34:11-16

a. From what you learned in Judges, were they obeyed?

b. What do you learn about God from this passage?

Lesson 4/Assignment 2
2. There's a victory that overcomes the world according to 1 John 5:4-5. Look up the following verse and then answer the related questions:

HEBREWS 12:1-4

a. What are you to lay aside?

> For whatever is born of God overcomes the world; and this is the victory that has overcome the world—our faith.
>
> Who is the one who overcomes the world, but he who believes that Jesus is the Son of God?
>
> - 1 John 5:4-5

Student Page 47

Unit two - Teacher's Guide

Judges

Jesus because He is the author and perfecter of faith and the prime example of someone who ran the race set before Him successfully.

c. Jesus endured the cross to accquire the joy set before Him.

d. Students should recognize that if Jesus was able to endure the cross then they have a role model to help them endure the race set before them. No obstacle, trial, testing, or temptation is too great.

U-2, Lesson 4, Chapter 3

b. What will help you run the race set before you? Why?

c. What did Jesus endure in order to succeed?

d. Even if the race is difficult, how do you know it's possible to finish well?

> The nations were left there to test Israel; all they had to do was listen to God, do what He said, obey Him, and then they would have triumphed over the enemy. But they did not "hear" (obey). In the days of Joshua they had victory through faith and consequently they did great works for God. They were strong and courageous and knew how to wage war God's way. If you are not experiencing victory, you need to learn war. There's no compromise with the enemy – you're called to kill the body of sin. Don't allow the enemy to remain. Yield the members of your body to the Lord as instruments of righteousness. Refuse to compromise, even if you think you will die! You will find life in putting sin to death.

Unit two - Teacher's Guide

Judges

World View Project – Death to Sin, Life for You

This project provides students with an opportunity to solidify their understanding of the cycle of sin and practically apply what they learned about being set free from it. The discussion you had on the previous lessons will help them complete this project.

World View Project U-2, Lesson 4, Chapter 3

DEATH TO SIN, LIFE IN CHRIST - PROJECT

For this assignment you will need the following:

Paper
Crayons and markers
Bible
Poster-board or card-board box
Pictures
Bible dictionary

a.
Read Colossians 3:1-10 in your Bible. If you do not know the definitions for some of the sins listed, look them up in a Bible dictionary or ask your teacher for help.

First, choose one of the sins listed that you know is still a struggle for you to overcome. On a scratch sheet of paper, think of things you participate in (perhaps by what you watch on television, listen to on the radio, look at on the internet, read in books or magazines, think or talk about) that entice you to fall into the sin you chose. Write them down.

Then ask God to help you walk in the freedom Christ bought for you with His death. Ask God to help you consider the members of your body as dead to that sin and to stop participating in things that tempt you to sin in this area again.

If you're not sure you're a believer, take this opportunity to decide if you're ready to be set free from sin. Read Romans 10:9-11 and talk with your teacher, parent, or leader about making today the day you ask the Son to set you free!

Next, using a card-board box or poster-board cut out a tombstone like this ▮, write on it the sin you are asking God to put to death. Also list on it the activities that tempt you in this area. Use whatever materials you want to make the tombstone look as realistic as possible.

Finally, share your conclusions with someone else. Ask this person to pray for you and help hold you accountable to obey what God has shown you through His Word and prayer. Keep this tombstone somewhere you can see it everyday to remind you that you are dead to sin and free in Christ.

Student Page 49

//
Unit Two - Teacher's Guide

Judges

UNIT TWO - TEACHER'S GUIDE

Judges

DISCUSSION GUIDE LESSON THREE AND FOUR:

Begin your discussion reviewing the cycle of sin students identified in Lessons 1 and 2.

Question your class regarding what they learned from Judges 2:11-19 and Judges 3. Let them reason together about Israel's downward spiral.

> Israel did evil, forsook the Lord, served other gods.
>
> The anger of the Lord burned against them – He gave Israel to their enemies.
>
> When their enemies distressed them, Israel cried to the Lord.
>
> He raised up a judge to deliver them.
>
> After the judge died Israel did evil, and the cycle started over.
>
> Israel lived this way for more than 300 years.

Your class can discuss the New Testament cross-references at this point. Help them understand that there Christians cannot live in cycles of sin; they have been set free from sin. Even though some teach that Christians can live like Israel did in Judges, that is not what the New Testament teaches.

> Matthew 1:21 and John 8:34-36 teach that Jesus Christ sets free from slavery to sin, making unbelievers believe He is Lord and Savior. He saves from sin's bondage not just its penalty (death).
>
> Romans 6 says believers *died* to sin; so they cannot still *live* in it. Believers are raised to walk in newness of life. When believers sin, it is a choice, not a result of slavery, bondage, or being unable to prevent it. The flesh (old man) still chooses sin, but the spirit (new man) is free from slavery (Romans 7:25; 2 Corinthians 4:16).
>
> Accordingly, sin is not master over Christians. Before Jesus freed them, believers were slaves to sin; when He greed them, He enslaved them to righteousness.
>
> First John 5 says faith, that Jesus Christ is the Son of God, overcomes the world. The faith believers have is the victory that overcomes the things of the world. Keeping the Lord's commandments is not burdensome; it is our love to Him.
>
> This was not true for Israel in the Old Testament because they were under the old covenant of the Law, not part of the new covenant of grace, salvation.

UNIT TWO - TEACHER'S GUIDE

Judges

Hebrews 12 encourages believers to run with endurance the race set before them. Don't become entangled in sin.

If Israel had done what the Lord commanded in Exodus 34, not making covenants with foreign peoples in the land, they would not have become entangled with the sin around them. Their enemies became snares in their midst.

Ask your class how this happened.

When Israel grew strong, they did not drive enemies out of the land; instead they became forced labor.

The Lord knew the Canaanites would lead Israel astray to their gods – one of the reasons He commanded Israel to completely destroy them. He also intended to use Israel as His arm to judge the wickedness of Canaan and the Amorites.

Even though Joshua completely conquered the major cities, the tribes of Israel did not completely drive the remaining nations out.

These peoples led the Lord's holy nation astray.

Ask your students to share what they learned from these lessons.

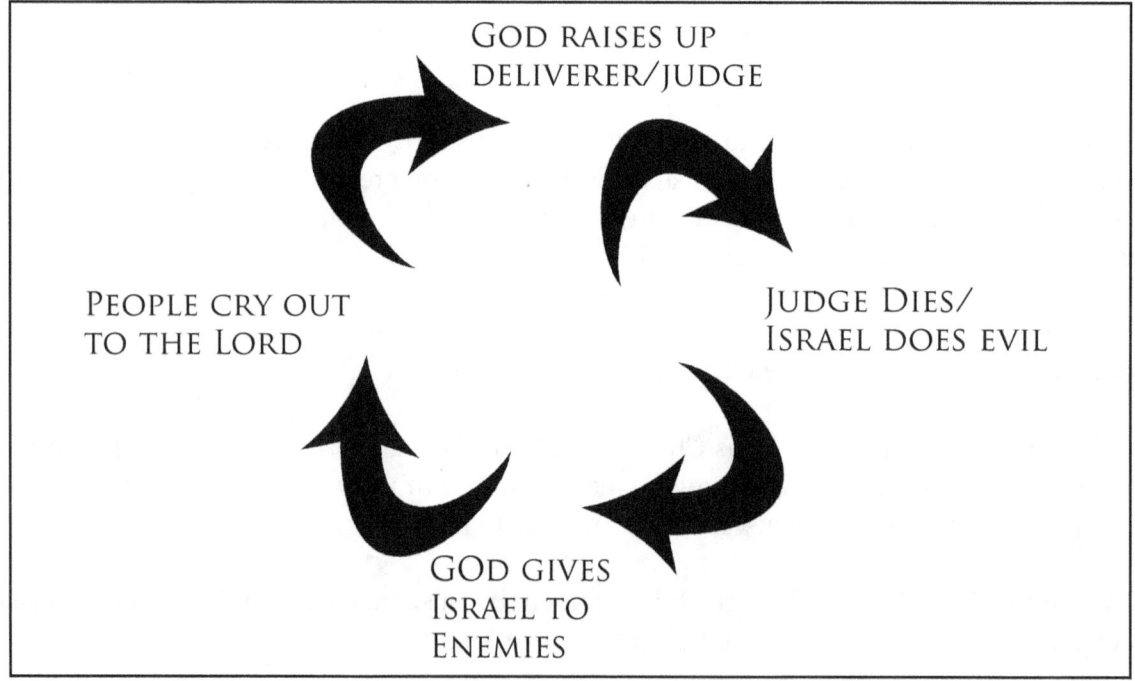

UNIT TWO - TEACHER'S GUIDE

Judges

LESSON FIVE:

 Judges 1 and 3 Observation Worksheets, "The Judges of Israel" chart from the Appendix

OBJECTIVES:

In this lesson, students will observe the text and record what they learn about Othniel, the first judge mentioned in the book of Judges.

Lesson 5/Assignment 1 - Observation
Students will need to re-read Judges 1 and 3 to familiarize themselves with Othniel.

 Remind your students that even though they have already read these chapters, reading them again will help them complete the assignments in this lesson and help them retain the information contained in these chapters.

Lesson 5/Assignment 2 - Observation
Students will record what they learn about Othniel from Judges 1 and 3 on "The Judges of Israel" chart located in the Appendix. You'll find a blank copy of the chart in the Teacher's Helps. You may want to make a transparency and fill in the information with your students for the first few judges they study. You'll find a completed chart at the end of the Teacher's Guide.

LESSON FIVE

Lesson 5/Assignment 1
U-2, Lesson 5, Chapter 3

The book of Judges gives an account of a number of men and one woman whom God raised up to deliver His people. Each judge differs from the others. Although God tells more about some than others, don't miss one bit of information He has preserved in respect to who they were and how He used them. From this point on until chapter 17 look at the judges and the times and situations they lived in.

1. Othniel is the first judge mentioned in Judges 3, but he is mentioned in Judges 1 as well as in Joshua 15 (which almost parallels what is written in Judges). Therefore, read Judges 1 and 3 to observe all the information on this judge and the times he served God.

Lesson 5/Assignment 2
2. Summarize all you learn about him on the chart "The Judges of Israel" which you'll find in the Appendix of your workbook. Be sure to ask the 5Ws and H!

While the scriptures don't give much description of Othniel, it's evident that his devotion to the Lord led to freedom for an entire nation from the bondage of sin and from its oppressors. Why do you think God raised up Othniel? Who may have been a direct influence on him? Remember, he was Caleb's younger brother – Caleb one of only two men in the entire nation to stand for God's truth and believe His promise of land. Think of how God used one generation to impact another. What legacies has God given you to succeed and are you faithfully carrying on that **legacy**?

Student Page 51

Unit two - Teacher's Guide

UNIT TWO - TEACHER'S GUIDE

Judges

LESSON SIX:

 Judges 3 and 5 Observation Worksheets, Bible, "At A Glance" chart from the Appendix

OBJECTIVES:

Students will record their observations on Ehud and Shamgar, the second and third judges mentioned in Judges 3. They will also look at cross-references to better understand the times and relevance of these judges to their lives.

Lesson 6/Assignment 1 - Observation
Students will record what they learn about Ehud and Shamgar from Judges 3 on "The Judges of Israel" chart found in the Appendix.

Lesson 6/Assignment 2 - Interpretation/Application
Students will learn that Ehud was a "left-handed" man.

a. Students will learn from "The More You Know..." box on Ehud that this feature enabled him to rid Israel of its oppressor.

b. Help your students understand that God uses what some people call a "weakness" or "abnormality" to accomplish His will.

LESSON SIX

Lesson 6/Assignment 1 *U-2, Lesson 6, Chapter 3*

1. Today you'll study the next two judges mentioned in this third chapter: Ehud and Shamgar. Record what you learn on the chart "The Judges of Israel."

Lesson 6/Assignment 2
2. What was unique about Ehud?

   a. Was this "uniqueness" important in his story? Read "The More You Know..." box below for additional insight.

   b. Think about this...some people falsely label a "unique" trait as a weakness or flaw, but Ehud's "uniqueness" helped him carry out God's plan. What does that teach you about God's design and plan for you? Does He ever make mistakes?

Ehud's left-handed allowed him to carry out his plan to assassinate Eglon. The guards would have noticed that he had no dagger on his left hip (the usual place); since he was left-handed, he had it at his right side where it could be easily concealed.

THE MORE YOU KNOW...

Unit two - Teacher's Guide

Lesson 6/Assignment 3 - Interpretation
a. According to Judges 5:6-11 in the days of Shamgar the highways were deserted, people were afraid to travel, and there was no peasantry. (Apparently field workers were so afraid they didn't risk leaving the walled city to tend fields and herds.)

b. Students can record that although there is little information recorded about Shamgar, his killing 600 Philistines single-handedly is impressive.

Lesson 6/Assignment 4 - Interpretation/Application
Students will describe Ehud and Shamgar. They may include things like:
- *Courageous*
- *Bold*
- *Willing to rise up when no one else was*
- *Served the Lord's purposes*
- *God used them in their low positions (Ehud was a tribute carrier, Shamgar was probably a herdsman)*

Lesson 6/Assignment 5 - Interpretation/Application
Students should learn that God doesn't need men with long lists of accomplishments; He uses men who are willing to stand up and fight for Him and His people.

Lesson 6/Assignment 3   U-2, Lesson 6, Chapter 3
3. There is only one short verse on Shamgar, but he is mentioned again in Deborah's song in Judges 5.

   a. Read Judges 5:6-11 for additional understanding of Shamgar's times. Record what you learn below.

   b. When you think of Shamgar, what will you remember him for?

Lesson 6/Assignment 4
4. How would you describe Shamgar and Ehud to others?

Lesson 6/Assignment 5
5. What point does God want you to grasp as you look at these men, and Othniel?

> The ox goad is mentioned only in Judges 3:31, the weapon Shamgar used to kill 600 Philistines. Used by a ploughman, this weapon is apparently more fitted for the hand of the soldier than for the peaceful husbandman. It often measured up to 10 feet in length. One end had an iron spear, the other, a piece of the same metal flattened. One can well understand how a warrior might use such a weapon effectively in the battlefield.
>
> THE MORE YOU KNOW...

Unit two - Teacher's Guide

Lesson 6/Assignment 6 - Interpretation/Application
a. According to 1 Corinthians 1:26-2:1-5, God chooses weak, foolish and base things of the world. Because God is the same yesterday, today and forever, He did the same during the times of the judges.

b. Students should learn that God does not need an impressive list of credentials to be used by God to accomplish great things.

Lesson 6/Assignment 7 - Application
Students will think about and record how their knowledge of the judges from chapter 3 can help them and others.

Lesson 6/Assignment 8 - Observation/Interpretation
Students will list what they learn about God from these chapters. Their lists may include:
- *His anger is kindled by disobedience.*
- *He is faithful to His Word both of promise <u>and judgment</u>.*
- *He is compassionate.*
- *He does not tolerate idolatry.*
- *He uses ordinary people to accomplish His will.*

Lesson 6/Assignment 6   U-2, Lesson 6, Chapter 3
6. Read the following verses and then answer the questions below:

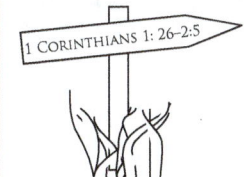

   a. If God is the same yesterday, today, and forever, what does this cross-reference tell you about the men God raised up in Judges?

   b. What does this mean to you when it comes to serving the Lord?

Lesson 6/Assignment 7
7. Are there any life application lessons in the three brief accounts of these judges for us? List them below.

Lesson 6/Assignment 8
8. What do you learn about God from Judges 2 and 3? What kind of a God do you see in these chapters?

UNIT TWO - TEACHER'S GUIDE

Judges

Lesson 6/Assignment 9 - Interpretation

Students will identify the main point of Judges 3 and write a chapter theme on the "At A Glance" chart in the Appendix. A possible theme for this chapter is:

Judges 3 – Othniel, Ehud, and Shamgar

Unit two - Teacher's Guide

Judges

DISCUSSION GUIDE LESSONS FIVE AND SIX:

Review the information concerning the judges from Judges 2 and then ask your students to discuss the first judge mentioned.

JUDGES 3
Verses 7-11 – Othniel

    Ask your students what they learned about Israel's first enemy and judge mentioned in Judges.

    Cushan-rishathaim, king of Mesopotamia, made Israel serve him for eight years.

    Show Mesopotamia on a map to help students understand that this enemy was not part of the land of Canaan.

    Israel cried to the Lord and He raised up a deliverer for them.

    Ask your group what this says about God's character.

    Discuss the first judge.

    Othniel was Caleb's nephew and son-in-law.

Give students opportunities to share what they remember from Joshua, if they studied it previously, and what they learned from Unit 1 about Caleb. What was he like? What kind of man did he give his daughter to? How well did he know Othniel?

    Caleb was one of the two men who came out of Egypt, lived in the wilderness 40 years, and entered the Promised Land. He fully followed the Lord and was zealous to take the land.

    In order to marry Achsah, Caleb's daughter, Othniel had to conquer Kiriath-sepher, which was within Judah's land inheritance.

    Caleb then gave his daughter to Othniel.

    Verse 10 says that the Spirit of the Lord came upon Othniel.

    He delivered Israel from the king of Mesopotamia.

    The land of Israel then had rest 40 years.

    It seems from verse 11 that Othniel was alive for the 40 years, then died. Compare this with Judges 2:18 – the Lord was with the judge and delivered Israel all the days of the judge.

UNIT TWO - TEACHER'S GUIDE

Judges

So for eight years Israel suffered because of its evil ways; then the Lord sent a deliverer and the land rested for 40 years.

Verses 12-30 – Ehud
Discuss Israel's second enemy and judge.

Israel did evil again.

The Lord strengthened Eglon the king of Moab against Israel.
The Lord sold Israel to Moab.

Ammon and Amalek took part in defeating Israel.

Moab and Ammon are part of modern Jordan. They were the two sons of Lot by his two daughters, born after the destruction of Sodom and Gomorrah. Amalek was the grandson of Esau.

The Lord used the ungodly nations around Israel to correct them.
Stimulate discussion of how the Lord corrects His people today.

Moab, like Mesopotamia, was not part of the land of Canaan. Beyond the borders of Israel, these two were not among the nations God instructed the tribes to destroy. But they were equally ungodly – idol-worshiping nations.

Israel served Eglon of Moab for 18 years, 10 years longer than they had served Mesopotamia.

Israel cried to the Lord. Isn't it interesting how oppression got their attention? Does the same happen today?

The Lord raised up a left-handed deliverer, Ehud of the tribe of Benjamin.

Ask your class why they think the text mentions that he was left-handed. Ask them for the details of how he single-handedly delivered Israel from Eglon.

Ehud made a two-edged sword and hid it by binding it on his right thigh under his cloak. When he took the tribute from Israel to the king of Moab, he cleverly grabbed his sword with his left hand without suspicion. Most likely he presented the tribute with his right hand, as Eglon would expect.

He arranged a private meeting by saying he had a secret message for Eglon. His cleverness extends to how he escaped after killing the king.

UNIT TWO - TEACHER'S GUIDE

Judges

After returning from his mission, he led Israel in the defeat of Moab – 10,000 valiant and robust Moabite men.

Ask your class what verse 30 says about the land and if they think it relates to Ehud. Compare this with Judges 2:18.

> The land was undisturbed for 80 years.
>
> It's very possible Ehud lived that 80 years.

Verse 31 – Shamgar
Discuss the judge who came after Ehud. Some do not think Shamgar was a judge, but what does the text say?

> The enemy was the Philistines, the people who lived with Israel in Canaan. Israel should have completely destroyed them, but they didn't.
>
> The Bible gives little information about Shamgar, but if he killed 600 Philistines with only an oxgoad for a weapon, he was a mighty man. The text clearly says that he "saved" Israel. The Hebrew word for "saved" is also translated "delivered." As with the other judges, the Lord was with him and delivered Israel all the days he was alive.
>
> The only other mention of Shamgar is in Judges 5:6, which indicates that he may have been a contemporary of Deborah. He may have been busy with the Philistines on the western part of the land as she was judging elsewhere. We'll learn more about her in the next lesson.

Let your students discuss what kind of men Ehud and Shamgar were. Were they outstanding warriors like Othniel? Were they "regular guys"?

They were both valiant in what the Lord did through them.

> Even if they were just "regular guys," 1 Corinthians says the Lord uses such people to accomplish His purposes.
>
> Encourage your class to be "deliverers" by giving the gospel to people. The truth delivers from sin's slavery. Jesus is the Savior, the Deliverer of men.

It doesn't matter what kind of people we are; we should just do what the Lord raises us up to do. He is with us to take truth to the world and overcome "enemies."

Ask them to share what they learned from this unit.

Unit two - Teacher's Guide

Unit Two - Teacher's Guide

Judges

Enrichment Words:

Besetting – troubling or harassing enough to agitate mentally or spiritually.

Cyclical – moving in a cycle; a course or series of events or operations that recur regularly and usually lead back to the starting point.

Enslaved – reduced to slavery; to be governed, controlled or made submissive.

Ensnare – to take in or as if in a snare; trap.

Entrenched – solidly established.

Inerrancy – freedom from error.

Legacy – something transmitted by or received from an ancestor, a predecessor, or the past.

Mythology - an allegorical narrative dealing with the gods, demigods, and legendary heroes of a particular people; popular beliefs or assumptions that have grown up around someone or something.

Opposition – hostile or contrary action or condition by a person or body of persons.

Unit two - Teacher's Guide

Unit Two - Teacher's Guide

Judges
Unit Two Quiz

Name: _____ Date: _____

Unit Two - Quiz Key

Multiple choice – Circle one.

1. Who is the first judge mentioned in Judges?
   a. Ehud
   b. Othniel
   c. Joshua
   d. Shamgar

2. Who is the second judge mentioned in Judges?
   a. Ehud
   b. Othniel
   c. Joshua
   d. Shamgar

3. Who is the third judge mentioned in Judges?
   a. Ehud
   b. Othniel
   c. Joshua
   d. Shamgar

4. According to Judges 3, why did God leave some of the nations in Israel?
   a. To point out Joshua's disobedience
   b. To frustrate the sons of Israel and test their faith in God
   c. To test Israel and provide forced labor
   d. To test Israel and teach them war

5. What evil did Israel do in the sight of the Lord during Othniel's time?
   a. They killed Ehud and Shamgar.
   b. They forgot the Lord and served the Baals and Asheroth.
   c. They destroyed the tabernacle.
   d. They did not bury Joshua where the Lord commanded.

6. As a result of Israel's sin, whom did God sell them into the hands of during Othniel's time?
   a. Eglon, king of Moab
   b. Cusham-rishathaim, king of Mesopotamia
   c. The Philistines
   d. Pilate, king of the Romans

UNIT TWO - TEACHER'S GUIDE

Judges
Unit Two Quiz

7. Who did God strengthen against Israel during the time of Ehud?
   a. *Eglon, king of Moab*
   b. Cusham-rishathaim, king of Mesopotamia
   c. The Philistines
   d. Pilate, king of the Romans

8. Who did Shamgar save Israel from?
   a. Eglon, king of Moab
   b. Cusham-rishathaim, king of Mesopotamia
   c. *The Philistines*
   d. Pilate, king of the Romans

9. Which left-handed judge used his sword to kill the king of Moab?
   a. Othniel
   b. *Ehud*
   c. Shamgar
   d. Joshua

10. Which judge killed 600 Philistines with an ox goad?
    a. Othniel
    b. Ehud
    c. *Shamgar*
    d. Joshua

Unit Two - Teacher's Guide

Judges
Unit Two Test

Name: _____ Date: _____

Unit Two - Test Key

Matching - Choose one and write the letter in the blank.

___c___ 1. Freedom from error

___d___ 2. Reduced to slavery; governed, controlled or made submissive

___b___ 3. To take in or as if in a snare

___e___ 4. Hostile or contrary action or condition by a person or body of persons

___a___ 5. Troubling or harassing so as to agitate mentally or spiritually

a. Besetting
b. Ensnare
c. Inerrancy
d. Enslaved
e. Opposition

True or False

___F___ 6. A believer can never be free from the bondage of sin.

___T___ 7. Eglon was a very fat king!

___F___ 8. Israel was never delivered from the king of Mesopotamia.

___T___ 9. The children of Israel failed God's test.

___T___ 10. The five lords of the Philistines were some of the inhabitants left by God to test Israel.

Multiple Choice - Circle one.

11. Who is the first judge recorded in Judges?
    a. Ehud
    b. *Othniel*
    c. Joshua
    d. Shamgar

© 2008 Precept Ministries International

UNIT TWO - TEACHER'S GUIDE

Judges
Unit Two Test

12. Who is the second judge recorded in Judges?
    a. *Ehud*
    b. Othniel
    c. Joshua
    d. Shamgar

13. Who is the third judge recorded in Judges?
    a. Ehud
    b. Othniel
    c. Joshua
    d. *Shamgar*

14. According to Judges 3, why did God leave some of the nations in Israel?
    a. To point out Joshua's disobedience
    b. To frustrate the sons of Israel and test their faith in God.
    c. To test Israel and provide forced labor
    d. *To test Israel and teach them war*

15. What evil did Israel do in the sight of the Lord during Othniel's time?
    a. They killed Ehud and Shamgar.
    b. *They forgot the Lord and served the Baals and Asheroth.*
    c. They destroyed the tabernacle.
    d. They did not bury Joshua where the Lord commanded.

16. As a result of Israel's sin, whom did God sell them into the hands of during Othniel's time?
    a. Eglon, king of Moab
    b. *Cusham-rishathaim, king of Mesopotamia*
    c. The Philistines
    d. Pilate, king of the Romans

17. Who did God strengthen against Israel during the time of Ehud?
    a. *Eglon, king of Moab*
    b. Cusham-rishathaim, king of Mesopotamia
    c. The Philistines
    d. Pilate, king of the Romans

18. Who did Shamgar save Israel from?
    a. Eglon, king of Moab
    b. Cusham-rishathaim, king of Mesopotamia
    c. *The Philistines*
    d. Pilate, king of the Romans

UNIT TWO - TEACHER'S GUIDE

Judges

19. Which left-handed judge used his sword to kill the king of Moab?
    a. Othniel
    b. Ehud
    c. Shamgar
    d. Joshua

20. Which judge killed 600 Philistines with an ox goad?
    a. Othniel
    b. Ehud
    c. Shamgar
    d. Joshua

21. Which of the following is a possible theme for Judges 3?
    a. Be strong and courageous
    b. No king in Israel and every man did what was right in his own eyes
    c. Did not drive out the inhabitants of the land
    d. Othniel, Ehud, and Shamgar

22. What were the days of Shamgar like according to Judges 5?
    a. Israel was a land of wealth and prosperity.
    b. There was civil war between Dan and Ephraim.
    c. Peace ruled the land.
    d. The highways were deserted and peasantry ceased.

23. According to 1 Corinthians 1, what does God choose to use?
    a. The strong, wise, and superior things of the world
    b. The weak, foolish, and base things of the world
    c. Only the highly credentialed
    d. Only the rich

24. Which of the following is a possible theme for Judges 1?
    a. Be strong and courageous
    b. The inhabitants of the land not driven out
    c. Joshua's final words
    d. The cycle of sin

25. Which of the following is a possible theme for Judges 2?
    a. Be strong and courageous
    b. The inhabitants of the land not driven out
    c. Joshua's final words
    d. The cycle of sin

UNIT TWO - TEACHER'S GUIDE

Judges

SHORT ANSWER

26. Draw and label a diagram depicting the cycle of sin:

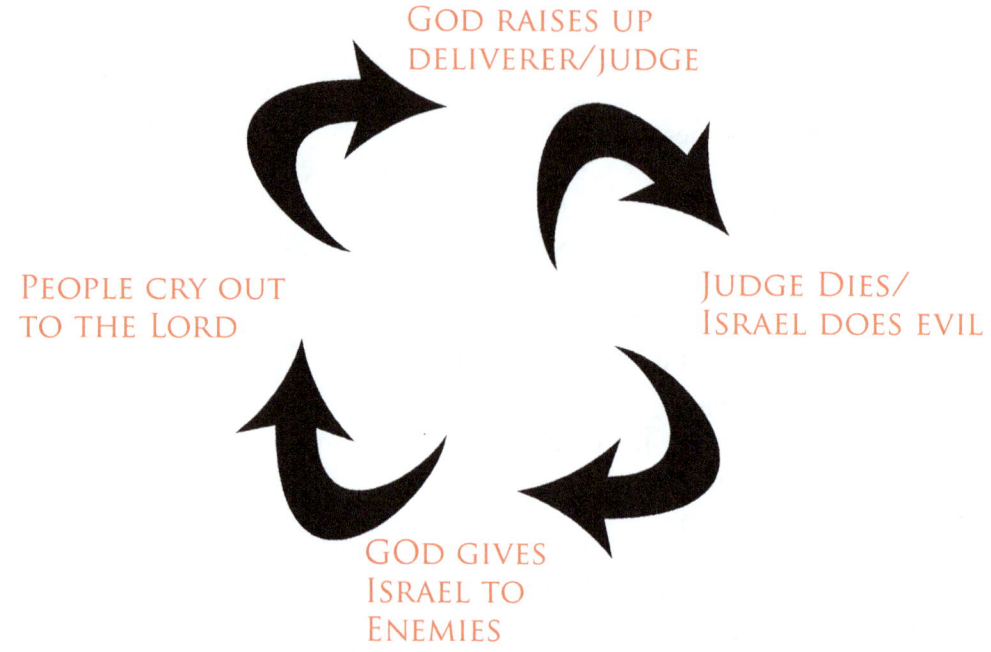

27. List at least three things you learned from marking the key word "nations."

Students can have any three of the following:
- 2:21 - God will no longer drive out the nations because Israel transgressed His covenant.
- 2:23 - Lord allowed these nations to remain by not driving them out quickly – did not give them into the tribes' hand.
- 3:1 - Nations left to test Israel and teach it war.
- 3:2 - The nations left were:
    - five Lords of the Philistines
    - Canaanites, Sidonians, and Hivites who lived in Mount Lebanon from Mount Baal-hermon as far as Lobohamath
- 3:4 - God used these to test Israel's obedience to the Law given through Moses.

28. Explain the difference between hearing and obeying.

Hearing God's commandments alone is not enough; truly hearing God's commands is to obey them.

UNIT TWO - TEACHER'S GUIDE

Judges

29. According to Exodus 34, what did God command the children of Israel not to do with the Canaanites, Hittites, Perizzites, Hivites, and the Jebusites?

According to Exodus 34:11-16, God commanded the children of Israel to not make any covenants with these peoples (nations). He commanded His people to tear down their altars, smash their sacred pillars, and cut down their Asherim because He is jealous. If they did not, they would play the harlot with their gods and intermarry with their daughters.

30. List at least three things you learned about God in Judges 3.

Answers should include characteristics about God found in Judges 3.

ESSAY

Choose one of the following topics; briefly summarize it and discuss how it applies to your life:

a. How someone today is delivered from the cycle (slavery) of sin (Matthew 1:21; John 8:34-36; and Romans 6).

b. What God uses to accomplish His will as shown by the examples of Ehud and Shamgar (c.f. 1 Corinthians 1:26-2:5).

c. What you learned about God in Judges 2-3

Students will identify the main points of these topics and discuss how the truths they learned apply to their lives.

Unit two - Teacher's Guide

Unit Three - Teacher's Guide

Judges

Leaders and Volunteers

Unit Objectives:

Students will recognize the same cycle of sin identified in Unit 1, in Judges 4 and 5; they will critically evaluate the prominent roles Deborah and Jael play in Scripture; and they will compare and contrast other roles women played in the Old and New Testaments. As they identify historical events in these chapters, students will also compare Deborah and Barak's times with our own. Students will also carefully observe and interpret Judges 4 and Deborah's song in Judges 5 to competently discuss the battle described in both chapters. Lastly, they will observe God'ssovereignty over this battle.

Introduction/Prayer
Encourage your students to begin this unit with prayer, specifically asking God to show them His will for their lives.

Unit Three

Leaders and Volunteers
U-3, Chapters 4-5

Leadership. Where does it come from? What happens when there is no **leader**? What's so important about leadership anyway?

It has been said, "Everything rises and falls on leadership." Why? Because leaders have the power to build or destroy people and nations. They can lead others to victory or defeat. History testifies to that. Libraries are filled with volumes that tell the stories of the power of leadership – or the lack of it.

> "The leaders led...
> the people volunteered"
> – Judges 5:2

The absence of leadership results in anarchy – everyone doing what is right in their own eyes. The last chapters of Judges are a clear warning against the destructiveness of this kind of mind set. People need leaders – godly leaders!

These are the days when young men and women, just like you, must wake up and rise to the needs of the time. **Volunteers** are needed so that your generation and those to follow will benefit even as Israel did in the days of Deborah, Barak, and Jael. God is looking for someone like you to see the need at hand, grasp the gravity of the situation, and lead others to accomplish His will. He needs someone who is able to lead others in obedience because he has learned it in his life .

Read through the following prayer before you begin this unit. Remember, your goal in studying God's Word is to KNOW HIM and as a result of knowing Him to live differently from those who are ignorant of His Word. As you read this prayer, make it the desire of your heart.

Introduction/Prayer
ONE ON ONE:

I come to You today, Elohim, Creator, to tell You that I want to be all that You created me to be. I know from the scriptures that there's a purpose for everyone's existence. You even use evil people to accomplish Your will, but my desire is to be righteous in Your sight, to know the good purpose for my existence, and to fulfill that purpose.

Father, You have not created everyone to be leaders – some will be followers or like Joshua, followers for a while, then leaders. All I want to know is what You would want me to do. If I follow, may I have the discernment and wisdom to know whom to follow and how to support him or her. If You have ordained me to lead, then may I understand that it is a servant leadership, not serving myself, but Your purposes. And may I never forget that You keep books (records and accounts) and that someday I will give an account to

Student Page 59

Unit Three - Teacher's Guide

Judges

> U-3, Chapters 4-5
>
> *You of my faithfulness and service.*
>
> *Father, awake Your Church from apathy. Teach us Your Word so that we hold fast to truth no matter what the cost is rather than apostatize as they did in the days of the Judges. Remind us over and over that anarchy, the fruit of apathy and apostasy unchecked, is poisonous – that it can destroy a people, culture, nation, and world.*
>
> *Whether we are called to be leaders or volunteers, may we hear Your call and come to the place of Your appointment.*
>
> *I ask all this in the name of our Servant Leader, Your only begotten Son, the Lord Jesus Christ. Amen.*

UNIT THREE - TEACHER'S GUIDE

Judges

LESSON ONE:

 Judges 4 Observation Worksheets, key word bookmark, colored pencils, and "The War of Deborah and Barak Against Sisera" map located at the end of the unit

OBJECTIVES:

Students will observe Judges 4 by using their key word bookmarks to identify and mark key words and phrases in this chapter. They will also identify main events and their locations on the map.

Lesson 1/Assignment 1 - Observation

 As you begin this assignment, ask your students to briefly discuss the importance of observation and the tools they will use to complete this assignment. They should remember that observation is foundational to inductive study. They will read with a purpose by asking the 5W and H questions and marking key words.

Reminding students of these inductive study components will help retain the process in their memory.

Lesson 1/Assignment 2 - Observation

Your students can either list main events in this chapter in the space provided or in the margins of their Observation Worksheets. They should include the following events:

- *4:1-3 – Sons of Israel cry out to God concerning Jabin and the 900 chariots.*
- *4:4-10 – Deborah summons Barak and gives him God's directions.*
- *4:12-16 – The battle between Israel and Sisera*
- *4:17-22 – Jael kills Sisera*
- *4:23-24 – God subdues Jabin*

Remember, their answers don't have to match these exactly. They may include details not listed in these summaries. However, the goal is to learn how to identify main events in a chapter.

LESSON ONE

U-3, Lesson 1, Chapter 4

You've seen a lot of men throughout your study of God's Word, but this lesson will focus on two women mightily used by God! You are about to meet a woman judge! What a rarity! When you read the Bible, you seldom find a woman in the place of leadership. Yet here she is, Deborah, and there is much for us to learn from her life and the days when she served the nation of Israel. You're really going to enjoy this week's study; you'll find much that is applicable to the needs of every generation.

If you sincerely prayed the prayer in the introduction to this unit – wow, you had better get ready for what God will do. Remember, in Judges 3 you saw that this new generation did not know God or the mighty works He had done for Israel. How similar to your generation today!

God left other nations in the land for two reasons: first, to see if this new generation would follow the Lord as their fathers had done under Joshua; and second, so that the new generation could learn war! It's time to know our God, take a stand, and fight.

Lesson 1/Assignment 1
1. Observe Judges 4 today. Mark key words and phrases on your bookmark.

Lesson 1/Assignment 2
2. List the main events in order and the main characters.

Lesson 1/Assignment 3
 3. You'll find a map at the end of this unit: "The War of Deborah and Barak Against Sisera." Using one color for Israel and another for Sisera, show movements of the two armies. Then, in another color, draw a line showing the flight of Sisera from the battlefield to Jael's tent.

Student Page 61

Unit Three - Teacher's Guide

Judges

Lesson 1/Assignment 3 - Observation

Students will locate the places mentioned in this chapter on "The War of Deborah and Barak Against Sisera" map located at the end of this unit in the Student Guide (pre-marked map in the Teacher's Guide at the end of this unit). Locations mentioned in the text but not on the map are not precisely known to scholars.

 Finding locations mentioned in Scripture on maps will help your students in two ways. First, it helps students clearly understand, remember, and visualize events discussed. Second, it reinforces the historical validity of God's Word.

UNIT THREE - TEACHER'S GUIDE

Judges

LESSON TWO:

 Judges 4 Observation Worksheets, "The Main Characters of Judges 4-5" chart located at the end of this unit, "At A Glance" chart located in the Appendix

OBJECTIVES:

Students will continue to observe Judges 4 to identify main characters and attributes of God. They will also begin interpreting after identifying Israel's fear of Jabin's army.

Lesson 2/Assignment 1 - Observation/Interpretation

 This assignment is an observation *and* interpretation assignment; as students complete their charts they will evaluate what they learn.

This chart is completed for you at the end of this unit.

Lesson 2/Assignment 2 - Observation/Interpretation

- *4:3 – 900 iron chariots, sons of Israel oppressed severely for 20 years*
- *4:7 – chariots and many troops*
- *4:13 – 900 iron chariots*

Lesson 2/Assignment 3 - Observation/Interpretation

Remind your students that the goal of all Bible study is to KNOW GOD – His character, attributes, and will. Emphasize to students to always note what they learn about God in their studies.

- *4:2 – God sold His people into the hand of Jabin.*
- *4:6 – He commanded Israel to march to Mt. Tabor with 10,000 men from Naphtali and Zebulun.*
- *4:6 – He drew out Sisera and his army to the Kishon River and gave them into Israel's hand.*

LESSON TWO

Lesson 2/Assignment 1 *U-3, Lesson 2, Chapter 4*
1. Read through your Observation Worksheets on Judges 4. Then on the chart at the end of this unit, "The Main Characters of Judges 4-5," record insights you get on Deborah and others.

Lesson 2/Assignment 2
2. According to the text, why were the sons of Israel so afraid of Sisera? Go back and underline in orange each reference to things they were afraid of.

Lesson 2/Assignment 3
3. Just as in the battles of Jericho and Ai, God does some amazing things in the battle against Sisera and Jabin. Note all the things God does in this chapter and record your insights below.

Lesson 2/Assignment 4
4. Record the main event or theme of Judges 4 on the "At A Glance" chart.

Chapter Theme – Don't forget, this is just a summary of main event(s) in the chapter. When you record a theme for each chapter you are building your own table of contents for the Bible! This exercise will also help you remember what this chapter was about when you look back at a later date.

Student Page 63

UNIT THREE - TEACHER'S GUIDE

Judges

- *4:9 – He sold Sisera into the hands of a woman.*
- *4:14 – He gave Sisera into Israel's hands; He went before Israel.*
- *4:15 – He routed Sisera, his chariots, and army with the edge of the sword.*
- *4:23 – He subdued Jabin, the king of Canaan.*

Lesson 2/Assignment 4 - Interpretation
Help students determine the main point of chapter 4 and a summary statement to help them remember the chapter. A possible summary of this chapter is:

Judges 4 - Deborah and Barak vs. Jabin and Sisera

UNIT THREE - TEACHER'S GUIDE

Precept Upon Precept

Judges

DISCUSSION GUIDE LESSONS ONE AND TWO:

Begin by reviewing the main points of Judges 1-3 and 17-21. This will give your students historical context while the maps will provide geographical context.

> Judges 1   Israel did not drive out the Canaanites
> Judges 2   Israel did evil; enemies oppressed them; cried to Lord; the Lord raised up a judge
> Judges 3   Othniel, Ehud, and Shamgar
> Judges 17-21   Every man did what was right in his own eyes

JUDGES 4

To establish the setting of Judges 4, question your students about verse 1 and compare it with Judges 3:12-30 and 31.

> Events in Judges 4 occurred after Ehud, the second judge of Israel, died. The land was undisturbed for 80 years, but after Ehud died Israel did evil again. Relate this to Judges 2:11-13; 3:7 and 12.
>
> The enemy in this chapter (the Canaanites) is within Canaan. They oppressed Israel for 20 years because Israel did not destroy them (Judges 1).

You can show on the map that two other enemies, Mesopotamia and Moab, were not within the land of Canaan. But, the Philistines and the Canaanites should not have been there at that time; Israel should have wiped them out.

Ask students who studied Joshua if they remember anything about the city of Hazor.

> Joshua took the city of Hazor (Joshua 11). He defeated the leaders of the Canaanites but because Israel did not completely drive the Canaanites out, Hazor recovered to become the city of the king of Canaan – Jabin.

Discuss main characters in these two chapters as you talk about events. You can write them on a visual aid with a descriptive note or two; however, it's not vital since students completed a chart of the main characters in the lesson. You *can* show the location of each one on a map if you want.

> Jabin, king of Canaan, reigned in Hazor.
>
> Sisera, commander of his army, lived in Harosheth-hagoyim.
>
> Deborah the prophetess judged Israel at this time.
> She lived between Ramah and Bethel in the hill country of Ephraim.

© 2008 Precept Ministries International

UNIT THREE - TEACHER'S GUIDE

Judges

    Barak, from Kedesh-naphtali, became the leader of Israel's army.
    Jael the Kenite woman killed Sisera.

Let your class discuss the main events of Judges 4.

    Jabin severely oppressed Israel for 20 years. His army, commanded by Sisera, had 900 iron chariotts, which seem to have frightened Israel. Compare this with Judges 1:19. The Lord had drowned the Egyptian army and its chariots so Israel should have defeated Jabin sooner than they did. Twenty years is a long time to be oppressed.

    Verse 3 says Israel cried to the Lord, part of the cycle we studied in the last lesson. Review the cycle and relate it to Judges 4:
- Israel did evil
- The Lord sold Israel to an enemy
- Israel cried to the Lord
- The Lord raised up a judge

    In Judges 4, the judge is a woman, which was very unusual. No woman had led Israel up to this point in its history.

    Deborah the prophetess speaks from the Lord – the people go to her for wisdom and counsel.

    She tells Barak to take 10,000 men and go to Mount Tabor – that the Lord will draw out Sisera and give him into Barak's hand.

    Barak says he will not go without her, so she tells him that the honor will go to the woman who kills Sisera.

    They gather the men at Kedesh-naphtali, and then go to Mount Tabor.

    Sisera with his men and chariots come from Harosheth-hagoyim and meet Barak in battle at the river Kishon.

    The Canaanites fall to Israel, but Sisera flees on foot.

    Jael goes out to meet him and suggests that he hide in her tent. She then kills him by driving a tent peg through his temple. She receives honor for killing this enemy of Israel.

    Jabin is destroyed by Israel. Judges 5:31 says the land was undisturbed for 40 years.

Ask students what they learned about God and how the principles apply to their lives.

UNIT THREE - TEACHER'S GUIDE

LESSON THREE:

Judges 5 Observation Worksheets, colored pencils, key word bookmark, "The Main Characters of Judges 4-5" chart located at the end of this unit, "At A Glance" chart, Bible, "The Judges of Israel" chart located in the Appendix

OBJECTIVES:

Students will observe Judges 5 by marking the key words from their bookmarks and including *curse*, *bless(ed)*, and any mention of the *12 tribes of Israel*. They will identify this chapter's purpose in conveying the story of Deborah and Barak. Finally, students will interpret this chapter while recording main characters and events in this chapter and other parts of Scripture.

Lesson 3/Assignment 1 - Observation
Remind your students to look for and mark the words that are listed on their bookmarks plus *curse*, *bless(ed)* and *12 tribes of Israel*. The insight box in the student workbooks lists the 12 tribes for their reference.

Lesson 3/Assignment 2 - Observation/Interpretation
a. This chapter is a poetic song.

Identifying types of literature establishes context so the text can be more accurately interpreted. Direct students to the insight box in the student workbook for more information.

b. Judges 5 gives more detailed information concerning the war in chapter four. Among other things, it tells what each tribe did or didn't do in the war.

Lesson 3/Assignment 3 - Observation/Interpretation
This chart is completed for you at the end of this unit.

LESSON THREE

Lesson 3/Assignment 1
U-3, Lesson 3, Chapter 5

Judges 5 is unique in the book of Judges. For the rest of this unit, you will look more closely at this chapter to see how its information will help you understand Judges 4.

1. Observe Judges 5. Mark the following words in distinctive ways:

   a. *curse* with an orange cloud shaded brown like this 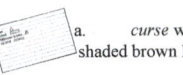.

   b. *bless(ed)* with a blue cloud shaded pink like this ☁.

   c. any mention of one of the 12 tribes of Israel (underline it in blue).

Tribes of Israel			
Reuben	Judah	Dan	Naphtali
Simeon	Zebulun	Asher	Benjamin
Levi	Issachar	Gad	
Ephraim and Manasseh (Joseph's sons)			

Lesson 3/Assignment 2
2. Now, take a closer look at this incredible chapter.

   a. What type of literature is Judges 5?

   b. After reading the historical account of Judges 4, what purpose does Judges 5 serve?

Type of literature – It's important to identify the type of literature you are studying since this will determine how you handle the text. For example, Hebrew poetry and songs (such as the Psalms) are different from the historical books (such as Kings and Chronicles), and the historical books are different from the epistles (such as 1 Peter or 1 Timothy), in style and content. History books give background, tell of real events, and reveal how God dealt with people, but you don't build **doctrine** on historical events. Most doctrine for the Church is contained in the epistles. So determine if the text is: **historical**, **biographical**, **poetic**, **proverbial**, **prophetic**, an **epistle** or a combination.

Lesson 3/Assignment 3
3. Record new information about main characters in Judges 4 on the chart you began yesterday.

Lesson 3/Assignment 4
4. Record a Judges 5 chapter theme on the "At A Glance" chart.

Student Page 65

Unit Three - Teacher's Guide

Lesson 3/Assignment 4 - Interpretation
Help students determine the main point of chapter 5 and a summary statement to help them remember it. A possible summary statement for this chapter is:

Judges 5 – Deborah's Song

Lesson 3/Assignment 5 – Interpretation
Barak is listed with other men of faith who "conquered kingdoms, performed acts of righteousness, obtained promises, escaped the edge of the sword, from weakness were made strong, became mighty in war, put foreign armies to flight."

Lesson 3/Assignment 6 - Observation/Interpretation
This chart is completed for you at the end of the Teacher's Guide.

Lesson 3/Assignment 5
U-3, Lesson 3, Chapter 5

5. Record what this passage says about Barak.

HEBREWS 11: 32-34

Lesson 3/Assignment 6
6. Fill in the information about Deborah on "The Judges of Israel" chart.

> Judges 5 is the only song recorded in the book of Judges. After God led Israel to victory against Jabin and Sisera, Deborah and Barak sing a song of **praise** recounting God's mighty works.
>
> What has God done that you can praise Him for? Given you victory over sin? Restored a relationship that seemed unsalvageable? Answered your prayer? The next time God accomplishes something miraculous in your life – praise Him! Just like Deborah and Barak, write or sing a song about what He has done on your behalf. If you can't write or sing, at least tell someone... you never know how hearing about God's mighty works will impact his life.

Student Page 66

UNIT THREE - TEACHER'S GUIDE

Judges

LESSON FOUR:

 Judges 4 and 5 Observation Worksheets

OBJECTIVES:

Students will learn more about the battle described in Judges 4 in chapter five, then study the historic setting of Deborah. They will then consider how to apply what they learned from these chapters and Deborah's leadership style.

Lesson 4/Assignment 1 - Observation
- v. 6 – Highways deserted
- v. 7 – Peasantry ceases
- v. 8 – New gods chosen
- v. 8 – War in the gates
- v. 8 – No shield or spear seen among 40,000 in Israel

Lesson 4/Assignment 2 - Interpretation
You may need to help your students interpret the circumstances in Israel given in Judges 5. Remind them to read the insight box in the student workbook.

a. Israel was so oppressed under the rule of Jabin that the highways were no longer safe for Israelites to travel. They were stuck in their cities.

b. Choosing new gods could indicate two things: first, Jabin may have forced Jews to worship Canaan's gods; or second, the people may have reached out to any god they thought could provide relief from their persecution.

c. The leaders spent time talking about what they should do. No action was taken; it was a war of words only.

© 2008 Precept Ministries International

UNIT THREE - TEACHER'S GUIDE

d. Jabin took the Israelites' spears and shields from them. They had no defense and no way to attack.

Lesson 4/Assignment 3 - Application
a. Students should learn that leadership was extremely vital. Israel had no hope until Deborah arose (5:7) and called Barak (5:12). No man stepped up so God used a woman to call the nation to fight and motivate a man to lead.

b. It was extremely rare for women to hold positions of leadership. But here even Barak was unwilling to fight unless Deborah was with him. And another woman, Jael, was given the honor of ultimately defeating Israel's oppressor.

c. The people were oppressed and hopeless. They lived in fear – no man was willing to lead.

d. Students should recognize that nothing is impossible with God – He overrules circumstances and uses those willing to follow His lead.

U-3, Lesson 4, Chapters 4-5

d. What can you conclude about the lack of shields or spears?

Lesson 4/Assignment 3
3. Now, take a closer look at leadership from these two chapters. Support your answers from the text.

   a. How vital was leadership in this situation?

   b. When it came, where did it come from? Was this usual?

   c. What does this tell you about the times?

   d. What does this tell you about God? Do circumstances limit what He does? Explain your answer.

When circumstances are bad and it seems like all hope is lost... remember, you serve a God with whom NOTHING is impossible!

UNIT THREE - TEACHER'S GUIDE

Judges

DISCUSSION GUIDE LESSONS THREE AND FOUR:

JUDGES 5

Ask students how Judges 5 relates to Judges 4. Encourage them to discuss the details of the times and the battle within the song of Judges 5.

> Deborah and Barak sang a song of praise after the Lord delivered Israel from the Canaanites. Ask your class if they praise God for victories He gives them.
>
> The song includes praise and thanks for leaders and volunteers. Contrast the leaders' confidence with Barak's reluctance to lead. (He did not want to go into battle without Deborah. When she agreed to go with him, then he led the army.)

Ask your students who verses 3-5 credit for the victory.

> The Lord, the God of Israel
>
> > Is remembered for His appearance at Sinai and for His miraculous ways
> >
> > Brings earthquakes, clouds, and rain.

Discuss the times in Israel before the battle against the Canaanites.

> Verses 6-11 say that fear of the highways made people find roundabout ways to travel.
>
> Village life and peasantry disappeared because the open country was unprotected.
>
> Israel chose new gods, and then there was war and oppression.
> No weapon was found among 40,000 people in Israel.
> Enemies and fear enslaved them.
>
> But, from verses 9-11, these people joyfully volunteered as they recount the righteous deeds of the Lord.
>
> Verses 12-13 recount God's call of Deborah and Barak.
> Verses 14-18 describe the tribes that volunteered and those that did not.

Verses 19-23 recount the battle. Ask your group to discuss the details.

> The main fighting was done at Taanach near Megiddo. The waters of Megiddo are mentioned. Relate this reference to the 900 iron chariots of the Canaanites – how well do iron chariots

Unit Three - Teacher's Guide

function in water or mud?

The stars fought from heaven against Sisera, and the Kishon River swept away the enemy.

The Lord sent a downpour from heaven that overflowed the Kishon River and drowned the Canaanites. Their iron chariots were a hindrance – not the advantage they expected.

The Lord fought this battle. According to Judges 4:7 Deborah told Barak God will draw out Sisera's army and chariots to the Kishon River and give them into Barak's hand.

Judges 4:6 says God told Barak to "march to" (draw toward—KJV) Mount Tabor, about 10 miles from the Kishon River. The Hebrew word for "march" is trasnslated "draw out" in verse 7; *mashak* simply means "to draw" (***New American Standard Concordance***).

The Lord tells Barak if he marches with his 10,000 men to Mount Tabor, He will draw Sisera's army to the battle site.

The Lord used the heavens and earth in the fight. Judges 4:15 says the Lord "routed Sisera and all his chariots." The Hebrew word translated "routed" means "confused," (***New American Standard Concordance***).

So God confused the army and the chariots. Sisera left his chariot and fled the battleground on foot.

Ask students if they've been in the place of Israel – oppressed and fearful to the point that it hampers their lives. What causes this kind of fear? Do they need to rise up the way Deborah did? Do they need to stop fearing and put their faith in the God who can even use the elements to fight for His people? The Lord confused the enemy! He gave Barak victory as Deborah said He would. Help your students evaluate their faith. How much do they trust the Lord? Do they trust Him in the everyday battles of life?

Verses 24-27 tell of a woman living in a tent who killed the commander of the Canaanite army. Encourage your students to discuss what they learned about her.

Jael was married to Heber the Kenite who had separated from the Kenites and lived within Israel. There was peace between Jabin and Heber. The Lord used Jael in a mighty way to deliver His people.

She was not fearful; she knew what to do and did it.
She knew the enemy and destroyed him completely. Fear did not stop her, even when she was face-to-face with the commander of an army with 900 iron chariots.

Unit Three - Teacher's Guide

Judges

Sisera's knowledge of the peace between Heber and King Jabin may have caused him to trust the refuge of Heber's wife.

Discuss with your students what they learned from verses 28-30.

Sisera's mother wondered why it took so long for him to return. She repeated her questions about his delay and wondered about the spoils of his victory.

Ask your class to discuss what they learned that applies to their lives.

UNIT THREE - TEACHER'S GUIDE

Judges

UNIT THREE - TEACHER'S GUIDE

LESSON FIVE:

 Judges 1 and 5 Observation Worksheets, colored pencils

OBJECTIVES:

Students will observe Judges 5 to discover which tribes fought under Deborah and Barak in the battle against Jabin and Sisera.

Judges 5 can be difficult for students to interpret since it recounts in song Israel's victory over Jabin and Sisera. But the time spent interpreting will not only help students understand these details, but also give them experience in interpreting this type of literature.

Lesson 5/Assignment 1 - Observation
Students will mark the tribes who fought with a star and those who didn't with an X.

Lesson 5/Assignment 2 - Observation/Interpretation
See student page for chart information.

Lesson 5/Assignment 3 - Interpretation
Students will think about statements

LESSON FIVE

Lesson 5/Assignment 1 *U-3, Lesson 4, Chapter 5*
The song of Deborah reveals who fought and who didn't on behalf of Israel. In this lesson, you'll look more closely at who fought with Deborah and Barak, who didn't, and why.

1. In the margin of your Observation Worksheet put a star next to the tribes that fought with Deborah and Barak and an "X" next to those who didn't fight.

Those who yield the staff of office is a reference to scribes, writers.

Lesson 5/Assignment 2
2. List the tribes mentioned in the song of Judges 5 on the chart below in the appropriate column. Leave space by each name for the next assignment.

THE TRIBES FROM SONG IN JUDGES 5

TRIBES THAT FOUGHT	TRIBES THAT DIDN'T
Ephraim *Those whose root was in Amalek came down (14)*	*Reuben* *Great resolves of heart, sitting in the sheepfolds piping for the flocks (15,16)*
Benjamin *Followed Ephraim, both people and commanders came down (14)*	*Gilead* *Remained across the Jordan (17)*
Zebulun *Those who yield the staff of office came down (14)*	*Dan* *Stayed in the ships (17)*
Issachar *Princes came down with Deborah (15)*	*Asher* *Sat at the seashore and landings (17)*
Naphtali *Despised lives even to death on the field (18)*	

Student Page 69

UNIT THREE - TEACHER'S GUIDE

Judges

concerning the tribes that did not fight. You may need to help them think through each of the scenarios.

Reuben, even though "there were great searchings of heart," did not come to fight.

"Gilead remained across the Jordan" is probably a reference to the one-and-a-half tribes on the east of the Jordan, Gad and half of Manasseh. Even though "Gilead" was the son of Manasseh, the tribe of Gad inherited most of the land called "Gilead" on the east side of the Jordan River.

Dan and Asher it seems were more concerned about the shipping trade and their industry than fighting with their brothers.

Lesson 5/Assignment 4 - Application

a. Encourage your students to choose the tribe whose actions best match their Christian walk.

b. In 2 Timothy 4:1-8, Paul says he has "fought the good fight." In other words, he finished the work he was now calling Timothy to do, "preach the word, reprove, rebuke, exhort with great patience and instruction, be sober in all things, endure hardship, and do the work of an evangelist." Believers are called to imitate Paul's fight.

In 2 Timothy 2:3-4, Paul compares the Christian life to that of a soldier in service to Jesus Christ. Believers should not entangle themselves in the affairs of everyday life so that they will please the one who "enlisted" them.

c. Students will examine their lives to determine if they are actively participating in the call to please the Lord and minister to others.

Lesson 5/Assignment 3
U-3, Lesson 5, Chapter 5

3. Now evaluate what was written about the tribes who didn't fight. What was more important than fighting with their brothers (which by the way was God's command)? Next to the tribe's name on your chart, write out why they didn't fight.

Lesson 5/Assignment 4

4. Now, think about what you observed about the tribes and how they responded to the battle against Sisera.

   a. If you were to apply this scenario to your life today, what tribe best describes the way you are living? Why?

   b. Read these passages Paul wrote and answer this question: has God called you to battle?

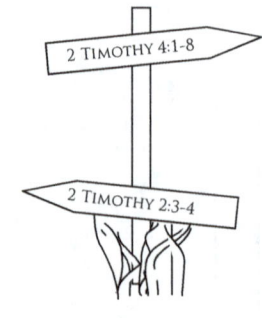

2 TIMOTHY 4:1-8

2 TIMOTHY 2:3-4

Student Page 70

UNIT THREE - TEACHER'S GUIDE

Judges

d. Students will evaluate if they, like the tribes who did *not* fight, are more concerned with worldly matters than God's commands.

U-3, Lesson 5, Chapter 5

c. Are you responding to the call to fight or are you talking about it without doing anything? Explain.

d. Are you more concerned with your possessions than the battle? How do you know?

> Isn't it fascinating to get a glimpse of history through the song of this woman of God? What did it reveal to you? Did you find yourself challenged to answer the battle cry?
>
> Share what you learned with others; ask God to show you how to get them excited about studying the Bible inductively. But above all, do it in humility. When you've dug into the Word of God for yourself and uncovered many of its truths, its easy to sound superior and boastful. That is pride and God resists the proud. If your life is not being changed and you are not becoming more like Jesus Christ, then you're not applying what you know, and knowledge alone puffs up. Unless you exhibit Christ's character, people will resist studying <u>with</u> you...or <u>as</u> you do.

UNIT THREE - TEACHER'S GUIDE

UNIT THREE - TEACHER'S GUIDE

DISCUSSION GUIDE LESSON FIVE:

JUDGES 5

The people volunteered (5:2). Relate this to verses 14-18 and 23 to show that ***not all*** tribes fought.

Zebulun and Naphtali are mentioned in Judges 4 as participating in the battle. Judges 5 lists others who fought with Barak. They are:

Ephraim

Benjamin

Machir (the oldest son of Manasseh and father of Gilead. This probably is a reference to Manasseh on the west of the Jordan, because the half tribe of Manasseh on the east side is "Gilead" and Gad.)

Issachar

Those who did not come to battle are condemned in the song:

Reuben (though "there were great searchings of heart," perhaps considering whether to fight in the battle or not, did not come to fight.)

"Gilead remained across the Jordan" (probably a reference to the one-and-a-half tribes on the east of the Jordan – Gad and half of Manasseh. Even though Gilead was the son of Manasseh, the tribe of Gad inherited most of the land called "Gilead" on the east of the Jordan River.)

Dan

Asher

Meroz (most likely a reference to a city about seven miles south of Kedesh that did not fight, though in the middle of the battle area. "Utterly curse" implies this city will be destroyed for not helping Israel against its enemy.)

Ask your students to discuss what they learned from these verses that applies to their lives.

UNIT THREE - TEACHER'S GUIDE

Unit Three - Teacher's Guide

Lesson Six:

 Bible

Objectives:

In this lesson, students will evaluate cross-references to identify prophetesses other than Deborah.

Lesson 6/Assignment 1 - Observation/Interpretation
a. According to Exodus 15:20-21 Miriam, Aaron's sister was a prophetess. She led women in praising God after He parted the sea.

b. According to 2 Kings 22:8-20 and 2 Chronicles 34:22-28, Josiah sent his high priest, scribe, and servants to Huldah, a prophetess, after the book of the law was found in the house of the Lord. Huldah speaks the word of the Lord to them and prophesies God's wrath to Judah because of their idolatry. She tells them His judgment will not occur until after the king's death because he humbled himself before the Lord.

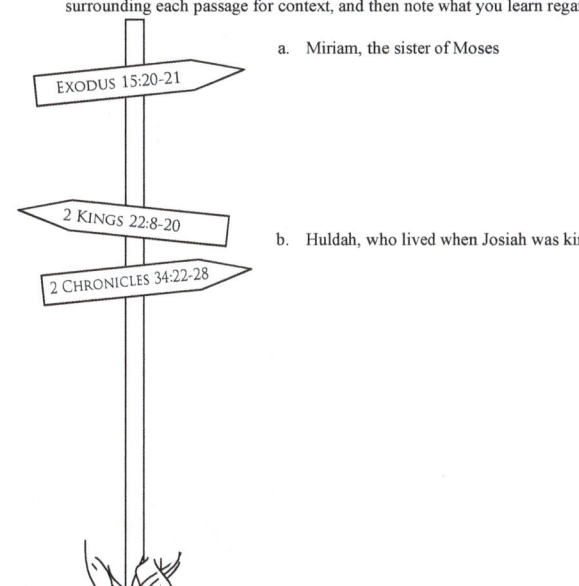

UNIT THREE - TEACHER'S GUIDE

Judges

c. According to Isaiah 8:3, Isaiah's wife was a prophetess.

d. According to Luke 2:35-38, Anna was a prophetess. She knew the infant Jesus was the Messiah, gave thanks to God, and continued to speak of Him to those looking for Israel's redemption.

e. According to Acts 21:7-9, Phillip's daughters were prophetesses.

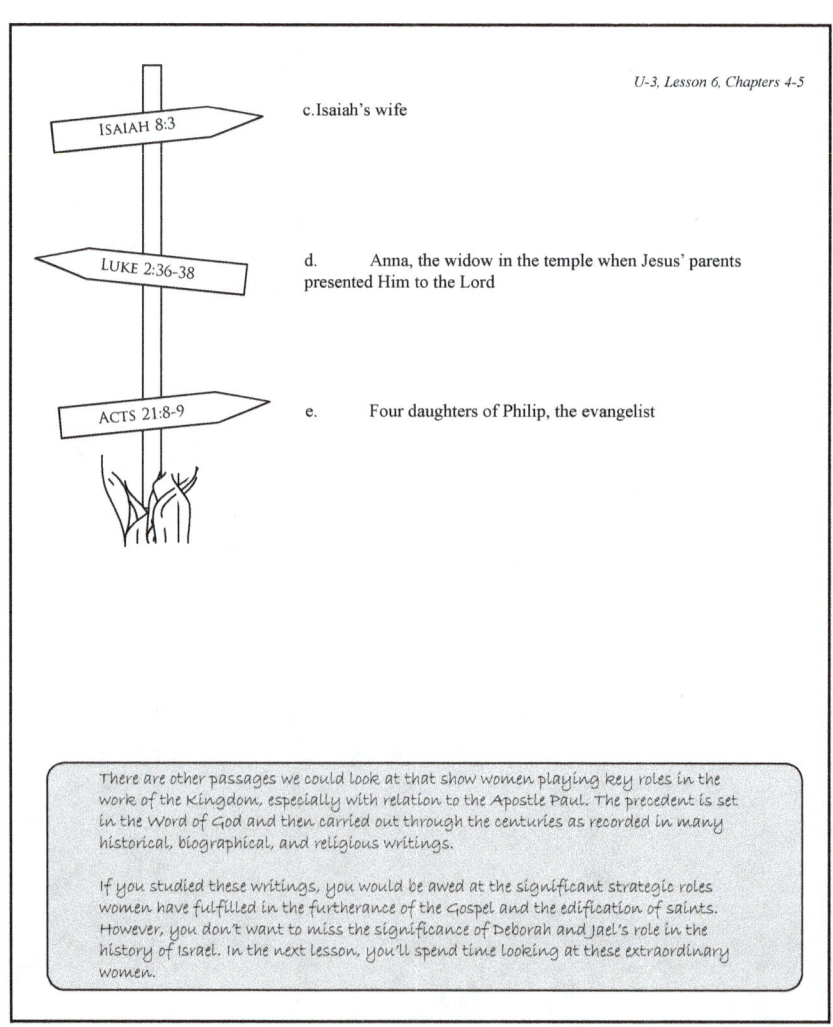

UNIT THREE - TEACHER'S GUIDE

LESSON SEVEN:

 Judges 4 and 5 Observation Worksheets

OBJECTIVES:

In this lesson, students will look more closely at the roles Deborah and Jael played in the defeat of Sisera. They will learn that God uses whomever He chooses to accomplish His will.

Lesson 7/Assignment 1 - Observation/Interpretation

Students will record insights on Deborah and Jael on the chart from previous observations of Judges 4 and 5. This information should include who they were, how they are described, and what role they played in the battle with Sisera.

Lesson 7/Assignment 2 - Application

a. Students will determine if they believe God uses anyone, male or female, to accomplish His will and specifically if they believe God is using them.

LESSON SEVEN

Lesson 7/Assignment 1
U-3, Lesson 7, Chapters 4-5

You have filled in the chart, "The Main Characters of Judges 4-5." Now you need to take time to reflect on who Deborah and Jael were, where they were, and what happened in their lives. What caused Deborah to compose such a masterful song and Jael to take the honor Barak could have had? Both of these women served God in powerful but different ways.

1. Think through the facts you recorded about them from the text – how they differed yet God used them. What lessons have you learned from these women? Write out your insights.

DEBORAH	JAEL

Lesson 7/Assignment 2

2. As you looked at Deborah and Jael, undoubtedly you noticed that Deborah, an Israelite, publicly fought with Barak while Jael, a Gentile, privately dealt a fatal blow to the enemy of Israel in the confines of her home. Though vastly different, God used both women because they made themselves available to God and did what was necessary. How can you apply this to your life?

   a. Do you realize that male or female, God made you and desires to use you to further His kingdom? Is He using you? What are you doing?

Student Page 75

Unit Three - Teacher's Guide

Judges

b. Students should ask if they are like Sisera's mother or Deborah. Encourage them to contrast these two women and determine whom they are more like and why. Remind them that application begins with prayer, asking God to reveal how principles they learn apply to their lives.

World View Project - Taking a Stand

Students will consider situations where someone publically stood for truth. Encourage your students to consider their responsibility to be "lights" to the world by standing for truth in their community.

U-3, Lesson 7, Chapters 4-5

b. Have you become apathetic, consumed by your own world even as Sisera's mother was? Like Deborah, do you need to awake, arise, and be about God's business? Write your response to these questions below.

World View Project

TAKING A STAND - PROJECT

For this assignment you will need the following:

Internet   Magazine   Newspaper

Have you ever watched television or read a newspaper or magazine and thought, "This shouldn't be!" or "They shouldn't get away with this!"? Have you heard of or seen people in your city that need someone to stand and fight on their behalf? Maybe you were appalled at children left on their own or terribly abused. Perhaps senior citizens were mistreated and neglected in a nursing home. Or have you ever been outraged at pornography in magazines and on the Internet and television that was easily accessible to those in your community?

Have you ever asked yourself why certain special interest groups got their way – when they opposed the moral values Scripture clearly defines?

Find an example of this kind of situation on the Internet or in a magazine or newspaper. Cut or print out the article and write a summary of the event. (If you know of a situation first hand, gather the facts or interview the people involved and write out the story yourself.) If some took a stand, like Deborah or Jael, write out how they addressed it. Did others rise up to support them or did they stand alone?

Now think of a situation where you can take a stand for truth, perhaps in your school, community, or even in your family. Write out how you can get involved in standing up for what's right – then do it! It's as easy as writing a letter to a government official, participating in a demonstration, or volunteering with an organization already fighting immorality or injustice.

Finally, discuss with your class your experience with this project.

Unit Three - Teacher's Guide

U-3, Lesson 7, Chapters 4-5

> Do you see how relevant the Word of God (even the Old Testament) is for your times? There are principles and precepts for life in the Bible. When you take the time to study and understand why God preserved such truths for you, they can radically impact the way you live and the choices you make.
>
> It is so awesome that you are studying and thinking through these truths at a young age. You are building a framework of godly wisdom that will guide and bless you if you live by it. We commend you for honoring the Word of God, applying yourself and disciplining yourself so that you know your God and understand His ways.

Unit Three - Teacher's Guide

UNIT THREE - TEACHER'S GUIDE

Judges

DISCUSSION GUIDE LESSONS SIX AND SEVEN:

Ask your students to discuss what they learned about women in the scriptures they studied.

It was unusual for the Lord to use a woman to lead His people, but Deborah is not the only prophetess mentioned in Scripture.

Judges 4-5 events occur when the men of Israel are immobilized by fear. Deborah and Jael are the most courageous. Barak leads the army by faith (Hebrews 11), but he wants Deborah to go with him.

Miriam, Aaron and Moses' sister, was another prophetess. She sang and danced before the Lord and led Israel in worship for His deliverance from Egypt's army.

Josiah, the king of Judah, consulted a prophetess named Huldah in Jerusalem.

Isaiah was married to a prophetess.

Anna the prophetess served in the temple at the time of Jesus' birth – night and day with fastings and prayers. When Jesus was brought into the temple, she gave thanks to God and proclaimed Jesus to those looking for Israel's redemption. She knew He was the Messiah.

Philip the evangelist had four prophetess daughters.

Even though the Lord usually communicated with His people through men, He used some women to speak for Him. Now that His Word is complete, it is the only inerrant source of truth.

It's vital to know His Word to evaluate what others say. Caution students against those who say they "speak for the Lord." He speaks for Himself through His Word and His Spirit who indwells believers.

Ask them to share what they can apply to their lives from these lessons.

Unit Three - Teacher's Guide

Unit Three - Teacher's Guide

Judges
U-3, Chapters 4-5

The War of Deborah and Barak Against Sisera

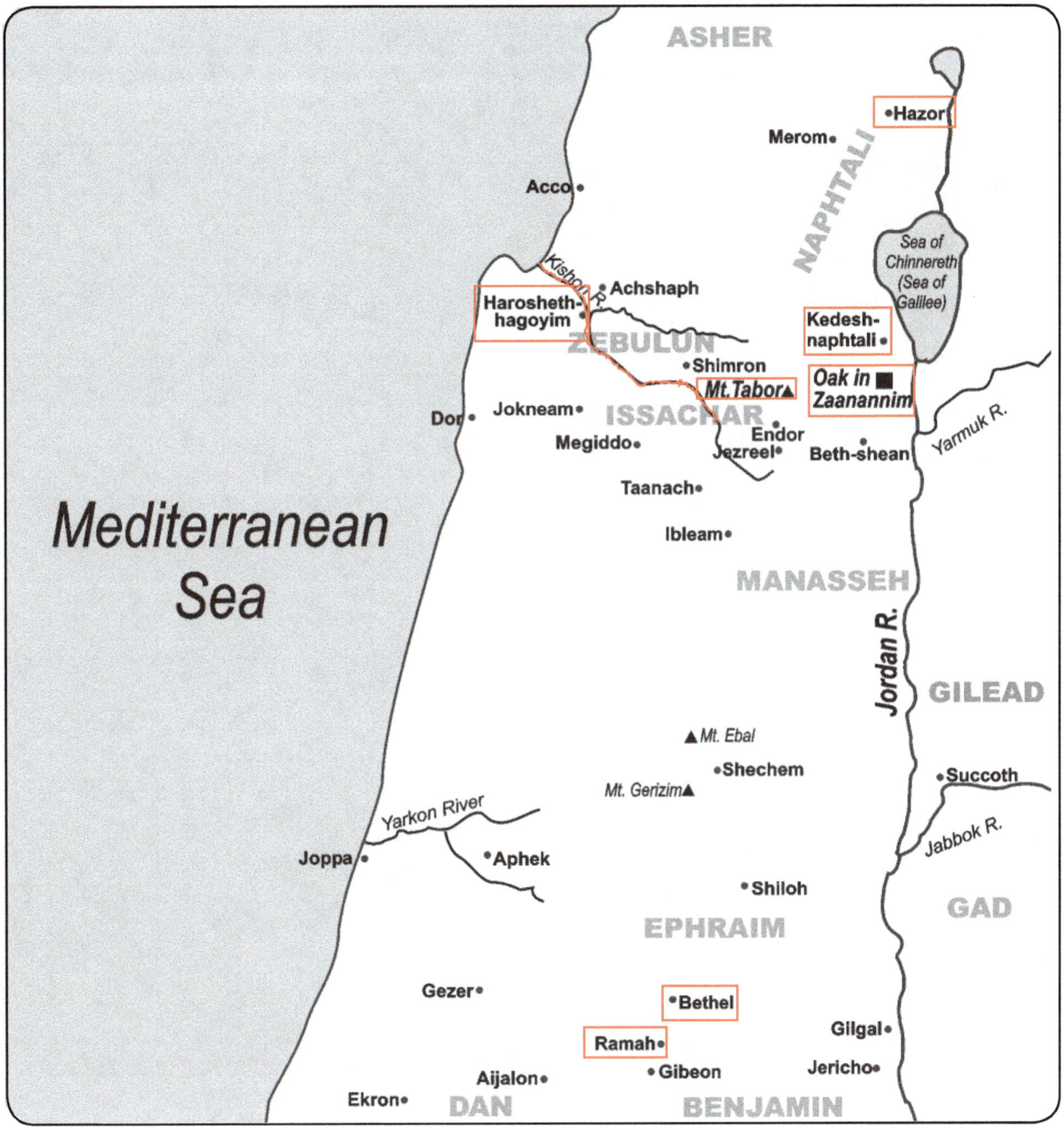

UNIT THREE - TEACHER'S GUIDE

Unit Three - Teacher's Guide

Judges
U-3, Chapters 4-5

The Main Characters of Judges 4–5

DEBORAH	BARAK	SISERA	JAEL
v.4:4 - prophetess, wife of Lappidoth, judge	v.4:6 - son of Abinoam of Kadesh-naphtali	v.4:2, 7 - commander of Jabin king of Canaan's army, lived at Harosheth-hagoyim	v.4:17 - a Kenite, Gentile, wife of Heber
v.4:5 - lived under palm tree of Deborah in Ephraim; sons of Israel came to her for judgment	v.4:8 - would not go to battle without Deborah	v.4:3 - had 900 iron chariots and multitudes of troops	v.4:18 - met Sisera, invited him into tent, covered him with a blanket
v.4:6 - summoned Barak, gave Lord's orders	v.4:10 - called Naphtali and Zebulum to fight	v.4:15 - confused by the Lord, fled chariot on foot to Jael	v.4:19 - gave him milk instead of water
v.4:8-9 - went to Kadesh with armies	v.4:14 - had 10,000 men	v.4:21 - killed by Jael	v.4:21 - drove tent peg through his skull
v.4:14 - told Barak the Lord was with him	v.4:16 - pursued Sisera's chariots and army, defeated them		v.5:24 - blessed among women
v.5:7 - a mother in Israel			
Insights: She spoke God's Word, led His people when no man stepped up, went fearlessly into battle recognizing the Lord's power.	Insights: Though victory and honor went to Jael, Barak obediently led the army. He followed the command of the Lord even though he had the weaker army.	Insights: Though stronger militarily, Sisera was defeated because the Lord was not with him.	Insights: A Gentile woman God used to defeat king's commander.

UNIT THREE - TEACHER'S GUIDE

Unit Three - Teacher's Guide

Judges

Enrichment Words

Biographical – consisting of the written history of a person's life.

Doctrine – a principle or the body of principles in a system of belief.

Epistle – one of the letters adopted as books of the New Testament.

Historical – based on history.

Leader – a person who has commanding authority or influence.

Poetic – writing that formulates a concentrated, imaginative awareness of an experience in language chosen and arranged to create a specific emotional response through meaning, sound, and rhythm.

Praise – to express a favorable judgment of, to recommend as worthy of confidence or notice.

Prophetic – consisting of the inspired declaration of divine will and purpose or a prediction of something to come.

Proverbial – a collection of moral sayings and counsels forming a book of canonical Jewish and Christian Scripture.

Volunteers – people who voluntarily undertake or express a willingness to undertake a service.

UNIT THREE - TEACHER'S GUIDE

Unit Three - Teacher's Guide

Judges
Unit Three Quiz

Name: _____ Date: _____

Unit Three - Quiz Key

MATCHING - Choose one and write the letter in the blank.

___g___ 1. The place God commanded Israel's army to wait until He drew out the army of Canaan

___a___ 2. A judge and prophetess of Israel

___e___ 3. The King of Canaan

___d___ 4. The Gentile woman who hid Canaan's army commander and killed him with a tent peg

___b___ 5. The man from Kadesh-naphtali who wouldn't fight Jabin unless Deborah went with him

___c___ 6. The commander who fled from battle on foot and was killed with a tent peg

___f___ 7. A torrent of this river swept away the army of Canaan

a. Deborah
b. Barak
c. Sisera
d. Jael
e. Jabin
f. Kishon
g. Mount Tabor

SHORT ANSWER

8. List three descriptions of the situation in Israel during the days of Deborah from Judges 5.

Can be any of the following:
  Highways were deserted
  Travelers went in roundabout ways
  Peasantry ceased
  New gods were chosen
  War in the gates
  Not a shield or a spear was seen

© 2008 Precept Ministries International

Unit Three - Teacher's Guide

Unit Three - Teacher's Guide

Judges
Unit Three Test

Name: _____ Date: _____

Unit Three - Test Key

MATCHING - Choose one and write the letter in the blank.

__c__	1. A principle or the body of principles in a belief system	a. Epistle
		b. Biographical
__b__	2. Consisting of the written history of a person's life	c. Doctrine
		d. Proverbial
__d__	3. A collection of moral sayings and counsels forming a book of canonical Jewish and Christian Scripture	e. Prophetic
		f. Deborah
		g. Barak
__e__	4. Consisting of the inspired declaration of divine will and purpose or a prediction of something to come	h. Sisera
		i. Jael
		j. Jabin
__a__	5. One of the letters adopted as books of the New Testament	k. Kishon
		l. Mount Tabor
__l__	6. The place God commanded the army of Israel to wait until He drew out the army of Canaan	
__f__	7. The judge and prophetess of Israel	
__j__	8. The King of Canaan	
__i__	9. The Gentile woman who hid Canaan's army commander and then killed him with a tent peg	
__g__	10. The man from Kadesh-naphtali who wouldn't fight Jabin unless Deborah went with him	
__h__	11. The commander who fled from battle on foot and was killed with a tent peg	
__k__	12. A torrent of this river swept away the army of Canaan	

© 2008 Precept Ministries International

UNIT THREE - TEACHER'S GUIDE

Judges
Unit Three Test

MULTIPLE CHOICE - Circle one.

13. Which of the following is a possible theme for Judges 4?
    a. Cycle of sin
    b. Tribes of Israel did not drive out the inhabitants
    c. Deborah's Song
    d. *Deborah and Barak versus Jabin and Sisera*

14. Which of the following is a possible theme for Judges 5?
    a. Cycle of sin
    b. Tribes of Israel did not drive out the inhabitants
    c. *Deborah's Song*
    d. Deborah and Barak versus Jabin and Sisera

15. What type of literature is Judges 5?
    a. Biography
    b. Epistle
    c. *Song (Poetic)*
    d. Narrative

16. Why did the sons of Israel cry out to the Lord in Judges 4?
    a. The King of Mesopotamia had oppressed them for eight years.
    b. *The King of Canaan had 900 iron chariots and had severely oppressed them for 20 years.*
    c. The King of Moab had oppressed them for 18 years.
    d. The King of Midian struck down 600 Israelites with an ox goad.

17. All of the following occurred when God fought for Israel (Judges 4 and 5) EXCEPT:
    a. *He threw large hailstones from heaven.*
    b. He caused the earth to quake and clouds to drip water.
    c. He subdued the king of Canaan.
    d. He gave Sisera into their hands.

18. Who was looking out the window waiting for Sisera's return?
    a. Sisera's wife
    b. Sisera's sister
    c. *Sisera's mother*
    d. Sisera's daughter

Unit Three - Teacher's Guide

Judges
Unit Three Test

Short Answer

19. Describe the circumstances and the situation in Israel during the days of Deborah.

Highways were deserted
Travelers went in roundabout ways
Peasantry ceased
New gods were chosen
War in the gates
Not a shield or a spear was seen

20. What information does Deborah give about the tribes of Israel in her song?

She lists the tribes that volunteered to fight against Sisera and the ones that stayed home.

21. How does the problem in Judges 5 connect with the action the tribes took in Judges 1?

According to Judges 5, Israel is oppressed by the Canaanites – inhabitants they did not drive out as God commanded (Judges 1).

22. List at least three other women prophetesses in the Bible.

Isaiah's wife, Miriam (Moses' sister), Anna, and Phillip's daughters

23. Why didn't the honor for Sisera's defeat go to Barak?

In Judges 4:8-9, Deborah tells Barak the honor for Sisera's defeat will go to a woman because he did not go into battle without her support.

24. Describe Jael's role in the defeat of Sisera.

Jael invited Sisera into her tent. When he asked for water, she gave him milk. After he fell asleep she hammered a tent peg into his temple. Later, Barak came and saw what she had done. God gave the honor for defeating Sisera to this woman, as Deborah predicted.

© 2008 Precept Ministries International

UNIT THREE - TEACHER'S GUIDE

Judges
Unit Three Test

25. Briefly summarize how Israel defeated Canaan in Judges 4 and 5.

Students should include most of the following:
- *4:15 - The LORD routed Sisera, his chariots, and army with the edge of the sword before Barak.*
- *4:23 - God subdued Jabin the king of Canaan before the sons of Israel.*
- *5:4 - The earth quaked, the heavens dripped, the clouds dripped water.*
- *5:5 - The mountains quaked.*
- *5:21 - A torrent of the Kishon River swept them away.*

ESSAY

Choose one of the following topics, briefly summarize it, and discuss how it applies to your life:

1. What you learned about God from Judges 4 and 5
2. The tribes that did not volunteer and why
3. Principles from the story of Deborah and Barak

Unit Four - Teacher's Guide

Judges

From Ordinary to Extraordinary

UNIT OBJECTIVES:

In this unit, students will observe Judges 6-8. They will analyze the context of God's name *Yahweh-Shalom* – The Lord is Peace. They will also continue to identify cycles of sin in these chapters. They will look at cross-references to interpret Gideon's life events and identify significances. Lastly, students will apply the truths to their lives.

UNIT FOUR

From Ordinary to Extraordinary
U-4, Chapters 6-8

Do you think God wants to use you to accomplish His purposes? If so, what keeps you from following when you hear Him call? Maybe you read something in His Word, heard a message that revealed an opportunity for ministry, or heard God speak His Word directly to your heart yet failed to act. What stopped you from obeying? Fear? Uncertainty? Doubt? Laziness? Do you believe God is setting you up to fail because you lack abilities nessesary to follow through?

> Did you know God has chosen the foolish, the weak, the base things of the world, and the despised (1 Corinthians 2:26-31)? He loves to raise up the **inadequate** to demonstrate His power through them!

You've seen God raise up bold, courageous, and faithful judges to lead Israel out of sin and into victory but do you discount God's ability to use you the same way? Maybe the judges were natural leaders with a lot of education, training, and strong families that offered them encouragement and wisdom to succeed. Surely it was easy for them to assume those roles, right?

Well, meet Gideon – eventually a warrior, but originally an **ordinary** man with the same struggles, family issues, and difficulties of everyone else! This week you'll see God grow within the heart of this fearful man, the confidence, strength, and determination to be all God called him to be. You will see what happens when a fearful man encounters a mighty God! It doesn't matter who you are, only Who is with you! Fear does not have to keep you from obedience.

Student Page 85

Unit four - Teacher's Guide

Judges

Introduction/Prayer

Encourage students to write what they want to know about God's will for their lives in their prayer. Remind them that because God already knows what's in their hearts, they should honestly express their questions and doubts.

Introduction/Prayer

U-4, Chapters 6-8

ONE ON ONE:

No study of the Word of God should begin without a cry to God to speak to your heart. In light of the Introduction and all you studied so far in Judges, what is the cry of your heart? Write it out – you will be encouraged when you read it later? Perhaps it will be found among your possessions as a **legacy** to those who follow you.

UNIT FOUR - TEACHER'S GUIDE

LESSON ONE:

 1. Judges 6-8 Observation Worksheets, colored pencils, "Locations in Judges 6-8" map at the end of the unit

OBJECTIVES:

Students will observe Judges 6-8 by reading the chapters with purpose and identify geographical locations.

Lesson 1/Assignment 1 - Observation
Students will read Judges 6-8 to get an overview of Gideon.

 Observation begins by reading the text purposefully. Remind your students that when they are studying inductively, they should not read as quickly as they can to complete the assignment; they should read with purpose. Asking the 5W and H questions as they read helps them understand and retain the text they're examining.

Lesson 1/Assignment 2 - Observation
Students will mark geographical locations in these chapters and locate them on the map at the end of this unit. There's a map in the Teacher's Helps for you to make a transparency of to help your students identify these locations.

Note: Discuss main events in this chapter when your students complete their observations.

LESSON ONE

Lesson 1/Assignment 1
1. Your assignment today is simply to read Judges 6–8. You need to gain a broad understanding of Gideon – who he is and what he does. In the remainder of the unit, we will take a deeper look at the text.

Lesson 1/Assignment 2
2. For today, mark only the geographical locations in the text. When you find one, look up the place on the map at the end of this unit and mark it. Be sure to identify where the Midianites lived.

U-4, Lesson 1, Chapters 6-8

Overview – An overview of a book or section of Scripture will help you see the message of the book as a whole; gain an understanding of the author's purpose for writing; identify themes; become aware of the structure or progression of events; and give you a sound basis for accurate interpretation and correct application. Be sure to ask the 5Ws and H as you read!

A CLOSER LOOK AT MIDIAN:

According to Genesis 25:2, Midian was a descendent of Abraham through his **concubine** Keturah after the death of Sarah. A concubine is a wife whose children have no inheritance rights. Midian, a personal and clan name, comes from the word "madon" meaning "strife." Interesting, isn't it?

THE MORE YOU KNOW!...

Pretty cool, huh? Isn't it amazing to see God take an average person and use him in such a mighty way? When God looks at you, He knows all of your faults and fears, but can also see past them to the new man He creates to use for His kingdom. Whether you characterize yourself as a doubter, an introvert, or a timid person, remember, it's simply a matter of taking God at His Word and trusting that He will equip you with His strength, wisdom and power to accomplish what He wants you to do.

Unit Four - Teacher's Guide

Judges

UNIT FOUR - TEACHER'S GUIDE

Judges

LESSON TWO:

Judges 6 Observation Worksheets, colored pencils, key word bookmark, "A Profile on Gideon" chart at the end of the unit

OBJECTIVES:

Students will continue to observe Judges 6 by marking the key words from their bookmarks including *afraid (fearful)*. Students will also identify verses referring to idolatry in this chapter and study key characteristics of Gideon and how they relate to him.

Lesson 2/Assignment 1 - Observation
Students will read Judges 6 and mark key words from their bookmarks found in this chapter including *afraid (fearful)*.

You can decide together how to mark the new key word for this chapter or let students decide for themselves. Remind them that there is no "wrong way" to mark. They can highlight or use a symbol or picture. However, key words should be marked in ways that distinguish them from others.

Lesson 2/Assignment 2 - Observation/Interpretation
Students will identify verses that refer to idolatry and write "idolatry" in the margins next to the verses they appear in.

Lesson 2/Assignment 3 - Observation/Interpretation
Students will identify chapter six's main events and record summary statements about them in the margins of their Observation Worksheets (wherever they are mentioned).

LESSON TWO

Lesson 2/Assignment 1 *U-4, Lesson 2, Chapter 6*
In Lesson 1, you saw the big picture of Gideon's life. Today you will begin to focus on the details.

1. Observe Judges 6. In addition to marking the key words on your bookmark, also mark references to being afraid of others. You can mark it with a brown box.

Lesson 2/Assignment 2
2. Continue to mark references to idolatry by simply writing the word "idolatry" in the margin of the text next to the verse it appears in.

Lesson 2/Assignment 3
3. Note the progression of events in this chapter. In the margin of your Observation Worksheets, write a brief summary statement of what happens next to the verse in which the event begins.

   For example:

   "Israel given to Midian" - v. 1
   "God sends a prophet" - v. 7

Lesson 2/Assignment 4
4. List all you learn about Gideon in the chart "A Profile on Gideon" at the end of the unit, instead of the "The Judges of Israel" chart since there are so many details.

Lesson 2/Assignment 5
5. As you look at Gideon, think about whether you relate to him in any ways. Put a star beside this information on your chart and then write out how you relate to him in that way in the appropriate column.

> Think about it...
> If God could use a young man with these shortcomings, He can use you with all your shortcomings too!

© 2008 Precept Ministries International

Student Page 89

UNIT FOUR - TEACHER'S GUIDE

Judges

 Recording main events helps students observe and interpret chapters. Additionally, it will strengthen their reading comprehension skills including determining a theme for the chapter.

Lesson 2/Assignment 4 - Observation/Interpretation

Students will list what they learned about Gideon on the "A Profile on Gideon" chart found at the end of this unit. You can make a transparency from the blank chart in the Teacher's Helps to use in class. Help students determine the first few characteristics of Gideon.

 In this listing assignment, students will ask the 5W and H questions to determine what the text tells them about Gideon. Who was he? Where was he from? etc. As they find answers, they should record them on the chart.

Lesson 2/Assignment 5 - Application

Students will evaluate what they learned about Gideon and how they relate to him or his life.

UNIT FOUR - TEACHER'S GUIDE

LESSON THREE:

 Judges 6 Observation Worksheets

OBJECTIVES:

In this lesson, students will continue to observe Judges 6, particularly the significance of Gideon's encounter with the angel of the Lord and Gideon's strengths and weaknesses.

Lesson 3/Assignment 1 - Observation/Interpretation/Application

Students should learn the following from Gideon's encounter with the angel of the Lord in Judges 6:11-24:

Verses 12-13
- *Angel's Words – The Lord is with you, O valiant warrior.*

- *Gideon's Reponse – If the Lord is with us, why has this happened? Where are all His miracles? The Lord has abandoned us and given us into the hand of the Midian.*

Verses 14-16
- *Angel's Instruction – Go and deliver Israel from the hand of Midian – I have sent you.*

- *Gideon's Excuse – How can I deliver Israel? My family is the least in Manasseh. I am the youngest in my father's house.*

- *Angel's Response – Surely I will be with you, you shall defeat Midian as one man.*

Verses 17-24
- *Gideon's Request – If I have found favor in your sight, show me a sign that it is You who speaks to me – don't depart until I return with an*

LESSON THREE

Lesson 3/Assignment 1
U-4, Lesson 3, Chapter 6

1. In Judges 6:11-24, the angel of the Lord came and spoke to Gideon and a big change happened in Gideon as a result. In the space provided below, write out what the angel of the Lord says and how Gideon responds. Note the excuses Gideon gives and how the angel of the Lord responds.

VERSES 12-13:

Angel's Words –

Gideon's Reponse –

VERSES 14-16:

Angel's Instruction –

Gideon's Excuse –

Angel's Response –

VERSES 17-24:

Gideon's Request –

Angel's Reponse –

Gideon's Action –

Angel's Action –

Student Page 91

UNIT FOUR - TEACHER'S GUIDE

offering to lay before you.

- *Angel's Reponse – I will remain until you return.*

- *Gideon's Action – Prepared a kid and unleavened bread, presented them.*

- *Angel's Response and Action – Told Gideon to lay meat and bread on the rock and pour out the broth; took his staff and touched the meat and bread; fire sprang from the rock and consumed the meat and bread; angel vanished.*

- *Gideon's Response – Alas, I have seen the angel of the Lord face to face.*

- *Lord's Response – Peace, do not fear – you will not die.*

a. According to the angel of the Lord, Gideon was a valiant warrior.

b. Students should learn that Gideon was fearful and hesitant, not the characteristics of a valiant warrior.

c. Students should learn that Gideon becomes a valiant warrior who defeats Midian.

d. Students should learn that God sees not just <u>what they are</u>, but <u>what they can be</u> when they follow His lead believing and obeying..

e. Students should consider that when they fear what others think instead of trusting what God thinks, they are implying that God is a liar.

U-4, Lesson 3, Chapter 6

Gideon's Response –

Lord's Response –

a. According to the angel of the Lord, what was Gideon?

b. Did Gideon act like a "valiant warrior" during this encounter? Why or why not?

c. Based on your observations from the overview, does Gideon ever fulfill this calling? How?

d. What does this tell you about God?

e. Even when God told Gideon what He was going to do through him, Gideon looked at his circumstances and what others said about him. Why is it dangerous to worry about what others say about you? How can it affect your obedience to God?

UNIT FOUR - TEACHER'S GUIDE

Judges

Lesson 3/Assignment 2 - Interpretation/Application

a. Students should see that the Lord (of) Peace, Yahweh-Shalom, was revealed in spite of the fact that there was no peace, only relentless attacks by the Midianites. The name is a promise of things to come (peace).

b. In Judges 6:11, Gideon was beating out wheat in the wine press, hiding from the Midianites so they would not come and take it.

c. After Gideon's encounter with the angel of the Lord, he obeys the Lord's command to remove the altar of Baal and the Asherah that belonged to his father. Although he is not completely free of fear, he trusts God and obeys His commands. Instead of continuing to hide in fear from his enemies, he takes action.

d. According to John 14:27, Jesus promises His peace to believers. He tells His disciples not to let their hearts be troubled or fearful. In Philippians 4:6-7 Paul tells believers to "be anxious for nothing, but in everything by prayer and supplication with thanksgiving let [their] requests be made known to God. And the peace of God, which surpasses all comprehension, will guard their hearts and minds in Christ Jesus."

e. Students will evaluate their response to enemies and confidence in God. They will determine if confidence makes them obey in difficult, intimidating circumstances.

Lesson 3/Assignment 2
U-4, Lesson 3, Chapter 6

2. Judges 6:24 includes the first mention of one of God's names – the "Lord is Peace" (Yahweh-shalom).

   a. When this name of God is given, what is taking place within Israel?

   b. Where was Gideon and how would you describe him when the angel of the Lord first appeared to him?

   c. What does Gideon do following his encounter with the angel of the Lord? What do you think he now understands about God?

   d. What are God's promises of peace to you? Look up the following verses and record what you learn.

   JOHN 14:27

   PHILIPPIANS 4:6-7

   e. How can knowing this about God change your life?

Student Page 93

Unit four - Teacher's Guide

Judges

Lesson 3/Assignment 3 - Interpretation
Help students determine the main point of chapter six and a summary statement that will help them remember it. A possible summary statement for this chapter is:

Judges 6 – The call of Gideon

World View Project - In Christ I am…
This project will help students identify what believers in Christ are despite what they or others think about them. When they have completed this project, you may want them to share with the class what they wrote on their poster board and how truth from God's Word impacted their lives.

Lesson 3/Assignment 3
U-4, Lesson 3, Chapter 6

3. Write the theme of Judges 6 on the "At A Glance" chart.

World View Project

WHAT'S YOUR WORLD VIEW?

IN CHRIST I AM… - PROJECT

For this assignment you will need the following:

"Who I Am in Christ" worksheet

In order to deliver Israel, Gideon needed to be confident that God was with him! To be all God wants you to be, you too need to know the God's promises. What are some of the things the Lord says in His Word that you need to understand and live in light of?

Using the worksheet "Who I Am in Christ," look up the cross references and fill in the blanks. Then read each dilemma below from a student like yourself.

"I'm a Christian but I am not very popular, and don't have very many friends. I don't fit into any group. Where do I belong when I feel like no one accepts me?"

"I want God to use me, but I have made some major mistakes. Will my past always define who I am? Can I ever be more than what I used to be?"

"I hear people talking about great things God has accomplished through them. I feel so ordinary. How and why would God want to use me?"

Write one of the quotes at the top of your paper, then respond to the question from what you just learned from God's Word. Be sure to reference the scriptures from the "Who I Am in Christ" worksheet.

> Knowing God's truth will help you overcome doubts and fear in your life. It will also give you the ability to encourage others in their personal struggles. The world offers lots of advice…. YOU can offer TRUTH!

Student Page 94

Unit four - Teacher's Guide

Judges

U-4, Lesson 3, Chapter 6

Who I Am In Christ

I AM ACCEPTED...

John 1:12	I am God's _____.
John 15:15	As a disciple, I am a friend of _____.
Romans 5:1	I have been _____.
1 Corinthians 6:17	I am _____ with the Lord, and I am _____ with Him in spirit.
1 Corinthians 6:19-20	I have been _____ with a price and I belong to _____.
1 Corinthians 12:27	I am a _____ of Christ's body.
Ephesians 1:3-8	I have been _____ by God and adopted as His child.
Colossians 1:13-14	I have been redeemed and _____ of all my sins.
Colossians 2:9-10	I am _____ in Christ.
Hebrews 4:14-16	I have direct access to the throne of _____ through Jesus Christ.

I AM SECURE...

Romans 8:1-2	I am free from condemnation.
Romans 8:28	I am assured that God works for my good in all circumstances.
Romans 8:31-39	I am _____ from any condemnation brought against me and I cannot be _____ from the love of God.
2 Corinthians 1:21-22	I have been _____, _____ and _____ by God.
Colossians 3:1-4	I am _____ with Christ in God.

Student Page 95

UNIT FOUR - TEACHER'S GUIDE

Judges

U-4, Lesson 3, Chapter 6

Philippians 1:6	I am confident that God will _____ the good work He started in me.
Philippians 3:20	I am a _____ of heaven.
2 Timothy 1:7	I have not been given a spirit of _____ but of _____, _____ and a sound _____.
1 John 5:18	I am born of _____ and the _____ cannot touch me.
I AM SIGNIFICANT...	
John 15:5	I am a _____ of Jesus Christ, the true vine, and a channel of His life.
John 15:16	I have been chosen and appointed to bear _____.
1 Corinthians 3:16	I am God's _____.
2 Corinthians 5:17-21	I am a minister of _____ for God.
Ephesians 2:6	I am _____ with Jesus Christ in the heavenly realm.
Ephesians 2:10	I am God's _____.
Ephesians 3:12	I may approach God with _____ and confidence.
Philippians 4:13	I can do all things through _____, who strengthens me.

Student Page 96

UNIT FOUR - TEACHER'S GUIDE

Judges

DISCUSSION GUIDE LESSONS ONE, TWO AND THREE:

Review the main points so far in Judges.

> The tribes of Israel had not obeyed the Lord by completely driving their enemies out of Canaan. Every man was doing right in his own eyes. Israel was in a cycle of evil, enemies, crying to the Lord, and God raising up a judge.
>
> Mesopotamia oppressed Israel eight years until Othniel delivered them.
> The land had rest for 40 years, presumably for the time Othniel was judge (2:18-19).
>
> Israel served Eglon, the king of Moab, for 18 years until Ehud killed him and told Israel to fight the Moabites. The land was then undisturbed for 80 years.
>
> After Ehud, came Shamgar, delivered Israel from the Philistines.
>
> After Ehud died, Israel returned to evil and the Lord sold them into the hand of Jabin, king of Canaan, who oppressed them severely for 20 years. The Lord raised up Deborah and Barak to deliver Israel from the Canaanites, and the land was undisturbed for 40 years.

JUDGES 6

Ask the 5W and H questions to stimulate discussion of the following:

> Israel again did evil and the Lord gave them into the hand of Midian for seven years. Show students on a map that Midian is not in the land of Canaan – its an external enemy outside Israel's borders.
>
> Verses 2-6 describe Midian's devastation in Israel like locusts destroying produce and animals.
>
> Amalek and the sons of the east are mentioned dwelling with the Midianites.
>
> Verses 7-10 say that Israel cried to the Lord at that time, and He sent a prophet. (This was not unusual. Deborah the prophetess spoke for the Lord during this time. Prophets reminded Israel who the Lord was and what He had done for them.) Relate this to 2:10. The Lord commanded them not to fear the gods of the Amorites, in whose land they lived. He reminded them that He was God and no other god could protect them.
>
> The prophet reminded Israel that they had not obeyed the Lord.

Unit Four - Teacher's Guide

Judges

Verses 11-24

> The Lord called Gideon to be His valiant warrior. Gideon was hiding in a winepress to save the wheat he was beating from the Midianites. Relate this to your students. Have they ever been afraid of God's enemies and hid in some way?
>
> Gideon was the youngest of the least family in the tribe of Manasseh. Perhaps some of your students feel just as insignificant.
>
> God chose a man who appeared to be "least likely a valiant warrior." He told Gideon to deliver Israel from the hand of Midian. The Lord assured Gideon that He would be with him to defeat Midian.
>
> Gideon asked God for a sign that He spoke to him. After the Lord consumed the sacrifice and vanished, Gideon knew he had seen the angel of the Lord face to face and thought he was going to die.
>
> The Lord reassured him (verse 23), and Gideon named the altar he built "The Lord is Peace." Today that name, Jehovah-Shalom, is used in songs and teachings. The context it is found in is reassuring – a man hiding because of fear after the Lord commissions him to defeat an enemy and fearing death because he saw the angel of the Lord face to face. Gideon conversed with the angel of the Lord, not knowing it was Him at first. He wondered why God had forsaken His people. Relate this to the cross-references on idolatry. Had the Lord forsaken Israel?

Verses 25-32

> The Lord told Gideon to tear down his father's idols. Even though he did this at night still fearful, he obeyed the Lord.
>
> Gideon's family was part of Israel, but involved in idol worship. His father wisely reasoned with men in the city who were upset with what Gideon did that if Baal is a god, let him contend for himself.
>
> Gideon was then given the name "Jerubbaal" which means, "Let Baal contend against him."

Verses 33-40

> The Midianites, Amalekites, and sons of the east assembled in the valley of Jezreel. Show this on the map. It is also sometimes called the valley of Megiddo. Where did Barak fight Sisera?
>
> The Spirit of the Lord came upon Gideon. He called together the Abiezrites and sent messengers

Unit Four - Teacher's Guide

Judges

to Manasseh, Asher, Zebulun, and Naphtali to plan for battle.

According to verses 36-40, Gideon asked the Lord to reassure him that he was called to deliver Israel from the Midianites. The Lord used a fleece to reassure Gideon that he was the one to deliver Israel.

This miracle reveals God's long-suffering and compassion to someone He had already appeared and spoken to very clearly. "Putting out a fleece" is not the way for New Testament believers to know the will of the Lord for their lives. The way to know His will is to know the Lord and His Word and to follow the leading of His indwelling Spirit.

Ask your students to share what they've learned from these lessons that they can apply to their lives.

Unit four - Teacher's Guide

Judges

UNIT FOUR - TEACHER'S GUIDE

Judges

LESSON FOUR:

Judges 1-6 Observation Worksheets, Bible

OBJECTIVES:

In this lesson, students will identify the various gods mentioned in the book of Judges and examine God's commands to the sons of Israel concerning these gods. They will look at cross-references about these commands to further understand God's instructions to Gideon concerning the altar of Baal and the Asherah.

Lesson 4/Assignment 1 - Observation/Interpretation
a. Students will identify the following gods:
- 2:11 – The Baals
- 2:13 – Baal and Ashtaroth
- 3:7 – Baals and the Asheroth
- 6:25 – Baal and Asherah

b. These were the gods of the inhabitants of the land and of the peoples around them.

Lesson 4/Assignment 2 - Interpretation
Students will look up each of the cross-references and record what they learn about idolatry and parallels they see to the times of Gideon or the judges.

a. According to Exodus 20:1-6, the sons of Israel were "to have no other gods before" God and were "not to make for themselves an idol, or any likeness of what is in heaven above or on the earth beneath or in the water under the earth." They were "not to worship them or serve them," because God is a jealous God.

b. According to Leviticus 26:1-18, the sons of Israel were "not to make for

---

LESSON FOUR

Lesson 4/Assignment 1   *U-4, Lesson 4, Chapter 6*

1. In Lesson 2, you noted the references to idolatry in the margin of Judges 6. This **recurring** sin throughout the days of the Judges (as you have already seen) is our subject for today.

   a. Look back through your Observation Worksheets on Judges 1-6 and list below the various gods people worshiped.

   b. Whose gods were these?

Lesson 4/Assignment 2

2. You have already looked at scriptures in Deuteronomy that warned the Israelites to not marry their enemies or worship their gods. Keeping this in mind, look up the following passages and see what God had taught His people about idols up to this point in their history.

   As you look up each passage, record what the verses say about idolatry and note contrasts and similarities to the times of Gideon or Judges in general.

> Baal is first mentioned in the Bible in Numbers 22:41.
>
> In Numbers 22:7 and Numbers 25, you learn that the Midianites associated with the Moabites to destroy Israel.
>
> Numbers 25 tells us the children of Israel "began to play the harlot with the daughters of Moab" and "Israel joined themselves to Baal of Peor." In this chapter you find one of the men of Israel sneaking a Midianite woman into his tent and God bringing a plague on the Israelites. Phinehas st**o**pped it by putting to death the man and woman. Do you remember reading about him at the end of Judges?

Student Page 97

Unit Four - Teacher's Guide

themselves idols, nor set up an image or a sacred pillar, nor place a figured stone in the land to bow down to it" (obviously, not a command obeyed during the times of the judges studied so far.) *If they kept his commands, God would "give them rains in their season, so that the land would yield its produce and the trees of the field would bear their fruit. Their threshing would last until grape gathering, and grape gathering would last until sowing time." They would be able "to eat their fruit and live securely in their land." God would also grant peace in the land, so that they could "lie down with no one making them tremble." God would eliminate harmful beasts from the land, and "no sword would pass through their land." The sons of Israel would be able "to chase their enemies and they would fall before them by the sword." However if they did not obey, God promised to "appoint over them a sudden terror, consumption and fever that would waste away the eyes and cause the soul to pine away;" also, they would "sow their seed uselessly, for their enemies would eat it up." God promised to "set His face against them" so that they would be "struck down before thier enemies;" they would be ruled by those who hated them. If they continued to disobey, God would punish them "seven times more for their sins." Students should recognize that since Israel didn't obey God concerning the idols, He brought about the punishments promised in these verses.*

c. According to Exodus 34:12-17, the sons of Israel were not to make covenants with the inhabitants of the land but instead to tear down their altars and smash their sacred pillars and cut down their Asherim. They were not to worship any other god, "for the LORD, whose name is Jealous, is a jealous God." If they didn't do this, they might make a covenant with the inhabitants of the land, "play the harlot with their gods and sacrifice to their gods, take daughters for wives and play the harlot with their gods." Students should recognize that the people defied the warnings in the times of the judges and God's judgment came to pass.

Lesson 4/Assignment 3 - Interpretation Students should learn that God commanded Gideon to do what He told the sons of Israel to do originally and Gideon was right to obey.

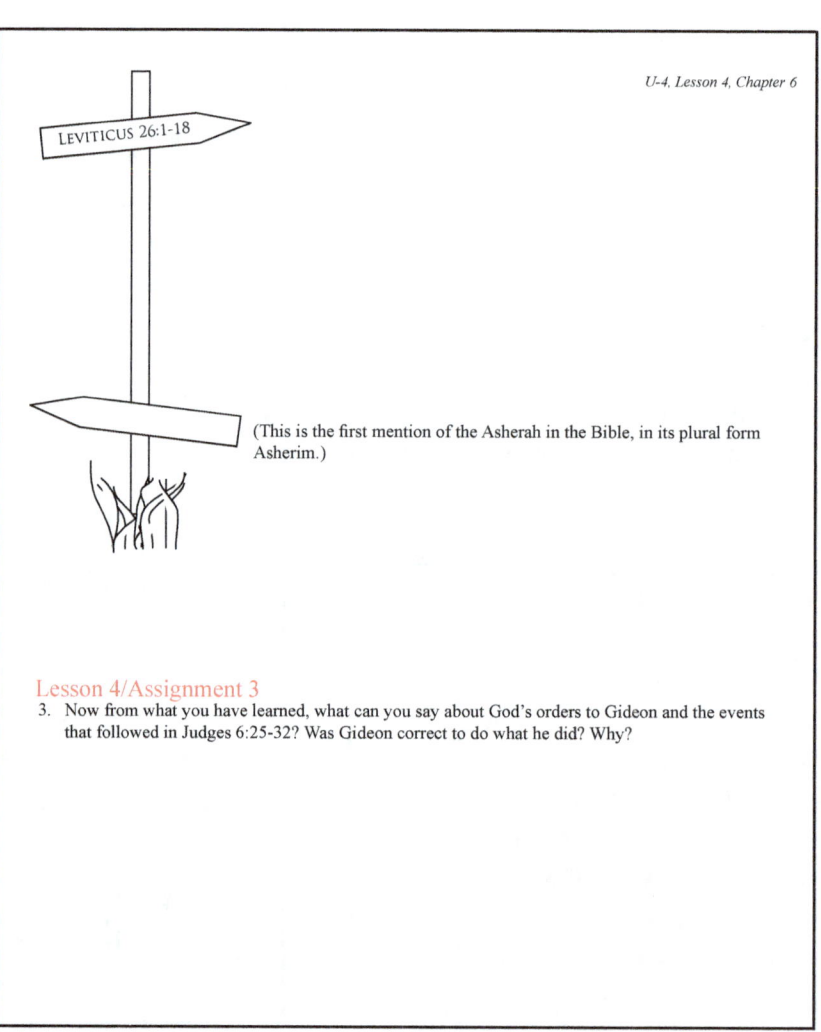

U-4, Lesson 4, Chapter 6

(This is the first mention of the Asherah in the Bible, in its plural form Asherim.)

Lesson 4/Assignment 3
3. Now from what you have learned, what can you say about God's orders to Gideon and the events that followed in Judges 6:25-32? Was Gideon correct to do what he did? Why?

Student Page 98
© 2008 Precept Ministries International

UNIT FOUR - TEACHER'S GUIDE

Judges

LESSON FIVE:

 Bible

OBJECTIVES:

In this lesson, students will examine cross-references to understand the uselessness of idols and the significance of God.

Lesson 5/Assignment 1 - Interpretation
a. From Isaiah 44:9-20, students should learn the following about idols:
- "Those who fashion a graven image are all of them futile, and their precious things are of no profit; they will be put to shame."
- "All his companions will be put to shame."
- "The craftsmen themselves are mere men. They use the same things they make into idols to eat, burn, and use as tools, but decide that some are worthy to be worshipped."
- "They do not understand they have a deceived heart."

b. Students should learn that no one made God; He is the only true God. He established the ancient nation and He knows the future. There is no God besides Him.

LESSON FIVE

Lesson 5/Assignment 1   U-4, Lesson 5, Chapter 6
Today you will uncover more about God's character in dealing with the sin of idolatry.

1. Isaiah 44:9-20 is a classic passage on idolatry. To put it in context, read verses 6-20.

   a.   List what you learn about idols and idolatry from this passage.

   b.   Now compare your observations on idols and idolatry with what God says about Himself in verses 6-8. List these comparisons.

Student Page 99

UNIT FOUR - TEACHER'S GUIDE

Judges

UNIT FOUR - TEACHER'S GUIDE

Judges

LESSON SIX:

 Bible

OBJECTIVES:

In this lesson, students will examine cross-references to understand the results of serving idols rather than God. They will also examine their lives for idolatry and how they should deal with this sin according to God's Word.

Lesson 6/Assignment 1 - Observation/Interpretation
Students will record what they learn about God, idols, and people who worship them on the "Romans 1:18-32: When People Serve Idols Rather Than God" chart. The chart key is available at the end of this unit. The Teacher's Helps has a blank chart for you to make a transparency to use in class.

Lesson 6/Assignment 2 - Interpretation/Application
According to Colossians 3:5, greed is idolatry and believers should consider the members of their bodies dead to it.

a. Students will record what they learned about idolatry and how they will define it for someone else. They should see that idolatry is worshipping created things and it includes greed.

b. Students will examine their desires for things they think are more important than God.

LESSON SIX

Lesson 6/Assignment 1 U-4, Lesson 6, Chapter 6

If God is the one and only true God, the first and the last, the Creator of all mankind who revealed Himself to man from the very beginning, where did idols come from and why does idolatry bring God's wrath and judgment? Why did He sell His people into the hands of their enemies as He did in Judges when they sinned and followed other gods?

1. Read Romans 1:18-32 very carefully. Summarize what you learn from this passage about God, idols, and those who worship them, on the chart at the end of this unit entitled "Romans 1:18-32: When People Serve Idols Rather Than God."

   As you observe this passage, watch for the key repeated phrase *God gave them over* and note what was exchanged for what in each occurance.

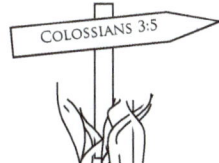

Lesson 6/Assignment 2
2. Look up the following verse (check footnotes in your Bible) and write out what you learn about idolatry.

   a. How would you describe idolatry to a person living in your country?

   b. Are there any idols in your life – anything tempting or **luring** you away from serving God and worshiping Him in spirit and truth?

Student Page 101

Unit four - Teacher's Guide

Judges

c. Students will consider what God would say to them about current times, their character, and the "job" He has for them to complete.

d. Students will think prayerfully about what they learned from this chapter and determine what truths they can take and apply to their lives.

U-4, Lesson 6, Chapter 6

c. If God spoke to you as He spoke to Gideon in Judges 6, what do you think He would say?

d. Based on all you've studied about Gideon in this unit so far, what has God taught you that you can apply to your life?

Student Page 102

UNIT FOUR - TEACHER'S GUIDE

Judges

DISCUSSION GUIDE LESSONS FOUR, FIVE AND SIX:

Ask your class to share what they learned about the gods of the Canaanites, Amorites, and nations of the land of Canaan.

> Even though there is only one God, Israel continually went after the gods of the wicked people around them: in Egypt, it was Baal of Peor in the wilderness; then the gods of the nations in Canaan.

Discuss with your students what they learned from the references to idolatry.

> Exodus 20:1-6 is part of what God Himself spoke to the people of Israel at Mount Sinai. They were so afraid that they asked Him not to speak anymore to them, but to speak to Moses and let Moses speak what He said to them.
>
> They entered into covenant with the Lord to do what He said – to obey His commands. That generation was killed in the wilderness for breaking His covenant. The second generation entered into the same covenant, agreeing to do what He commanded. They did well until Joshua, the elders, and the rest of that generation died. The following generations continually disobeyed the Lord's commands, especially the one to not worship other gods.
>
> Leviticus 26:1-18
> God told Israel repeatedly that He is the Lord their God. They were not to turn away to gods that were not gods at all, but to worship and obey Him, the only true God, who brought them out of Egypt, freeing them from slavery.
>
> He also warned them that if they reject His statutes and break His covenant, He will punish them. Their enemies will strike them down; those who hate them will rule over them. (This happened during the times of the judges.) If they repeatedly reject Him, He will punish them seven times more for their sins.
>
> Exodus 34:12-17 is another warning to Israel of the inhabitants of the land becoming a snare to them. The Lord, "whose name is Jealous," is a jealous God. Let your students discuss how this applies to New Testament believers as well.
>
> Isaiah 44:6-20 describes idols and those who make them. They are futile (no profit). Idols are made by men, not gods. The complete futility of idol worship is seen in this statement, "I fall down before a block of wood."
>
> In verses 6-8, the Lord reminds Israel of what He is.
> - King of Israel
> - Redeemer

© 2008 Precept Ministries International

Unit Four - Teacher's Guide

Judges

- Lord of hosts
- First and last
- Established the ancient nation – Israel
- Predicts future
- Rock

There is none other, and Israel is His witness.

Let your students discuss what they learned from these references about God and the futility of "idols."

Romans 1:18-32 and Colossians 3:5 tell more about idolatry. Greed, impure passions, exchanging the truth for a lie, a depraved mind.

Have your students discuss how they will apply the truths they learned in these lessons to their lives.

UNIT FOUR - TEACHER'S GUIDE

Judges

LESSON SEVEN:

 Judges 6-7 Observation Worksheets, colored pencils, key word bookmark, "At A Glance" chart from the Appendix, "A Profile on Gideon" chart

OBJECTIVES:

In this lesson, students will complete their observation of Judges 7 and determine its theme. They will also "discover" the characteristics of God in Judges 6 and 7.

Lesson 7/Assignment 1 - Observation
Students will observe Judges 7 marking the key words from their bookmarks including *worship*.

Lesson 7/Assignment 2 - Observation/Interpretation
Students will record new information they glean about Gideon on the "Profile of Gideon" chart.

Lesson 7/Assignment 3 - Interpretation
Help students determine the main point of chapter 7 and a summary statement to help them remember it. A possible summary statement for this chapter is:

Judges 7 – Gideon and the 300 against Midian

Lesson 7/Assignment 4 - Observation/Interpretation
Students will record what they learned about God from Judges 6 and 7. Their list should include some of the following:

- *God chose Gideon even though he was frightened and unsure.*
- *God is peace.*
- *God gave Gideon clear instructions.*
- *God provides for Gideon in his fear by allowing his servant to go with him and by letting Gideon hear the Midianite's dream.*

LESSON SEVEN

Lesson 7/Assignment 1
U-4, Lesson 7, Chapters 6-7

1. Read through Judges 6 again and then observe Judges 7. Gideon will later be called Jerubbaal, the name his father Joash gave to him after Gideon destroyed the altar to Baal and cut down the Asherah next to it.

   As you mark key words, mark *worship* in a distinct way. Although it is only used one time here, it's a good word to mark throughout your Bible. You can mark it with a green **W**.

Lesson 7/Assignment 2
2. Record new insights on Gideon on your "Profile" chart at the end of the unit.

Lesson 7/Assignment 3
3. Note on the "At A Glance" chart a theme for Judges 7.

Lesson 7/Assignment 4
4. What do you learn about God in Judges 6 and 7? Have you watched God meet with Gideon step-by-step? Have you gained new insights on His character and ways? List them below.

If you were raised in church or were read children's Bible stories as you grew up, undoubtedly you heard of the "sword for the Lord for Gideon." But did you realize how amazing the account of Gideon is or the lessons for life that can be gleaned from this historical account?

It's encouraging to see how God can take a man a "nobody" filled with fear, threshing wheat in a wine press where he cannot be easily seen, and use him so mightily! How often do you limit your faith with unbelief or fear? How often do you fail to listen, believe, dream?

Never forget that your God is the same God who moved with **extravagant** grace and patience in the life of a young man who battled fear, needing constant assurance that God would do what He said, ultimately delivering Israel through him.

Student Page 103

Unit four - Teacher's Guide

UNIT FOUR - TEACHER'S GUIDE

LESSON EIGHT:

 Judges 8 Observation Worksheets, colored pencils, key word bookmark, Bible, "At A Glance" chart and "The Judges of Israel" chart from the Appendix

OBJECTIVES:

Students will complete their observations of Judges 8, examining the people's desire to make Gideon king and his response. They will also identify the significance of the ephod Gideon makes and the people's response.

Lesson 8/Assignment 1 - Observation
Students will complete their observations of Judges 8 marking the key words from their bookmark and including *crescent* and *ephod*.

Lesson 8/Assignment 2 - Observation/Interpretation
a. According to Judges 8:22-23, Gideon said the Lord should rule over the people, not him.

b. Students should see that Gideon might have taken advantage of the situation and become king, but he knew God was ruler and he would not take God's place.

Lesson 8/Assignment 3 - Interpretation
According to Hebrews 11:32-34, Gideon was included with other men of faith, who "conquered kingdoms, performed acts of righteousness, obtained promises, escaped the edge of the sword, from weakness were made strong, became mighty in war, put foreign armies to flight."

LESSON EIGHT

Lesson 8/Assignment 1
Today you will conclude your study of Gideon in Judges 8. He won't be mentioned in any other book of the Bible except in Hebrews 11:32, where he's listed with those who pleased God and accomplished great things through faith.

1. Observe Judges 8. In addition to other key words on your bookmark, mark *crescent* with an orange half moon. Don't put it on your bookmark since the only other place it appears outside of Judges 8 is Isaiah 3:18.

   Also mark *ephod* and pronouns that refer to it with a blue shield like this ⬡. You can Put it on your bookmark because you'll come across it again in Judges.

> "And what more shall I say? For time will fail me if I tell of Gideon, Barak, Samson, Jephthah, of David and Samuel and the prophets, who by faith conquered kingdoms, performed acts of righteousness, obtained promises, shut the mouths of lions, quenched the power of fire, escaped the edge of the sword, from weakness were made strong, became mighty in war, put foreign armies to flight."
> - Hebrews 11:32-34

Lesson 8/Assignment 2
2. In Judges 8:22-23, the people seek to make Gideon their king.

   a. What do you think about his response?

   b. What does it show you about the man?

Lesson 8/Assignment 3
3. Note what this verse says about Gideon.

   HEBREWS 11:32-34

UNIT FOUR - TEACHER'S GUIDE

Judges

Lesson 8/Assignment 4 - Observation
Students should record the following about the ephod from this chapter:
* *Gideon made it.*
* *Gideon put it in his city.*
* *Israel played the harlot with it.*
* *It became a snare to Gideon and his household.*

Lesson 8/Assignment 5 - Interpretation
a. According to Exodus 25:7 and 28, the ephod was part of Aaron's holy garments; it was made of gold and precious stones. Aaron carried "the names of the sons of Israel in the breastpiece of judgment over his heart when he [entered] the holy place for a memorial before the LORD continually. The breastpiece of judgment, the Urim and the Thummim, [were] to be over Aaron's heart when he [went] in before the LORD; and Aaron [was] to carry the judgment of the sons of Israel over his heart before the LORD continually." It was to be a part of Aaron and his sons' holy garments so that when they entered the tent of meeting, they did not incur guilt and die.

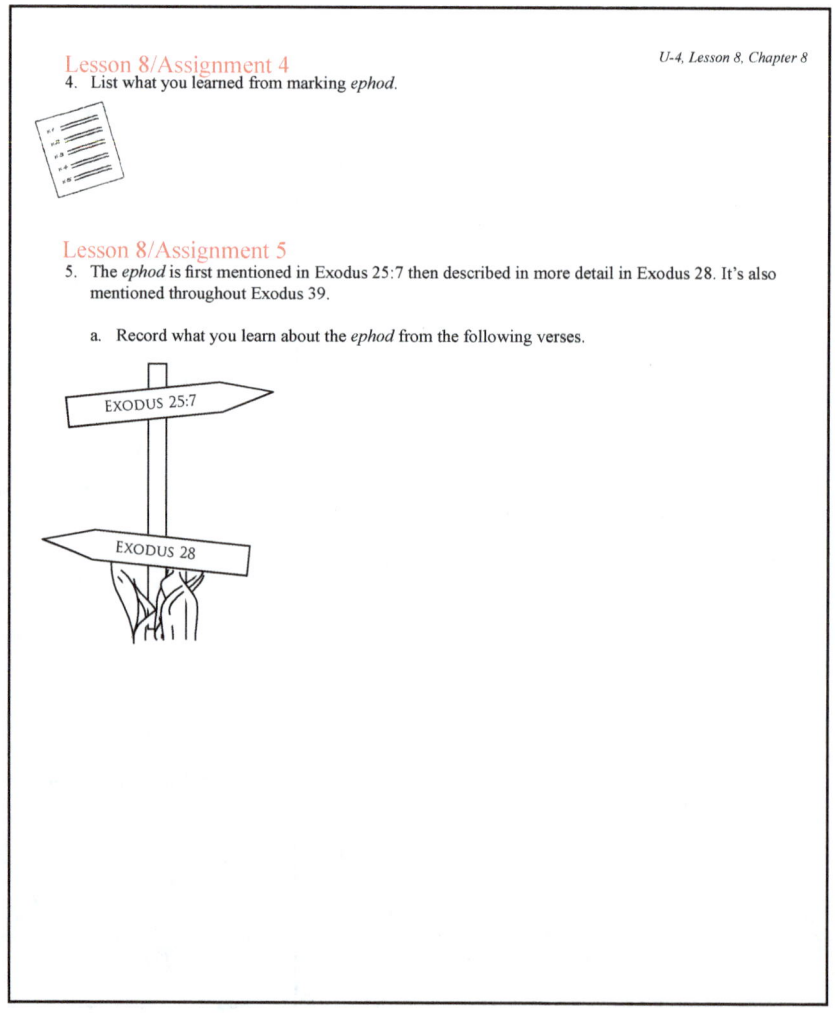

UNIT FOUR - TEACHER'S GUIDE

b. The ephod Gideon made (8:27) became an idol to the people.

c. Students should learn that after Gideon died the sons of Israel again played the harlot with the Baals and made Baal-berith their god. This shows that their hearts were intent on worshipping idols, not the one true God.

d. Students should see that Gideon was attempting to make a memorial piece as the priests were commanded to do in Exodus and did not intend for it to become an idol.

Lesson 8/Assignment 6 - Observation/Interpretation
Students should record relevant information about Gideon on "The Judges of Israel" chart in the Appendix.

Lesson 8/Assignment 7 - Interpretation
Help students determine the main point of chapter 8 and a summary statement to help them remember it. A possible summary statement for this chapter is:
Judges 8 – People want Gideon as king, and the ephod

Lesson 8/Assignment 8 - Interpretation
If commentaries are available, students can read about Judges 6-8.

Remind students that a commentary is a valuable tool they should use only after they complete their own examination of Scripture. Looking at commentaries prior to observing, interpreting, and applying Scripture for yourself can cause you to approach the text with a bias and ruin the joy of discovering truth on your own.

U-4, Lesson 8, Chapter 8

b. What happens to Gideon's ephod?

c. Do you see a correlation between this and what people do after Gideon dies? Does this tell you anything about their hearts?

d. From what you observed about Gideon in Judges 8, do you think he ever intended for the ephod to become an idol?

Lesson 8/Assignment 6
6. Record new insights about Gideon you gain from Judges 8. Then add his name and relevant information to the chart "The Judges of Israel."

Lesson 8/Assignment 7
7. Record the theme of Judges 8 on your "At A Glance" chart.

> Well, you have come to the end of the longest account of any of the Judges. How what does God want you to learn? What insights do you have from this man's life that you can apply to yours? What has God taught you? How has He spoken to your heart? Write your thoughts out on the following page in a creative way such as a song, poem, or journal entry. However you feel led to respond, remember, God has a purpose for your life, even as He had for Gideon's.

Unit four - Teacher's Guide

Unit Four - Teacher's Guide

Discussion Guide Lessons Seven and Eight:

Judges 7
Ask your students to discuss the main events of this chapter.

> The Lord wanted Israel to know their deliverance from Midian was not their own doing; He told Gideon to decrease the number of men from 32,000 to only 300.
>
> First those who were afraid and trembling returned home. Fear is infectious.
>
> Then those who lapped water instead of kneeling to drink were chosen to fight. (Perhaps they were more alert.)
>
> Gideon needed further reassurance from the Lord before the battle.
>
> He got it from an unlikely source. Gideon had the faith and strength to go to the Midianite camp, and he heard a man interpret his friend's dream that the Lord had given Midian into Gideon's hand.
>
> Israel didn't even have to fight in the battle. The Lord won the victory just as He did with Deborah and Barak in the battle against the Canaanites' iron chariots.

Relate this to the ways other judges delivered Israel.

> Othniel was a warrior.
> Ehud was clever; he single-handedly killed Eglon.
> Shamgar used an ox goad to kill 600 Philistines.
> The heavens and earth fought Sisera's army and he was killed by a woman.
>
> The Lord delivered His people with judges (deliverers).
>
> The leaders of Midian were killed by the men of Ephraim Gideon summoned to help when Midian fled.

Judges 8
Ask your students what they learned from studying chapter 8.

> Ephraim was upset that they weren't called for battle, but Gideon diplomatically answered them: they had taken the leaders of Midian, a good lesson in "...a soft answer turns away wrath."
>
> When Gideon pursued the kings of Midian, the men of Succoth refused to help.

UNIT FOUR - TEACHER'S GUIDE

Judges

After capturing Zebah and Zalmunna, Gideon returned to Succoth and disciplined the men for not helping.

Gideon then killed the kings of Midian.

When asked if he would rule over Israel, Gideon said neither he nor his son would rule Israel; the Lord would rule.

Given this response, it is unlikely that Gideon led Israel to worship an ephod.

Ask your students what they learned from studying the ephod.

Gideon took the spoils and made an ephod.

According to Exodus, the priest wore the ephod when he went into the presence of the Lord to bear the names of the sons of Israel before the Lord. The ephod held the breastplate used to discern the will of the Lord, and only the priest was to wear it. Gideon could have known that since he knew of the ephod. He had access to God's Word because Moses and Joshua wrote it down. It was written on stones on Mount Ebal (Joshua 8:30-32).

After Gideon died, the people worshipped the Baals, but they played the harlot with the ephod even before his death, and this became a snare to Gideon and his household – a very sad ending for one who had grown in faith.

Verse 28 states that the land was undisturbed for 40 years during the days of Gideon.

Ask your group about Gideon's family.

He had many wives and 70 sons as well as Abimelech, the son of a concubine.
This is important information to remember for the next lesson.

Discuss with your students what they learned by studying the Lord and His dealings with Gideon and how this relates to Hebrews 11:32.

The Lord built Gideon's faith step-by-step. He did not expect Gideon to conquer Midian at first.

God increased Gideon's faith. Hebrews 11:32, 39 says Gideon's faith was approved by God.

Ask your students if God has done anything like this in their lives. Do they walk by faith or by sight? Are they willing to obey when God calls? It doesn't matter who you are, but Who is with you.

Unit Four - Teacher's Guide

Judges
U-4, Chapters 6-8

Romans 1:18-32: When People Serve Idols Rather Than God

What God Revealed to Unrighteous Men

- *Made that which is known about Himself evident within them*
- *Made his invisible attributes, His eternal power and divine nature clearly seen since the creation of the world – these things are understood through what has been made*

What Man Did

- *"Exchanged the glory of the incorruptible God for an image in the form of corruptible man and of birds and four-footed animals and crawling creatures."*
- *"Exchanged the truth of God for a lie, and worshiped and served the creature rather than the Creator."*
- *"Did not see fit to acknowledge God any longer."*

The Consequences of Idolatry

- *"Gave them over in the lusts of their hearts to impurity, so that their bodies would be dishonored among them."*
- *"Gave them over to degrading passions;" immorality and homosexuality*
- *"Gave them over to a depraved mind, to do those things that are not proper"*
- *(They are "filled with all unrighteousness, wickedness, greed, evil; full of envy, murder, strife, deceit, malice; they are gossips, slanderers, haters of God, insolent, arrogant, boastful, inventors of evil, disobedient to parents, without understanding, untrustworthy, unloving, unmerciful; and although they know the ordinance of God, that those who practice such things are worthy of death, they not only do the same, but also give hearty approval to those who practice them.")*

© 2008 Precept Ministries International

UNIT FOUR - TEACHER'S GUIDE

UNIT FOUR - TEACHER'S GUIDE

ENRICHMENT WORDS:

Extravagant – extremely or excessively elaborate, profuse, and lavish.

Inadequate – not adequate; insufficient.

Legacy – something transmitted by or received from an ancestor or predecessor or from the past.

Luring – attract actively and strongly.

Ordinary – of common quality, rank, or ability.

Recurring – occur time after time.

UNIT FOUR - TEACHER'S GUIDE

Judges

Unit Four - Teacher's Guide

Judges
Unit Four Quiz

Name: _____ Date: _____

Unit Four - Quiz Key

MULTIPLE CHOICE - Circle one.

1. How did the angel of the Lord first address Gideon?
   a. "Peace, do not fear – you will not die."
   b. *"The Lord is with you, oh valiant warrior."*
   c. "Surely I will be with you, you will defeat Midian as one man."
   d. "Go and deliver Israel from the hand of the Midianites."

2. What was Gideon doing when the angel of the Lord appeared to him?
   a. Sleeping in bed
   b. *Beating wheat in the wine press*
   c. Fighting the Midian army
   d. Sacrificing in the tabernacle

SHORT ANSWER

3. Why didn't Gideon think he could deliver Israel from Midian?

His family was the least in Manasseh
He was least in his family

4. Why did God give Israel over to Midian after His great victory through Deborah and Barak?

The sons of Israel did what was evil in the sight of the Lord.

5. What does Yahweh Shalom mean?

The Lord is Peace.

UNIT FOUR - TEACHER'S GUIDE

Unit Four - Teacher's Guide

Judges
Unit Four Test

Name: _____ Date: _____

Unit Four - Test Key

MATCHING - Choose one and write the letter in the blank

____e____ 1. Extremely or excessively elaborate, profuse, and lavish

____b____ 2. Something transmitted by or received from an ancestor or predecessor or from the past

____a____ 3. Attracting actively and strongly

____c____ 4. Of common quality, rank, or ability

____d____ 5. Occurring time after time

a. Luring
b. Legacy
c. Ordinary
d. Recurring
e. Extravagant

MULTIPLE CHOICE - Circle one

6. How did the angel of the Lord first address Gideon?
    a. "Peace, do not fear. You will not die."
    b. *"The Lord is with you, oh valiant warrior."*
    c. "Surely I will be with you; you will defeat Midian as one man."
    d. "Go and deliver Israel from the hand of the Midianites."

7. What was Gideon doing when the angel of the Lord appeared to him?
    a. Sleeping in bed
    b. *Beating wheat in the wine press*
    c. Fighting the Midian army
    d. Sacrificing in the tabernacle

8. According to John 14:27, why does Jesus tell His followers to not let their hearts be troubled or fearful?
    a. From the point of salvation, they have no more hardships.
    b. Believers have no enemies.
    c. Jesus will not let anything bad happen to them.
    d. *Jesus promised His peace to believers.*

9. What name of God is revealed in Judges 6?
    a. Jehovah Rapha—The Lord is My Healer
    b. Jehovah Nissi—The Lord is My Banner
    c. Jehovah Jireh—The Lord is My Providor
    d. *Jehovah Shalom—the Lord is Peace*

UNIT FOUR - TEACHER'S GUIDE

Judges
Unit Four Test

10. What is a possible theme for Judges 6?
    a. *The call of Gideon*
    b. Gideon and the 300 versus Midian
    c. People want Gideon as king, and the ephod
    d. Gideon rebels against the Lord

11. What is a possible theme for Judges 7?
    a. The call of Gideon
    b. *Gideon and the 300 versus Midian*
    c. People want Gideon as king, and the ephod
    d. Gideon rebels against the Lord

12. What is a possible theme for Judges 8?
    a. The call of Gideon
    b. Gideon and the 300 versus Midian
    c. *People want Gideon as king, and the ephod*
    d. Gideon rebels against the Lord

13. What did the people do with the ephod Gideon made?
    a. They gave it to the priests as a gift.
    b. They wore it when they worshipped God.
    c. They sold it to buy more idols from Midian.
    d. *They played the harlot with it.*

14. All the following gods mentioned in Judges 6-8 were worshipped EXCEPT:
    a. Asherah
    b. *Molech*
    c. Ashteroth
    d. Baal

15. How did Gideon respond when asked to be king?
    a. "Yes, I will be king over you."
    b. "Later, when the work of the Lord is finished."
    c. *"Neither I nor my sons will rule, but the Lord shall rule over you."*
    d. He did not answer them.

16. According to Isaiah 44:9-20, all of the following are true about idolators EXCEPT:
    a. Futile
    b. Deceived heart
    c. Will be put to shame
    d. *Will die by the hand of their enemy*

Unit Four - Teacher's Guide

Judges
Unit Four Test

17. According to Colossians 3:5, what is a form of idolatry?
    a. *Greed*
    b. Lying
    c. Murder
    d. Gossip

18. What did the angel of the Lord do to Gideon's offering?
    a. He ate it and gave thanks to God.
    b. He refused it and cursed Gideon for his disobedience.
    c. *He touched it with his staff and fire sprang from the rock and consumed the meat and bread.*
    d. He took it with him.

19. What name did Joash give Gideon after Gideon tore down his father's Baal?
    a. *Jerubbaal*
    b. Baaladon
    c. Abimelech
    d. Asher

20. How did Gideon ask God to confirm that Israel would be delivered through him?
    a. He asked God to part the Red Sea as He did for Moses and then close it again on the Midianites.
    b. *He asked God to put dew on the fleece of wool and not on the ground and then let the fleece be dry and the ground wet.*
    c. He asked God to send the angel of the Lord to confirm His word in person.
    d. He asked God to accept his sacrifices for seven days and seven nights.

SHORT ANSWER

21. Why did God give Israel to Midian after His great victory through Deborah and Barak?

The sons of Israel did what was evil in the sight of the Lord.

22. Describe the Midianite oppression of Israel.

The sons of Israel were living in mountains and caves.
The Midianites destroyed everything the Israelites planted. They devastated the land.

Unit four - Teacher's Guide

Judges
Unit Four Test

23. What command did the LORD give Gideon first?

The Lord commanded Gideon to pull down his father's altar to Baal, cut down the Asherah beside it, and build an altar to the Lord.

24. How did Gideon respond when he recognized the angel of the Lord? How did the LORD respond?

Gideon feared for his life and the LORD said, "Peace to you, do not fear, you shall not die."

25. How did God tell Gideon to reduce the number of people with him before engaging Midian?

First He told Gideon to send home those who were afraid. Then He told him to send home everyone who knelt down to drink water and take only those who lapped it up like a dog.

ESSAY

Choose one of the following topics, briefly summarize it, and discuss how it applies to your life:

a. Idolatry and its consequences (Romans 1)
b. God's character in Judges 6 and 7
c. Principles from the story of Gideon

Students will identify the main points of each of these topics and then discuss how they apply to their lives.

UNIT FIVE - TEACHER'S GUIDE

Judges

From Victory to Defeat

Unit Objectives:

In this unit, students will use observation tools to identify the main events and characters of Judges 9-12. As they observe, they will continue to recognize cycles of sin in these chapters. They will observe the lives of Abimelech, Jotham and Jephthah to identify the positive and negative character traits of each. Students will interpret Jotham's parable and Jepthah's vow. They will also define *theocracy* and observe God's desire to be king over Israel. After carefully observing the text and working to accurately interpret its meaning, students will discuss how the events in these chapters apply to their lives.

Unit Five

Who Rules You?

U-5, Chapters 9-12

In the days of the Judges there was no king! No one submitted to God's authority. Everyone did what was right in their own eyes. Each man became his own king – right and wrong were determined individually.

You've seen how Israel's rejection of God's commands led to **apostasy**. Not submitting to God led to **anarchy**. In this unit you will continue to see the downward spiral of sin.

You are going to meet a number of judges in this unit. As you study, focus where God puts emphasis – on three men: Abimelech, Jotham, and Jephthah.

As you study these three, think about your generation. Who sets the rules for them? Is there an **absolute** standard for right or wrong? Whom do young men and women today want to rule their lives? Who or what influences the decisions and choices they make?

What about you? Whom do you look to for leadership? What would God say about the people and things that influence your choices and decisions?

> "For My thoughts are not your thoughts, neither are your ways My ways," declares the Lord. "For as the heavens are higher than the earth, so are My ways higher than your ways, and My thoughts than your thoughts."
>
> - Isaiah 55:8-9

Think about these things as you begin your study of Judges 9-12.

Student Page 117

© 2008 Precept Ministries International

UNIT FIVE - TEACHER'S GUIDE

UNIT FIVE - TEACHER'S GUIDE

Judges

LESSON ONE:

 Judges 8-9 Observation Worksheets, key word bookmark, colored pencils

OBJECTIVES:

In this lesson, students will observe Judges 9 marking the key words from their bookmarks and mark *Abimelech*, *Jotham*, and the *men of Shechem*. They will identify and mark geographical locations on the map at the end of the unit. Students will also look at Judges 8:30-9:1 to identify the context of Judges 9 and list information they observe about Abimelech, Jotham and the men of Shechem.

Lesson 1/Assignment Prayer

Your students may be able to complete this assignment on their own at this point. It's good to remind them how essential it is to begin with prayer every time they open the Word of God.

You can remind them that according to Colossians 1:9-10, God's will for them is to "be filled with the knowledge of His will in all spiritual wisdom and understanding, so that [they] will walk in a manner worthy of the Lord, to please Him in all respects, bearing fruit in every good work and increasing in the knowledge of God." First John 5:14-15 says "This is the confidence which we have before Him, that, if we ask anything according to His will, He hears us. And if we know that He hears us in whatever we ask, we know that we have the requests which we have asked from Him." Remind them that because it is His will that they increase in their understanding of Him and His ways, they can ask confidently, assured that this will be done!!! This is an exciting truth for students to know!

Lesson 1/Assignment 1 - Observation/Interpretation

This assignment will establish the context for events that occur in Judges

---

LESSON ONE

U-5, Lesson 1, Chapter 9

Judges 9 is a long chapter, so it will take time to read. But the rewards of having the Word of God written on your heart are worth it! Don't rush through this chapter. In each paragraph you read, ask the 5W and H questions. Who were mentioned? What were they doing? What results came from their actions? When did events take place?

Lesson 1/Assignment Prayer

ONE ON ONE:

This is the longest chapter in Judges. God devoted a lot of space to these men and events – so there must be some important lessons here. In light of that, spend time in prayer asking God to show you what He wants you to learn and apply to your life and then write it out.

> Keep your prayer simple and to the point. You don't have to be "super spiritual" to communicate your requests to God. Ask Him to help you understand what you read. It is His will for you to know His Word.
>
> "Ask, and it will be given to you; seek, and you will find, knock, and it will be opened to you."
> – Matthew 7:7

Lesson 1/Assignment 1

1. Look at Judges 8:30-9:1. These verses are the context for Judges 9. **They will help you understand what is happening and why.**

   a. Who was Abimelech?

   > Remember! Jerubbaal is Gideon's other name. Jerubbaal = "let Baal contend." Gideon's dad gave him this name after Gideon tore down the altars in Ophrah, his hometown.

   b. How was Gideon's family treated after his death?

Student Page 119

UNIT FIVE - TEACHER'S GUIDE

Judges

Help your students remember who Abimelech was and how Gideon's family was treated after his death, as they observe and interpret Abimelech's actions in this chapter.

Remind students that Jerubbaal is Gideon's other name. Point out the pull-out box in the Student Guide.

a. Abimelech was Gideon's son by his concubine (Judges 9:31).

b. Israel was not kind to Gideon's household after his death (Judges 9:35).

Lesson 1/Assignment 2 - Observation
Students will observe this chapter marking the key words from their bookmarks including references to *Abimelech*, *Jotham*, and the *men of Shechem*. Marking instructions are given in the Student Guide. These words don't need to be added to bookmarks since they are key only to interpreting Judges 9-12.

Lesson 1/Assignment 3 - Observation/Interpretation
Students will identify the locations mentioned in Judges 9 on the map at the end of the unit and mark them.

Lesson 1/Assignment 4 - Observation/Interpretation
This assignment will help students identify the main people in Judges 9 and understand their roles. They do not need to list all of the details – only general facts about these men.

a. Abimelech – Jerubbaal's son; killed all his brothers except Jotham; made himself king of Israel; died fighting the men of Shechem.

b. Jotham – Jerubbaal's youngest son; escaped Abimelech; told men of Shechem parable of the olive tree, fig tree, vine and bramble.

c. The men of Shechem – some were Abimelech's mother's relatives; gave Abimelech 70 pieces of silver to hire men to kill his brothers; made

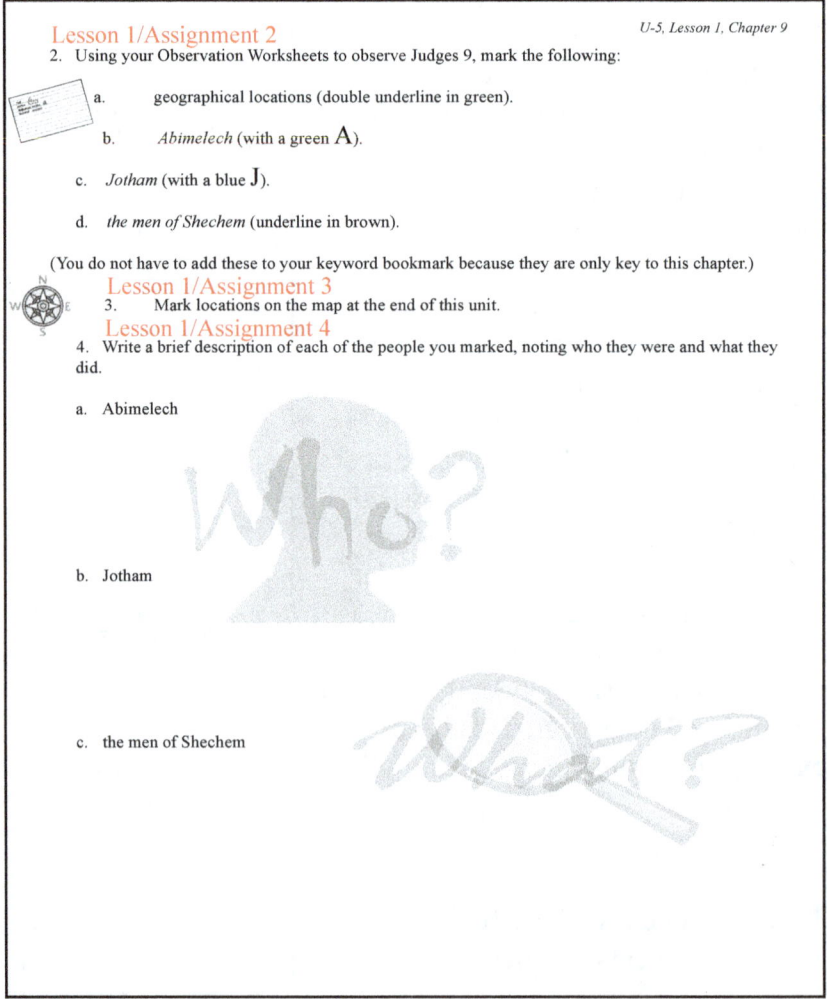

UNIT FIVE - TEACHER'S GUIDE

Abimelech king over them; dealt treacherously with Abimelech; betrayed him and tried to overthrow him.

UNIT FIVE - TEACHER'S GUIDE

UNIT FIVE - TEACHER'S GUIDE

Judges

LESSON TWO:

 Judges 8-9 Observation Worksheets

OBJECTIVES:

In this lesson, students continue their observation of Judges 9 looking more closely at Abimelech, Jotham, and key events. They will learn how Abimelech's actions resemble the key (repeated) phase in Judges 17-21. Students will then determine how they relate to Abimelech.

Lesson 2/Assignment 1- Observation
Students will look more closely at Abimelech and Jotham, key figures in Judges 9. They should carefully observe their actions and consider main points in this chapter.

Abimelech – Jerubbaal's (Gideon's) son; went to his mother's relatives in Shechem; offered to be their ruler instead of Gideon's 70 sons; used money the men of Shechem gave him to hire worthless men; killed all his brothers except one; was made king over the men of Shechem; ruled over Israel three years; laid in wait against Shechem when he heard about their betrayal; defeated Gaal and the men of Shechem; tried to destroy the leaders with fire when a woman dropped a millstone on his head; had armor bearer kill him so no one would say a woman killed him.

Jotham – Jerubbaal's (Gideon's) youngest son; hid from Abimelech; only son not killed; stood on Mt. Gerizim and told men of Shechem parable of olive tree, fig tree, vine, and the bramble, and compared it to how they treated his father, killed his brothers, and made Abimelech king; fled to Beer to escape Abimelech.

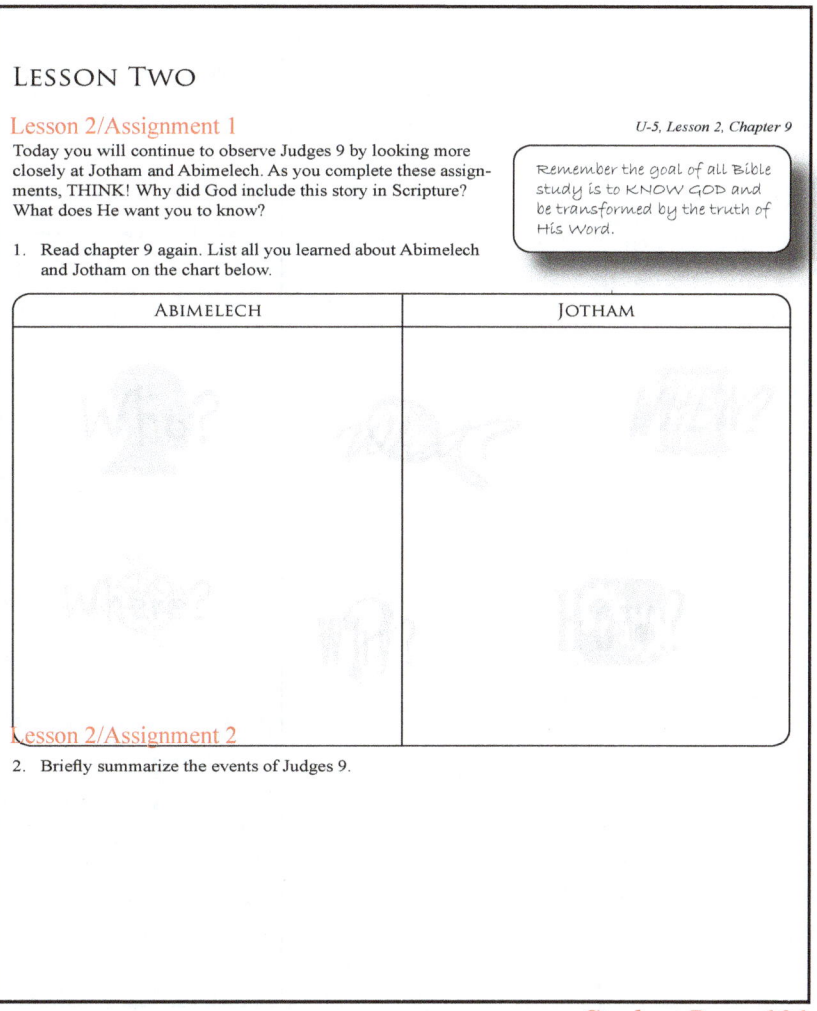

© 2008 Precept Ministries International

UNIT FIVE - TEACHER'S GUIDE

Judges

Lesson 2/Assignment 2 Observation
Students will briefly summarize main events in this chapter to help them remember what takes place and when. Some students will list more details than others.

 Although some of these assignments may seem repetitive, remind your students that it is important they do not miss any of the important details of this chapter. The more they observe the chapter, the less likely they are to misinterpret its meaning.

Abimelech offered to be king; men of Shechem gave him money; Abimelech killed his brothers; Jotham escaped; Abimelech was made king; Jotham told men of Shechem the parable of the olive tree, fig tree, vine and bramble; God sent an evil spirit between men of Shechem and Abimelech; men of Shechem rebel against Abimelech; Gaal the son of Ebed led them against Abimelech; Abimelech and his people went to lay in wait against Shechem; Shechem and Abimelech's people fought; Abimelech captured the city, razed it, and sowed it with salt; leaders of Shechem entered inner chamber of the temple of El-berith; Abimelech and his people took branches and set the inner chamber on fire, all die (about 1,000); Abimelech captured Thebez; the people shut themselves up in the tower; Abimelech approached the tower to burn it but a woman dropped a millstone on his head; Abimelech asked his armor bearer to kill him so no one will say that a woman killed him; all the men went home – thus God repaid Abimelech for killing his brothers and Shechem for their wickedness.

Lesson 2/Assignment 3 - Observation/Interpretation
According to Judges 8:33-35, "the sons of Israel again played the harlot with the Baals, and made Baal-berith their god. They did not remember the Lord their God, who had delivered them from the hands of all their enemies on every side; nor did they show kindness to the household of Jerubbaal (that is, Gideon) in accord with all the good that he had done to Israel."

U-5, Lesson 2, Chapter 9

Lesson 2/Assignment 3
3. What do you learn from Judges 8:33-35 about the spiritual condition of the sons of Israel?

Lesson 2/Assignment 4
4. What is the key repeated phrase in Judges 17-21? (You marked this in Unit 1, Lesson 1.)

   a. How was Abimelech doing this?

   b. How were the men of Shechem doing this?

   c. Have you ever done this? If so, how?

> As you answer this question think about this... Have you ever thought you knew more than your parents about how something should be done? Did you ever disregard a rule because it was "dumb?" How about disobey an authority because you just wanted your own way?

> There are two types of people in Scripture: those worthy of imitation and those who are not. Abimelech "did it all wrong." Will you learn from him?
>
> "My son, do not walk in the way with them. Keep your feet from their path, for their feet run to evil and they hasten to shed blood. Indeed, it is useless to spread the baited net in the sight of any bird; but they lie in wait for their own blood; they ambush their own lives. So are the ways of everyone who gains by violence; it takes away the life of its possessors." – Proverbs 1:15-19

Student Page 122

© 2008 Precept Ministries International

UNIT FIVE - TEACHER'S GUIDE

Judges

Lesson 2/Assignment 4 - Interpretation
The key repeated phrase in Judges 17-21 is:
"There was no king in Israel, every man did what was right in his own eyes."

a. Students should see that Abimelech wanted to be king because there wasn't one and "in his own eyes" he was best choice. He didn't consult or obey God. He even killed his brothers to get what he wanted.

b. The men of Shechem also did what was right in their own eyes and agreed to Abimelech's plan. But when they grew tired of him, they turned on him. Israel served idols during this time.

c. Students should ask themselves if they have done something right in their eyes, but contrary to God's command. The pull-out box in the Student Guide will help them consider their actions.

UNIT FIVE - TEACHER'S GUIDE

UNIT FIVE - TEACHER'S GUIDE

Judges

DISCUSSION GUIDE LESSONS ONE AND TWO:

REVIEW:
A quick review is a good way to begin your discussion.

>During the times of the judges, "every man did what was right in his own eyes."
>
>According to Judges 3-8, the Lord raised up five enemies to punish His people Israel and five judges to deliver them.
>
>>Othniel delivered Israel from Mesopotamia,
>>Ehud from Moab,
>>Shamgar from the Philistines,
>>Deborah from the Canaanites, and
>>Gideon (Jerubbaal) from the Midianites.
>
>Relate this to the sin cycle in Judges 2:11–3:6.
>Israel had not driven enemies out of their land; they became snares enticing them to follow their gods, which were not gods at all.

JUDGES 9:
Lead your class to discuss the main characters in this chapter by asking 5W and H questions.

>Abimelech was the son of Gideon through a concubine that lived in Shechem (8:31).
>
>Gideon had 70 other sons through several wives, Jotham the youngest.
>According to Judges 8:35 Israel not only forgot the Lord who delivered them from the above enemies, they also did not show kindness to the house of Gideon (Judges 9).

Question your students about main events in this chapter.

>Abimelech wanted to rule the leaders of Shechem. He appealed to the fact that he was their relative and better to have one ruling than 70.
>
>Gideon had said that neither he nor his son should rule over Israel; the Lord should rule.
>
>The men of Shechem gave 70 pieces of silver to Abimelech from the house of Baal-berith (Judges 8:33). He used them to hire worthless fellows to follow him.

Note: The Hebrew word *berith* is translated "covenant." Israel was not to make a covenant with Canaan's inhabitants.

UNIT FIVE - TEACHER'S GUIDE

Judges

Abimelech murdered all 70 of his brothers in Ophrah; Jotham the youngest escaped. Abimelech did this because he wanted to be ruler.

He was made the king in Shechem, but it was not the Lord's doing. Abimelech was not a judge raised up by the Lord. He seized leadership and became king.

Ask students how these kinds of things happen today in their homes, schools, churches, and nation.

UNIT FIVE - TEACHER'S GUIDE

Judges

LESSON THREE:

Judges 2, and 8-9 Observation Worksheets, Bible

OBJECTIVES:

In this lesson, students will continue to interpret Judges 9 looking at cross-references in Judges and 1 Samuel. They will learn that the people rejected God as king over Israel and chose Abimelech instead.

Lesson 3/Assignment 1 - Observation/Interpretation
a. Abimelech was king in Israel three years.

b. Abimelech presented himself to the men of Shechem to overthrow the rule of his brothers. He then killed his brothers.

Lesson 3/Assignment 2 - Observation/Interpretation
a. According to Judges 8:22-23, Gideon said "the Lord shall rule over you." He refused authority for himself and his sons.

b. According to Judges 2:16-18, the Lord raised up judges to deliver Israel from the hands of those who plundered them. Hebrew definitions will help students learn judges represented God and did His will. By contrast, kings headed up political, social, religious, and military authority.

Lesson 3/Assignment 3 - Observation/Interpretation
God's plan for Israel is a theocracy ruled by Him alone.

a. According to 1 Samuel 8:4-22, Israel requested Samuel to appoint a king so they would be like other nations.

LESSON THREE

Lesson 3/Assignment 1
U-5, Lesson 3, Chapter 9

1. You've carefully observed what Judges 9 says about Abimelech's rise to power. Today you're going to work on interpreting the text.

   a. What position did Abimelech hold in Israel and for how long?

   > Interpretation asks the question, "What does the text mean?" If you stopped with observing the text, you couldn't accurately apply it to your life.

   b. How did Abimelech rise to power?

Lesson 3/Assignment 2
2. The first mention of the soms of Israel asking for a ruler is in Judges 8:22.

   a. Read Judges 8:22-23 and write out Gideon's response.

   b. Read Judges 2:16-18. How does a judge differ from a king? Look at the Hebrew definitions for "king" and "judge" to help you answer this question.

   > **Judge** – a law-interpreter, judge, or **governor** of God.
   >
   > **King** – a governmental head of a embodied political, social, religious, and military authority.[1]

Lesson 3/Assignment 3
3. Was God's plan for His people a **theocracy** or **monarchy**? To answer this question read 1 Samuel 8:4-22 and 10:17-19 and answer the following questions:

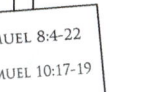
1 SAMUEL 8:4-22
1 SAMUEL 10:17-19

   a. Why did the people want a king?

   b. By choosing an earthly king, what king were they rejecting?

---
[1] Swanson, J. 1997. *Dictionary of Biblical Languages with Semantic Domains : Hebrew (Old Testament)* (electronic ed.). Logos Research Systems, Inc.: Oak Harbor

Student Page 123

UNIT FIVE - TEACHER'S GUIDE

Judges

b. According to 1 Samuel 8:4-22, they were rejecting God as their king over them by choosing a human king.

c. According to 1 Samuel 8:4-22, God decided when Israel had its first king and according to 1 Samuel 10:17-19, also chose the man.

d. Students should see that in trying to establish himself as king, Abimelech failed to usurp God's authority to determine when a king would be installed and who he would be.

World View Project - Being An Abimelech

This project will help students learn how to apply what they learned about Abimelech to their lives. Help them understand that "doing what is right in their own eyes" in the areas listed will lead to defeat, as it did for Abimelech.

U-5, Lesson 3, Chapter 9

a. Who decided when Israel was allowed to establish a king to rule?

d. In light of what you have learned, why was Abimelech wrong to make himself king?

World View Project

BEING AN ABIMELECH - PROJECT

Have you ever been like Abimelech? Could you ever be like him? Look at the following topics and choose one. In a one-page essay, describe how you would defy God's timing and authority and the consequences you would face by being like Abimelech in this situation.

Dating   Marriage   Church or school authority

Parental authority   Ambitions (e.g. class officer, team captain, etc.)

UNIT FIVE - TEACHER'S GUIDE

Judges

LESSON FOUR:

 Judges 8-9 Observation Worksheets

OBJECTIVES:
In this lesson, students will interpret Jotham's parable in Judges 9. They will study connections between the bramble and Abimelech. Finally, students will reason to apply Jotham's parable to their lives.

Lesson 4/Assignment 1 - Observation
Students will read Judges 9:7-21 again to observe Jotham's parable.

 They have read this chapter numerous times. Remind them that reading something repeatedly will help them see missed information and better retain what they are studying.

Lesson 4/Assignment 2 - Observation/Interpretation
a. According to Jotham's parable the trees were looking for a king.

b. The trees looked among their own kind (other trees and plants).

c. See student page for chart key.

d. Students should look at the definition of bramble at the end of the unit. The bramble was a thorny bush that did not produce any fruit. The trees were choosing a "weed" to rule over them.

Lesson 4/Assignment 3- Interpretation

LESSON FOUR

Lesson 4/Assignment 1
U-5, Lesson 4, Chapter 9

Today let's look at Jotham's **parable** since it relates to the people's choice of Abimelech as their king.

1. Read Judges 9:7-21 again, asking God for His insight into this parable.

Lesson 4/Assignment 2
2. What was Jotham trying to show the men through this parable? Let's examine it point by point.

   a. Who wanted a king?

   b. Where were they looking for a king?

   c. What four plants were appealed to and how did they respond? Fill in the chart below.

TREE OR PLANT	RESPONSE
Olive Tree	*'Shall I leave my fatness with which God and men are honored, and go to wave over the trees?'*
Fig Tree	*'Shall I leave my sweetness and my good fruit, and go to wave over the trees?'*
Vine	*'Shall I leave my new wine, which cheers God and men, and go to wave over the trees?'*
Bramble	*'If in truth you are anointing me as king over you, come and take refuge in my shade; but if not, may fire come out from the bramble and consume the cedars of Lebanon.'*

   d. How does the **bramble** compare with the others? (Hint: think about what each plant produces.)

Student Page 125

UNIT FIVE - TEACHER'S GUIDE

Judges

The trees and vine had something better to do than wave over the trees – a good purpose they were fulfilling. The bramble, which was good for nothing, accepted dominion over the trees.

Lesson 4/Assignment 4 - Interpretation
When the men of Israel asked Gideon to rule over them he said, "I will not rule over you, nor shall my son rule over you; the Lord shall rule over you. (Judges 8:23)" The bramble, which was good for nothing, took the position.

Lesson 4/Assignment 5 - Interpretation
It's important for students to see that the trees chose a bramble, a weed that did not produce anything valuable, to rule over them.

Lesson 4/Assignment 6 - Interpretation
The "bramble" was Abimelech. He had no right, merit, or authority to rule over them.

Lesson 4/Assignment 7 - Application
Students will think about all they learned in this lesson to answer these questions.

They should ask themselves if they are rejecting God as king of their lives for brambles (worldly influeneces) to rule.

Help them discern how various forms of media (TV, movies, radio, magazines, the internet) influence their decisions. The project at the end of this lesson will help them understand this.

Lesson 4/Assignment 8 - Observation

Lesson 4/Assignment 3   U-5, Lesson 4, Chapter 9
3. How does the bramble's response compare with the responses of the first three trees?

Lesson 4/Assignment 4
4. How does the the bramble's response compare with Gideon's response in Judges 8:22-23?

Lesson 4/Assignment 5
5. What did the trees choose to rule over them?

Lesson 4/Assignment 6
6. How does the ruler the trees chose compare with the one the children of Israel chose?

Lesson 4/Assignment 7
7. Who or what rules your life? Now do a little evaluation. Your answers to these questions will reveal who *really* rules your life.

   a. What or who determines what you talk about?

Student Page 126

UNIT FIVE - TEACHER'S GUIDE

Judges

Abimelech instructs his armor bearer to kill him after a woman from Thebez drops a rock on his head.

World View Project - Who's The Boss?

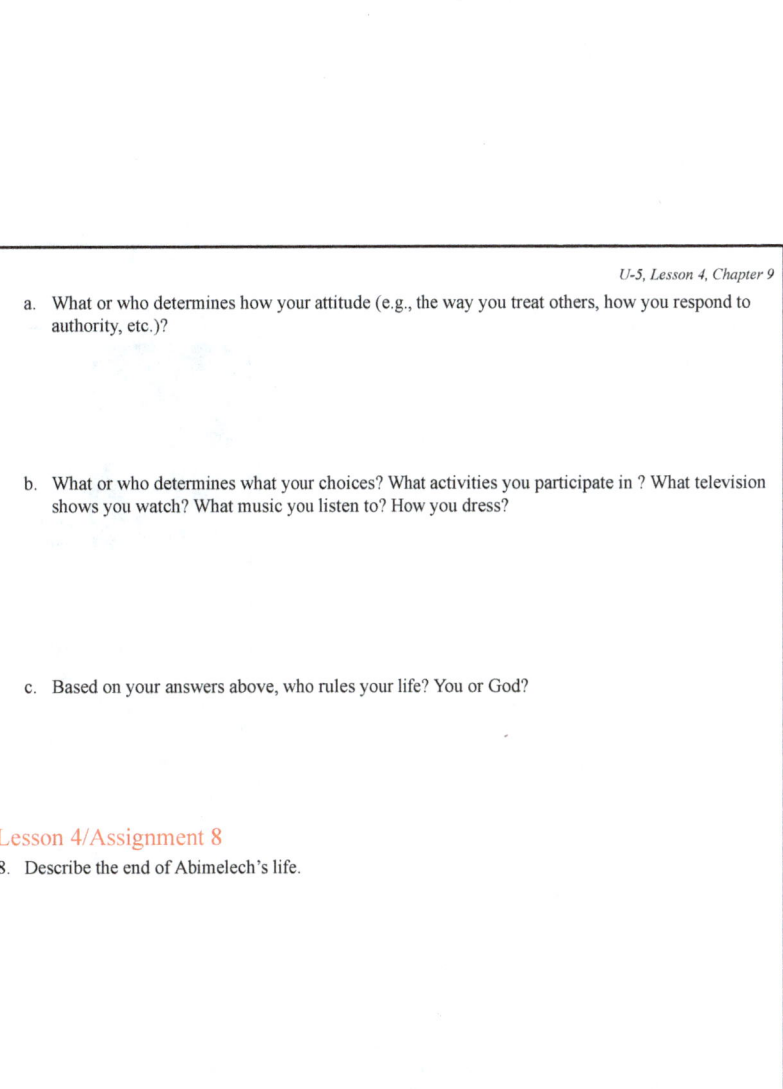

U-5, Lesson 4, Chapter 9

a. What or who determines how your attitude (e.g., the way you treat others, how you respond to authority, etc.)?

b. What or who determines what your choices? What activities you participate in? What television shows you watch? What music you listen to? How you dress?

c. Based on your answers above, who rules your life? You or God?

Lesson 4/Assignment 8
8. Describe the end of Abimelech's life.

At the beginning of this unit you were asked to think about why God included the story of Abimelech and Jotham in Scripture. Do you know why? Can you see the importance of learning from their examples? Who are you going to be like, Abimelech or Jotham?

Student Page 127

UNIT FIVE - TEACHER'S GUIDE

Judges

This project will help students recognize worldly influences that can take God's place in their lives. If they don't know where in the Bible God tells His people how to dress, talk, and act, look up verses with them or give them verses to look up on their own. A few examples follow:

Speech – Psalm 19:14, Ephesians 5:3,4, 1 Timothy 3:11
Dress – 1 Timothy 2:9, 1 Peter 3:3
Behavior – Ephesians 5:5-10

World View Project U-5, Lesson 4, Chapter 9

WHAT'S YOUR WORLD VIEW?

"WHO'S THE BOSS?" – PROJECT

1. For this assignment you will need the following:

   Poster board   Markers   Glue
   Scissors   Magazines

   Draw a line down the center of a piece of poster board. On one side draw a throne or crown, and on the other side a bramble. On the bramble side, find or draw pictures of influences that define a life ruled by the world or an authority other than God. On the throne side, find or draw pictures of influences that define a life ruled by God. Use your answers from question seven of this lesson to help you with this project.

   Now, write a half-page summary describing who rules your life and how others see this by looking at what you say and do.

Student Page 128
© 2008 Precept Ministries International

UNIT FIVE - TEACHER'S GUIDE

Judges

DISCUSSION GUIDE LESSONS THREE AND FOUR:

Begin by reviewing with your class the main event of Judges 9. Then discuss what they learned from the cross-references and word studies.

> The Lord Himself was to be the only king of Israel. Israel was to be a theocracy. Later when Israel asked Samuel (the last judge) to appoint a king, God said they were rejecting Him as king. They wanted a man to be king to be like the nations around them.
>
> Do Christians ever act like the unsaved – seek the things they seek, want what they have, live like they live?
>
> Ask your class if they have ever manipulated things to try to make something happen. Were they motivated by recognition (status) instead of by God's glory?

Now, ask questions that will help them discuss what they learned from Jotham's parable.

Verses 7-22:
> Jotham stood on the top of Mount Gerizim, the mountain of the blessings when Israel entered the promised land.
>
> Jotham presented a parable for the men of Shechem to judge their motives.
> The olive tree, the fig tree, and the vine all had something better to do than wave over trees. They all had good purposes they were fulfilling. The bramble, which was good for nothing, accepted dominion over the trees.
>
> The parable speaks of Abimelech. Jotham also prophesied what would happen to Abimelech and the men of Shechem.
>
> Ask your students how this can relate to them. Are they concerned with pleasing God or with prominence? Can we please God in prominent positions? What is most important?
>
> Jotham wanted the men of Shechem to consider if they had dealt in truth and integrity in making Abimelech king. You might ask your group if they have ever had to say "no" to an opportunity that threatened their integrity.
>
> Jotham fled to Beer and remained there, possible for the three years Abimelech ruled over Israel, and Shechem.

© 2008 Precept Ministries International

UNIT FIVE - TEACHER'S GUIDE

Judges

Have your students relate the rest of the chapter to Jotham's prophecy.

> Verses 23-24 say that the Lord caused treachery between Abimelech and the men of Shechem and the men of Shechem dealt treacherously with Abimelech.
>
> Abimelech was told the men ambushed and robbed people on the road. They also put their faith in Gaal, the son of Ebed.
>
> At a festival to their god, they cursed Abimelech. Gaal encouraged them to stop serving Abimelech and let him rule over them.
>
> This was reported to Abimelech so he ambushed Gaal and the men of Shechem, captured then razed the city, killed the people, and sowed salt in the ground so nothing would grow.
>
> Abimelech also killed people gathered in the tower of Shechem, about 1,000 men and women. But a woman in Thebez threw a millstone and crushed his skull; then his armor bearer stabbed him with his sword.
>
> Verses 56-57 say God repaid him for the wickedness he had done. Jotham's curse came on Abimelech and the men of Shechem for what they did to his brothers.
>
> "There was no king in Israel, and every man did what was right in his own eyes."

Your students may speculate that Abimelech's brothers' behavior caused him to strive for their acceptance of him as king (he was a concubine's son). But the past is no excuse for choices to sin today. Murdering his brothers to become king was inexcusable.

Ask students to discuss what they learned about who rules their lives and how others can tell.

UNIT FIVE - TEACHER'S GUIDE

Judges

LESSON FIVE:

 Judges 10-11 Observation Worksheets, key word bookmark, colored pencils, "The Judges of Israel" chart

OBJECTIVES:

In this lesson, students will observe Judges 10-11 marking key words and listing information about Jephthah. They will also think about what they can apply to their lives from Jephthah's example.

Lesson 5/Assignment 1 - Observation
Students will observe Judges 10 by marking the key words from their key word bookmark.

 Remind them to read with a purpose. Just looking for words to mark is NOT the point of this exercise. Marking slows us down to see what the text is saying.

Lesson 5/Assignment 2 - Observation
Students will record information they discovered about Tola the son of Puah and Jair the Gileadite on "The Judges of Israel" chart.

Lesson 5/Assignment 3 - Observation
Students will locate and mark Gilead on the map at the end of the unit and mark references to *Gilead* in Judges 10.

Lesson 5/Assignment 4 - Observation
Students will observe Judges 11 marking the key words on their bookmarks. They will also mark *Ammon* on the map at the end of the unit.

b. Students will list close to the following:

- *v. 1 - Jephthah was a Gileadite*
  a valiant warrior
  the son of a harlot
  his father was Gilead

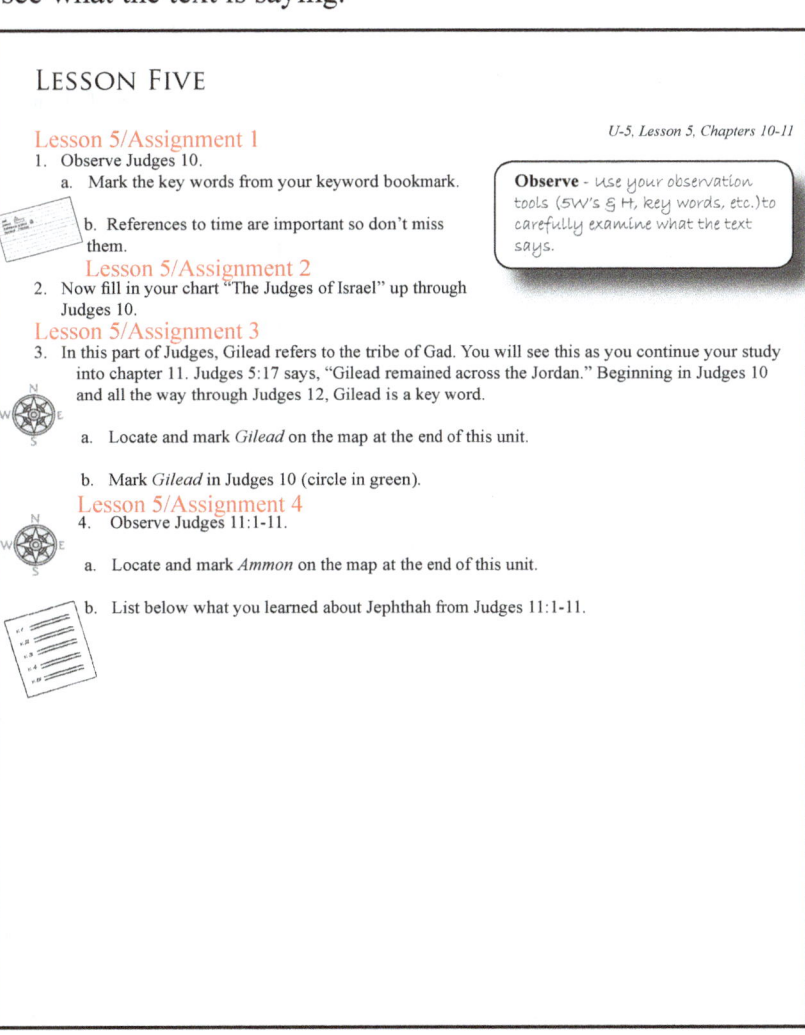

Student Page 129

© 2008 Precept Ministries International

223

UNIT FIVE - TEACHER'S GUIDE

Judges

- *v. 2 - his brother drove him out and did not give him an inheritance because of his mother*
- *v. 3 - Jephthah fled to Tob*
  worthless fellows gathered around Jephthah and went out with him
- *v. 5 - the elders of Gilead retrieved Jephthah from the land of Tob and asked him to be their chief*
- *v. 7 - Jephthah asks why*
- *v. 9 - Jephthah makes them promise that if he comes back and fights the Ammonites they will make him their head*
- *v. 11 - the elders of Gilead and the people made him head and chief over them*
  Jephthah spoke all his words before the Lord at Mizpah

Lesson 5/Assignment 5 - Application
Students should see that Jephthah didn't ask to lead and he spoke to God about everything he did. He also didn't retaliate against his brothers for driving him out.

Lesson 5/Assignment 5   U-5, Lesson 5, Chapters 10-11
5. What good things did Jephthah do that you can imitate?

Student Page 130

UNIT FIVE - TEACHER'S GUIDE

Judges

LESSON SIX:

 Judges 11-12 Observation Worksheets, key word bookmark, colored pencils, Bible

OBJECTIVES:

In this lesson, students will complete their observation of Judges 11:12-40 and 12 marking the key words from their bookmark and the word *Gilead*. They will identify and record new information about Jephthah. Students will examine Leviticus to understand Jephthah's vow and the actions he took to fulfill it. Students will determine how the information in these verses applies to their lives.

Lesson 6/Assignment 1 - Observation/Interpretation
a. Students will observe Judges 11:12-40 and 12 by marking the key words from their bookmark including *Gilead*.

b. Students will list close to the following:
- *v. 12-26 - in his discussion with the king of Ammon, Jephthah knows knows what God gave Israel when they acquired the land*
- *v. 27 - Jephthah is confident that God will judge and find that he and Israel have not sinned against Ammon*
- *v. 29 - the Spirit of the Lord comes upon Jephthah to go to the sons of Ammon*
- *v. 30 - Jephthah vows to give the Lord the first thing out of his door as a burnt offering if God gives the Ammonites into his hand*
- *v. 31-33 - Jephthah wins*
- *v. 34-53 - Jephthah's daughter is the first one to greet him. He keeps his vow*
- *12:7 - Jephthah judged Israel six years*

c. *Students should see that Jephthah was confident that he and Israel had*

© 2008 Precept Ministries International

UNIT FIVE - TEACHER'S GUIDE

not sinned against Ammon. He followed the leading of the Spirit and sacrificed his own daughter to fulfill his vow to the Lord.

Lesson 6/Assignment 2 - Application
Students should evaluate their family situation to see if they can relate to Jephthah's situation. Possibly some were conceived out of wedlock, never knew their fathers, or are part of blended families that don't accept them. But like Jephthah God can still use them to accomplish His purpose. They don't have to let their past define their future.

Lesson 6/Assignment 3 - Observation/Interpretation
a. Jephthah vowed (Judges 11:30-31) that if God gave the sons of Ammon into his hand, whatever came out the door of his house to meet him when he returned he would offer it up as a burnt offering.

b. According to Leviticus 1:3-9, a burnt offering was first cut into pieces, placed on the altar by the priest, then burned. God called this a soothing aroma.

c. Students should see that Jephthah took his vow seriously enough to sacrifice his only child.

d. Students should also see that Jephthah's daughter willingly submitted to the offering.

e. Students should observe in Jephthah's daughter's mourning the fact that she would never be married or have children.

f. This question helps students understand that Jephthah may have literally killed his daughter and burned her on the altar if he carried out the law concerning burnt offerings (Leviticus 1:3-9). Although scholars debate Jephthah's actions, Judges 12:39 says that Jephthah carried out his vow.

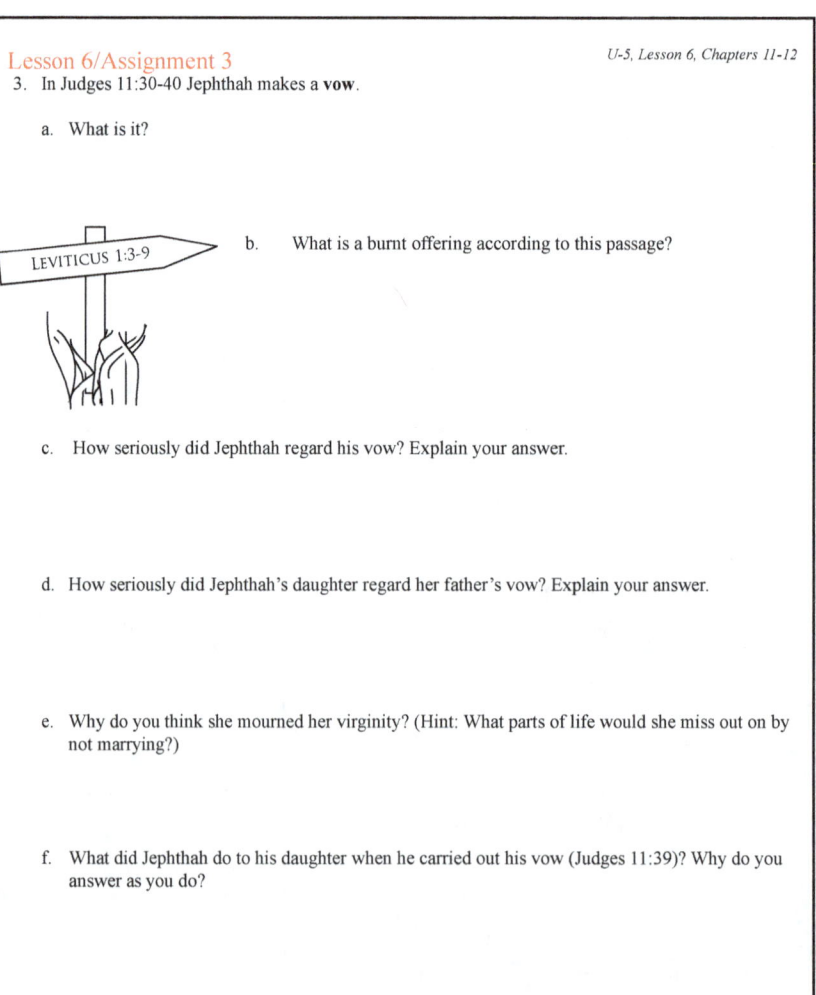

226

UNIT FIVE - TEACHER'S GUIDE

LESSON SEVEN:

 Judges 12 Observation Worksheets, Bible, "At A Glance" chart

OBJECTIVES:

In this lesson, students will look at cross-references to learn the importance of making vows and the options Jephthah might have chosen had he known the whole counsel of God's Word. Students will consider what they learn about vows and how to apply this knowledge to their lives.

Lesson 7/Assignment 1 - Observation/Interpretation
According to Numbers 30:1-2, the Lord commands "if a man makes a vow to the Lord, or takes an oath to bind himself with a binding obligation, he shall not violate his word; he shall do according to all that proceeds out of his mouth."

Lesson 7/Assignment 2 - Observation/ Interpretation
Leviticus 27 indicates that when a man made a difficult vow, then that one could be redeemed or exchanged for a price. But verses 28-29 state that one devoted, "set apart," to the Lord could not be redeemed.

If your class studied Leviticus and Joshua, they might share what they remember about things devoted to the Lord or "under the ban." The following excerpt from The Expositor's Bible Commentary may help:

"The death of this innocent girl came because of a rash vow. Jephthah knew that it was a sin to break a vow (Numbers 30:2), but in this case it was a greater sin to fulfill it. Jephthah was treating his daughter as a "person devoted to destruction" (Leviticus 27:29). This punishment was a strong curse reserved for the enemies of God

LESSON SEVEN

U-5, Lesson 7, Chapters 11-12

Wow! Jephthah took his vow seriously! He was willing to kill his own daughter rather than go back on his word. Why? Today you are going to look at what God's Word says about the importance of vows.

Lesson 7/Assignment 1
1. What does God's law say about making a vow, according to these verses in Numbers?

Lesson 7/Assignment 2
2. Read this chapter watching for the words "vow" and "consecrated." According to this chapter, could Jephthah have remained true to his vow and yet not offer his daughter as a burnt offering?

Lesson 7/Assignment 3
3. If there was a way out, why do you think Jephthah didn't take it?

> How important is it to know what the Bible says? How much sorrow and regret have God's people experienced because they didn't know the full counsel of God's Word?

Lesson 7/Assignment 4
4. Finally, read the verses in the sign post, which describe a period following the days of the judges. Do you see any parallels between this incident and Jephthah's? Any insight into what Jephthah did?

Student Page 133

UNIT FIVE - TEACHER'S GUIDE

Judges

(cf. Josh 6:17), but Jephthah's daughter had done nothing to deserve such a fate."[1]

Lesson 7/Assignment 3 - Interpretation
Jephthah either did not know a way out of his vow or he chose not to take it. Either way, his daughter was sacrificed.

Lesson 7/Assignment 4 - Observation/Interpretation
First Samuel 14 recounts another rash vow, made by King Saul. When his son Jonathan came under the curse of an oath Saul had taken, he was ready and willing to put him to death. Had the people not rescued Jonathan, his father would have killed him.

Students should see that Saul, like Jephthah, made a foolish vow. But, in Jonathan's case the people came to his rescue.

Lesson 7/Assignment 5 - Interpretation
Students may conclude that if Jephthah had known God's Word better he would not have made the rash vow.

Lesson 7/Assignment 6 - Observation/Interpretation
In Hebrews 11:32-34, Jephthah is listed among those who by faith "conquered kingdoms, performed acts of righteousness, obtained promises, shut the mouths of lions, quenched the power of fire, escaped the edge of the sword, from weakness were made strong, became mighty in war, put foreign armies to flight."

Lesson 7/Assignment 7 Observation/Interpretation
Matthew 5:33-37 and James 5:12 counsel making no oaths at all, but rather limiting our statements to, Yes and No.

Lesson 7/Assignment 5 — U-5, Lesson 7, Chapters 11-12

5. Do you think that if Jephthah had known the Word of God better, he might have handled his vow differently?

Lesson 7/Assignment 6

6. Read God's final word about Jephthah in Hebrews and note what you learn.

Lesson 7/Assignment 7

7. Read the following verses and write down what you learn about vows.

Student Page 134

---

[1] The Expositor's Bible Commentary, Volume 2, Frank E. Gaebelein, General Editor; Leviticus: R. Laird Harris, Zondervan Publishing House, Grand Rapids, Michigan 1990.

UNIT FIVE - TEACHER'S GUIDE

PRECEPT UPON PRECEPT
Judges

Lesson 7/Assignment 8 - Application
a. Students should understand that believers should not make vows. Their words should stand alone.

b. Students should understand that what they say is vitally important. They should not make rash promises they either can't or won't fulfill.

c. Students should evaluate if they are men of their word.

Lesson 7/Assignment 9 - Interpretation
Help your students determine the main point of chapters 9-12 and a summary statement that will help them remember these chapters. Remember, summary statements do not have to be the same, but they should all focus on the main events or points of chapters. Possible summary statements are:

Judges 9 – Abimelech made king, Jotham's parable
Judges 10 – Tola and Jair
Judges 11 – Jephthah and his vow
Judges 12 – Jephthah, Ibzan, Elon, Abdon

Lesson 7/Assignment 8
U-5, Lesson 7, Chapters 11-12

8. Take a few minutes for application.

    a. What place do vows have in a child of God's life?

    b. How important are your words?

    c. Are you a man or woman of your word, or do you speak rashly, flippantly, casually?

Lesson 7/Assignment 9
9. Finally, fill in your chart on the Judges and also the chapter themes for 9-12 on your "Judges At A Glance" chart.

> While you probably aren't engaged in literal battles for your life, face-to-face with enemies, you are engaged in a spiritual war against sin. You may have told God, "Lord, if you get me through this situation, I promise..." or "If you remove my consequences, then I will serve you fully."
>
> Jephthah's example has been recorded for your life! You have an opportunity to learn from it. Jephthah's words led to sacrificing something dear to him. How much are you willing to sacrifice for **ignorance**?

Student Page 135

UNIT FIVE - TEACHER'S GUIDE

Judges

UNIT FIVE - TEACHER'S GUIDE

Judges

DISCUSSION GUIDE LESSONS FIVE, SIX AND SEVEN:

JUDGES 10
Discuss main characters and events in this chapter and how they relate to life today.

"After Abimelech died" a man named Tola of Issachar arose to "save" (deliver) Israel. He judged Israel 23 years.

Not much is known about the judges mentioned in this chapter, but they each judged Israel for more than 20 years. Relate this to what Judges 2 says about all the judges the Lord raised up to deliver His people.

After Tola, Jair the Gileadite (possibly the tribe of Gad) judged Israel for 22 years.

Note: Judges 11:29 refers to Gilead and Manasseh, land east of the Jordan that the tribes of Gad and Manasseh possessed. Even though Gilead was the grandson of Manasseh, Gad and half of Manasseh possessed some of the land called Gilead.

The time phrase "then," in verse 6, indicates Israel's return to evil after Jair died. They forsook the Lord and served the Baals, the Ashtaroth, and the gods of Aram, Sidon, Moab, the sons of Ammon, and the Philistines. Relate this to what the Lord told Israel will happen when they tolerate nations within their land. They even followed the gods of those outside the land of Canaan.

Again the Lord's anger burned against Israel and He sold them into the hands of the Philistines and the sons of Ammon. If you show your students where these places are on a map, they will note that the Philistines were on the west coast of Canaan but the sons of Ammon on the east side of the Jordan – not part of the land the Lord gave to Israel. For 18 years Ammon greatly distressed Israel, not just Gilead on the east side of the Jordan.

Remind your students that the Lord sold His people into the hands of their enemies. They didn't conquer Israel without the Lord's help and knowledge. He brought this about because of His anger toward their sin. He still rules nations and peoples today.

Help your students understand that verses 10-16 are different from others in the book of Judges.

The Lord reminded Israel of the enemies He delivered them from in years past. Even though Israel confessed their sin, the Lord told them to destroy the gods they had chosen. He pointed out the cycle Israel lived in for about 300 years.

He delivered Israel from the Egyptians, the Amorites, the Ammonites, the Philistines, Sidonians,

UNIT FIVE - TEACHER'S GUIDE

Judges

Amalekites, and Maonites (possibly Midian).

When Israel told the Lord to do whatever seemed good to Him, and when they put away the foreign gods and served Him, He could bear their misery no longer. His long-suffering, mercy, and compassion are great indeed.

Verses 17-18

Ammon gathered in Gilead, and Israel gathered in Mizpah.

Note: The Mizpah in Gilead is not the Mizpah in Judges 20:1 – there were several Mizpahs (meaning watchtower or lookout) in Israel. The Mizpah in Gilead, however, is the one in Genesis 31:49.

But Israel had no leader to fight against Ammon.

JUDGES 11

This chapter introduces the valiant warrior the men of Gilead were looking for to lead them into battle against Ammon.

Compare this with the description of Gideon. The Lord called him a valiant warrior, but it wasn't until later that he actually became that. The first description given of Jephthah the Gileadite was that he was a valiant warrior.

Compare this with Abimelech, the son of a concubine. Jephthah was the son of a harlot; his brothers, sons of Gilead's wife, drove him away, and denied an inheritance to him. Worthless men gathered around Abimelech and Jephthah.

Jephthah became the head of the men of Gilead as Abimelech became king of the men of Shechem, but the way they became leaders was quite different.

Verses 4-11

When Jephthah consented to fight Ammon, he made an agreement with the men of Gilead. If the Lord gave Ammon into his hand, he would head them up.

From verse 11 it appears that they made him their head *before* going to battle – so he headed up the fight against Ammon as well as afterward.

Verses 12-28

These verses tell what Jephthah knew about the Lord. He recited the history of Israel from Egypt

UNIT FIVE - TEACHER'S GUIDE

Judges

to the present situation. Israel had not taken any of the land of the Ammonites. The Lord had told Israel not to provoke Edom, Moab, or Ammon to war (Deuteronomy 2) when He led them into the land of Canaan. The land of Sihon, an Amorite king of Heshbon, was taken because he had come against Israel.

Let your group discuss what they learned from Jephthah's statements about the Lord in verses 21-27.

He gave Sihon king of the Amorites and his land to Israel.
He drove out the Amorites.
He is the God of Israel – His people should possess what He drives out.
He is the Judge, the Deliverer of His people. He is the only completely righteous Judge.

Jephthah told the king of Ammon that during 300 years Israel possessed the land of the Amorites, no one had tried to take it from them. Jephthah and Israel had done no wrong, but Ammon did in its attempt to take land the Lord gave Israel.

The taking of Sihon and Og (Numbers 21) occurred just before Israel crossed the Jordan (beginning of Joshua). So from the taking of the land to Judges 11 spans about 300 years.

Verses 29-40
Ask your students what they learned from these verses and the cross-references about vows.

Even though the Spirit of the Lord came upon Jephthah to deliver Israel from Ammon, he still made a foolish vow to the Lord.

Since a burnt offering was killed and consumed by fire, some teach that Jephthah knew he was promising to sacrifice a person. Human sacrifice was practiced by some idolatrous nations surrounding Israel. And those in Israel were doing what was right in their own eyes.

Other Bible scholars believe that Jephthah's vow was to make his daughter a living sacrifice, to serve the Lord by never marrying or having children. That would have been a great sacrifice to Jephthah and his daughter since she was his only child. His name would end with his death.

The text says he did to her according to his vow. Since there's so much debate among scholars, don't let your class get carried away in debate.

Leviticus 27 indicates that when a man made a difficult vow, then it could be redeemed or exchanged for a price. But verses 28-29 say that one devoted, "set apart," to the Lord could not be redeemed. If your class studied Leviticus and Joshua, they might share what they remember about things devoted to the Lord or under the ban.

UNIT FIVE - TEACHER'S GUIDE

Judges

1 Samuel 14 recounts the foolish vow King Saul made. When his own son Jonathan came under the curse of the oath Saul had taken, he was ready and willing to put him to death. Had the people not rescued Jonathan, his own father would have put him to death.

Making a vow to the Lord is very serious. Jesus told his disciples to not vow or swear.

JUDGES 12

Continue to discuss Jephthah's life from verses 1-7.

The men of Ephraim complained to Jephthah, because he didn't call them to fight Ammon. Verse 2 says when he called them, they didn't help. Verses 4-6 records two tribes of Israel fighting each other. That had happened before (Israel and Benjamin in Judges 19–21). In the battle in Judges 12, 42,000 men of Ephraim are killed.

Verse 7 is the first reference to Jephthah as a judge. He judged Israel for only six years, yet the Lord devoted much of Judges to him. He wants people to learn from his life.

Verses 8-15 tell of three other judges of Israel.

Ibzan of Bethlehem judged after Jephthah for 7 years.
The only fact known about him is that he gave his sons and daughters to marry outside his family (either within or without his tribe).

Elon of the tribe of Zebulun judged Israel for 10 years after Ibzan.

After him, Abdon from the tribe of Ephraim judged Israel for eight years.

The enemies of Israel during the times of these judges are not mentioned.

The judges of Israel were not perfect people, but the Lord used them mightily to deliver His people. Ask your students how they can apply the truths in these lessons.

UNIT FIVE - TEACHER'S GUIDE

Judges

ENRICHMENT WORDS

Apostasy – abandonment of a previous loyalty.

Anarchy – absence or denial of any authority or established order.

Absolute – positive, unquestionable.

Bramble – a rough prickly shrub or vine.

Character – main or essential nature.

Ignorance – lacking knowledge or comprehension.

Judge – to act as law-giver or judge or governor of God.

King – a governmental head of a embodied political, social, religious, and military authority.

Governor – one that exercises authority especially over an area or group.

Monarchy – undivided rule or absolute sovereignty by a single person.

Parable – a usually short fictitious story that illustrates a moral attitude or a religious principle.

Theocracy – government of a state by immediate divine guidance or by officials who are regarded as divinely guided.

Vow – a solemn promise by which a person is bound to an act.

UNIT FIVE - TEACHER'S GUIDE

UNIT FIVE - TEACHER'S GUIDE

Judges

LOCATIONS IN JUDGES 9-12

U-5, Chapters 9-12

UNIT FIVE - TEACHER'S GUIDE

Unit Five - Teacher's Guide

Judges
Unit Five Quiz

Name: _____ Date: _____

Unit five - quiz key

MULTIPLE CHOICE - Circle one.

1. Which of the following is a possible chapter theme for Judges 9?
    a. Jephthah and his vow
    b. Jephthah, Ibzan, Elon, Abdon
    c. Tola and Jair
    d. *Abimelech made king, Jotham's parable*

2. All of the following are true about the sons of Israel after Gideon died EXCEPT:
    a. They did not remember the Lord.
    b. They used Gideon's ephod as an idol.
    c. They did not show kindness to the house of Gideon.
    d. *They were sold into the hands of the Midianites.*

3. All of the following are true about King Abimelech EXCEPT:
    a. He hired worthless and reckless men to kill his 70 brothers.
    b. He ruled Israel for three years.
    c. He was the son of Gideon by a concubine who lived in Shechem.
    d. *He told the men of Shechem a parable about trees.*

4. Who was Jotham?
    a. *Gideon's son*
    b. Jephthah's brother
    c. The king of Ammon
    d. A judge in Israel

5. How did Abimelech die?
    a. He died of old age.
    b. Jotham killed him.
    c. *His armor bearer killed him after a woman dropped a millstone on his head.*
    d. Jephthah offered him to the LORD to fulfill his vow.

© 2008 Precept Ministries International

UNIT FIVE - TEACHER'S GUIDE

Judges
Unit Five Quiz

SHORT ANSWER

6. Briefly explain Jotham's parable.

The trees looked for a king. First they asked the olive tree. When it refused they asked the fig tree. When it refused they asked the vine. When the vine refused they asked the bramble. The bramble warned that if they did not take refuge in its shade, fire would come out from it and consume the trees.

Jotham illustrates that Israel's chosen ruler, Abimelech, was a "bramble." He also cursed them for the way they treated his father's household. He told them fire would come from Abimelech and consume Shechem, and fire would come from the men of Shechem and consume Abimelech.

UNIT FIVE - TEACHER'S GUIDE

Judges
Unit Five Test

Name: _____ Date: _____

UNIT FIVE - TEST KEY

MATCHING

__d__	1. Abandonment of previous loyalty	a. Anarchy
		b. Vow
__a__	2. Absence or denial of any authority or established order	c. Absolute
		d. Apostasy
__c__	3. Positive, unquestionable	e. Bramble
		f. Abimelech
__b__	4. A solemn promise by which a person is bound to an act	g. Jotham
		h. Jephthah
__e__	5. A rough prickly stub or vine	i. Gideon
__i__	6. Refused to be king of Israel	
__g__	7. Told men of Israel a parable about trees and a bramble	
__f__	8. Killed his brothers in order to be the leaders of Israel.	
__h__	9. Vowed to offer the first thing out his door to the Lord if He gave the sons of Ammon into his hand	

MULTIPLE CHOICE - Circle one.

10. Which of the following is a possible chapter theme for Judges 9?
    a. Jephthah and his vow
    b. Jephthah, Ibzan, Elon, Abdon
    c. Tola and Jair
    d. Abimelech made king, Jotham's parable

11. Which of the following is a possible chapter theme for Judges 10?
    a. Jephthah and his vow
    b. Jephthah, Ibzan, Elon, Abdon
    c. Tola and Jair
    d. Abimelech made king, Jotham's parable

UNIT FIVE - Teacher's Guide

Judges

12. Which of the following is a possible chapter theme for Judges 11?
    a. *Jephthah and his vow*
    b. Jephthah, Ibzan, Elon, Abdon
    c. Tola and Jair
    d. Abimelech made king, Jotham's parable

13. Which of the following is a possible chapter theme for Judges 12?
    a. Jephthah and his vow
    b. *Jephthah, Ibzan, Elon, Abdon*
    c. Tola and Jair
    d. Abimelech made king, Jotham's parable

14. All of the following are true about the sons of Israel after Gideon died EXCEPT:
    a. They did not remember the Lord.
    b. They used Gideon's ephod as an idol.
    c. They did not show kindness to the house of Gideon.
    d. *They were sold into the hands of the Midianites.*

15. All of the following are true about King Abimelech EXCEPT:
    a. He hired worthless and reckless men to kill his 70 brothers.
    b. He ruled Israel for three years.
    c. He was the son of Gideon by a concubine who lived in Shechem.
    d. *He told the men of Shechem a parable about trees.*

16. Who was Jotham?
    a. *Gideon's son*
    b. Jephthah's brother
    c. The king of Ammon
    d. A judge in Israel

17. How did Abimelech die?
    a. He died of old age.
    b. Jotham killed him.
    c. *His armor bearer killed him after a woman dropped a millstone on his head.*
    d. Jephthah offered him to the LORD to fulfill his vow.

18. Who were the next two judges after Gideon?
    a. Jotham and Abimelech
    b. *Tola and Jair*
    c. Jephthah and Abimelech
    d. Saul and David

UNIT FIVE - TEACHER'S GUIDE

Judges
Unit Five Test

19. What did Jephthah ask God for in return for his vow?
    a. Make his family prosper
    b. Give him back the inheritance his brothers had stolen
    c. Spare his daughter's life
    d. *Give the sons of Ammon into his hand*

20. All the following are true about Jephthah EXCEPT:
    a. Son of a harlot
    b. Valiant warrior
    c. Abimelech's brother
    d. *Driven out of his father's house with no inheritance*

21. Why did Jephthah's daughter go away for two months?
    a. *To weep because of her virginity*
    b. To kill the men who had attacked her father
    c. To plead with the high priest to spare her life
    d. To visit her mother and sisters

SHORT ANSWER

22. Define monarchy and theocracy, and explain which was God's plan for Israel.

A monarchy is undivided rule or absolute sovereignty by a single person. A theocracy is a government of state by immediate divine guidance or by officials who are regarded as divinely guided. (Students can simply state that a monarchy is ruled by one person and a theocracy is ruled by God.) God's plan was for Israel to be ruled by Him alone.

23. Why did Israel want an earthly king, according to 1 Samuel 8:4-22? What did God say they were doing by choosing a man?

Israel wanted an earthly king to be like the nations around them. In doing so, they were rejecting God as their king.

24. Briefly explain Jotham's parable.

The trees looked for a king. First they asked the olive tree. When it refused they asked the fig tree. When it refused they asked the vine. When the vine refused they asked the bramble. The bramble warned that if they did not take refuge in its shade, fire would come out from it and consume the trees. Jotham illustrates that Israel's chosen ruler, Abimelech, was a "bramble." He also cursed them for the way they treated his father's household. He told them fire would come from Abimelech and consume Shechem, and fire would come from the men of Shechem and consume Abimelech.

© 2008 Precept Ministries International

UNIT FIVE - TEACHER'S GUIDE

Judges
Unit Five Test

25. Describe Abimelech's rise to power.

Abimilech went to Shechem and offered to rule over them instead of the 70 sons of Gideon. He reminded them he was their relative. They gave him seventy pieces of silver and he hired worthless and reckless fellows to go with him to kill his brothers. After he did this, the men of Shechem made him king.

ESSAY

Choose one of the following topics, briefly summarize it, and discuss how it applies to your life:

a. Principles you learned from Jephthah's vow
b. Principles you learned from Gideon's life
c. What you learned about God in Judges 9-12

Students will identify the main points of each of these topics and discuss how the truths they learned apply to their lives.

Unit Six - Teacher's Guide

PURSUIT OF PLEASURE

UNIT OBJECTIVES:

In this unit, students will observe Judges 13-16 to evaluate Samson' life and identify applications for their lives. They will work to comprehend the Nazirite vow by evaluating cross-references that describe this vow and those who participated in it. Students will also observe the role of the Spirit of the Lord in Samson' life and identify events surrounding his birth. They will continue to identify cycles of sin in Judges 13-16. Additionally, students will carefully observe and interpret Samson's character and choices to determine life principles for application. Finally, students will look at Proverbs 7 to identify how lust and naiveté lead to destruction.

Introduction/Prayer
Your students have probably heard the story of Samson before. Encourage them to ask God to show them things they can apply from Samson's life.

UNIT SIX

Pursuit of Pleasure
U-6, Chapters 13-16

Samson and Delilah – who doesn't know about these two! Even Hollywood was once captivated by this love affair!

Many people are familiar with Samson's story and weakness for beautiful woman. Few realize how often they are ensnared by the same lusts and end up with similarly devastating consequences.

As you study this unit, you may find you have more in common with Samson than you realize. For instance, do you ignore your parents rules and guidance if you don't agree with them? What about God's Word? Do you view the Bible as a menu of items to choose from? Do you ignore commandments that are inconvenient or "politically incorrect?" If so, then it's essential for you to observe Samson's life and learn from his mistakes before you discover from your own experience that poor choices bring life-changing consequences.

Introduction/Prayer
To begin, write a prayer asking God to help you understand His purpose in this account of Samson.

ONE ON ONE:

Student Page 141

UNIT SIX - TEACHER'S GUIDE

UNIT SIX - TEACHER'S GUIDE

Judges

LESSON ONE:

 Judges 13 Observation Worksheets, colored pencils, key word bookmark, "A Summary of the Life of Samson" found at the end of the unit

OBJECTIVES:

Students will observe Judges 13 marking key words from their bookmarks. Students will also identify main events in this chapter and record them on the "A Summary of the Life of Samson" chart at the end of this unit.

Lesson 1/Assignment 1 - Observation
Students will observe Judges 13 marking key words from their bookmarks including *Philistines*, *Nazirite*, instructions to Samson's parents, and *Spirit of the Lord*.

Remind them to interrogate the text with the 5W and H questions as they mark each word. They may have questions about Philistine and Nazirite vows. Remind them to focus on the obvious and future lessons will reveal details.

You may need to mark instructions to Samson's parents together if students have trouble identifying them.

Lesson 1/Assignment 2 - Observation
Students will list what they learn about Samson on the "A Summary of the Life of Samson" chart found at the end of the unit. A blank chart is in the Teacher's Helps for you to make a transparency of to use in class. Fill in the chart together for this chapter.

Remind students to summarize what the chapter says about each of the topics. They will identify chart information by asking the 5W and H questions to determine

---

LESSON ONE

U-6, Lesson 1, Chapter 13

Today you're going to observe Judges 13 – a significant chapter God devoted to part of the story of Samson's life. If you remember, of all the judges God gave the most attention to Gideon and then to Samson so you want to give this judge adequate attention. As you'll discover, Samson's story begins before he was born.

Lesson 1/Assignment 1
1. Your assignment today is to observe Judges 13.

   a. In addition to marking the key words on your bookmark, mark the word *Philistines* and add it to your bookmark (it's not necessary to mark pronouns. You can mark this word with a large black **P**.

   b. Another word to mark is *Nazirite*, its first use in Judges. Circle it in purple.

   c. As you come across instructions to Samson's parents, underline them in orange and number each guideline the angel of the Lord gives them.

   d. Mark the *Spirit of the Lord* with a blue cloud like this .

> Names and phrases that appear repeatedly throughout the Bible should be marked the same way from book to book. For example, you will find the "Spirit of the Lord" or "Holy Spirit." throughout Scripture. Other examples include God, Jesus, love, grace, and sin. When you mark and observe what the text says about these words in all the books you study, you will begin to build sound doctrine based on the whole counsel of God's Word.

Lesson 1/Assignment 2
2. Record the main events of Samson's life on the chart, "A Summary of the Life of Samson" found at the end of this unit.

 3. Record the theme of chapter 13 on the "Judges At A Glance" chart.

> **Chapter themes** help you remember the main point of the chapter. Key words are often used when determining appropriate themes. There are no "wrong" answers as long as they include the main point or event of the chapter. Simply summarize what you saw!

Student Page 143

Unit six - Teacher's Guide

Judges

what is said about the event – when it occurred, main participants, what happened to the Philistines, and how Samson lived out his Nazirite vow. Tell students to leave blanks where chapters don't provide information about topics.

Lesson 1/Assignment 3 - Observation

Help students determine the main point of chapter 13 and a summary statement to help them remember this chapter. A possible summary statement is:

Judges 13 – The angel of the Lord appears to Samson's parents

UNIT SIX - TEACHER'S GUIDE

Judges

LESSON TWO:

 Judges 13 Observation Worksheets, Bible

OBJECTIVES:

In this lesson, students will interpret the angel of the Lord's instruction for Samson to be a Nazirite. They will look at cross-references about the Nazirite vow to further comprehend the commands the angel of the Lord gave Samson's parents.

Lesson 2/Assignment 1 - Interpretation
Students will list instructions the angel of the Lord gave to Samson's parents on the chart entitled "The Nazirite Vow." See chart key at the end of this lesson.

Remind them of the reason to cross-reference – to look at scriptures that provide more information about the topic they are studying. This assignment will help students understand what the angel of the Lord meant when he instructed Samson to be a Nazirite.

Lesson 2/Assignment 2 - Observation/Interpretation
Students will look up each cross-reference and record what they learn about the Nazirite vow in the appropriate column on "The Nazirite Vow" chart.

See chart key at the end of this lesson.

Lesson 2/ Assignment 3- Interpretation
Students will use information from the cross-references to determine the purpose of the Nazirite vow, the restrictions involved, and how Samson's vow was different.

a. The Nazirite vow's purpose was to be separate, dedicated, and holy to the Lord (Numbers 6:2, 5, 8).

LESSON TWO

U-6, Lesson 2, Chapter 13

In this lesson you'll discover what Scripture teaches about the **Nazirite** vow. The Nazirite is referred to in only four books of the Bible: Numbers, Judges, Lamentations, and Amos. Since the reference in Lamentations is not significant to the study of Samson, you'll focus on Numbers, Amos, and Judges.

Lesson 2/Assignment 1
1. As you observed Judges 13, you were to underline and number the instructions the angel of the Lord gave to Samson's parents. Fill in the information you learned concerning the Nazirite vow on the chart "The Nazirite Vow" at the end of this lesson.

Lesson 2/Assignment 2
2. As you read the following cross-references, continue listing what you learn about the Nazirite vow in the appropriate column on the chart.

    a. Numbers 6 – (Identify the key repeated word in this chapter and write it below.)

    b. Amos 2:11-12

Lesson 2/Assignment 3
3. Now that you know more about the Nazirite vow, read Judges 13 again and interpret it in light of what you learned in Numbers 6. The following questions will help you walk through this process.

    a. What was God's purpose for Samson taking the Nazirite vow?

    b. What does this tell you about God's plan for Samson?

> **Interpretation** – "All Scripture is inspired (breathed) by God" (2 Timothy 3:16). In other words, God used men to write down His very words. He is the author of the Bible. The best way to understand God's Word is to interpret Scripture with Scripture. God doesn't always include all the information about a subject in one location. Other passages build up the subject. Some call this **progressive revelation**.

Student Page 145

UNIT SIX - TEACHER'S GUIDE

Judges

b. Students will see that God set Samson apart from birth for His purposes.

Lesson 2/Assignment 4 - Observation/Interpretation
The differences in Samson's vow from Numbers 6:

a. Samson was to be a Nazirite from birth until death; in Numbers 6, the person kept the vow until the specified time of separation ended.

b. The angel of the Lord told Samson's parents that he was to be a Nazirite; in Numbers 6, individuals make the vow themselves.

Lesson 2/Assignment 4   U-6, Lesson 2, Chapter 13
4. Use these questions to help you compare and contrast Sampson's vow with what you saw in Numbers 6.

> THINK! What or who determined the guidelines for Samson's vow?

  a. How long was Samson to be a Nazirite? How does this contrast with what you saw in Numbers?

  b. Who makes the choice to be a Nazirite according to Numbers 6? How about Judges 13?

> Nazirite means "consecrated" or "devoted" (one).

> Amazing! You've done groundwork that will help you better understand Samson' life. Your hard work has helped you understand the context of Judges 13. The Nazirite was to be set apart, separate for God. He did many things on the outside to show that he was dedicated, holy to the Lord on the inside. Be sure to have "The Nazirite Vow" chart you completed in this lesson out for the following lessons ahead. It will help keep you in context as you continue to look at the life of Samson, a man dedicated to God.

Student Page 146

UNIT SIX - TEACHER'S GUIDE

Judges
U-6, Lesson 2, Chapter 13

THE NAZIRITE VOW

	JUDGES 13	NUMBERS 6	AMOS 2:11-12
WHAT IS A NAZIRITE?	*Samson*	*A man or woman who makes a special vow* *Dedicated to the Lord*	*God raises up*
RESTRICTIONS ON THE NAZIRITE	*His mother was not to drink wine or strong drink, or eat any unclean thing* *No razor on his head*	*Abstain from wine and strong drink* *Drink no vinegar* *Not to drink any grape juice or eat fresh or dried grapes* *Not to eat anything produced by the grape vine, seeds or skin* *No razor on his head* *Not to go near a dead person – if a man next to him dies suddenly, he must shave head on 7th day; priest will offer a sin offering; must make a guilt offering*	*Not to drink wine*
LENGTH OF THE NAZIRITE VOW	*From the womb to the day of his death*	*Holy until the days of separation are fulfilled* *Until sacrifice is made before the priest at the doorway of the tent of meeting at the end of his days of separation*	

© 2008 Precept Ministries International

Unit Six - Teacher's Guide

Judges

UNIT SIX - TEACHER'S GUIDE

PRECEPT UPON PRECEPT
Judges

DISCUSSION GUIDE LESSONS ONE AND TWO:

REVIEW
Help your students understand the segment divisions listed in the "At A Glance" charts. Question them on what they learned so they can label the segments during the discussion.

    Judges 1-2 says Israel did not drive out its enemies.
    The sin cycle for the entire book is included in chapter 2.

    Judges 3-16 record the judges.

    Judges 17-21 describe events related to the tribes of Dan and Benjamin, which took place near the
     beginning of the times of the judges (but recorded at the end of the book).

Judges 3-16 contain the segments of the different judges.

3	Othniel, Ehud, Shamgar
4-5	Deborah and Barak
6-8	Gideon
9	Gideon's son Abimelech as king
10	Tola, Jair
11-12	Jephthah; 12 also mentions Ibzan, Elon, Abdon
13-16	Samson

JUDGES 13
Ask students for information from verse one only. Relate answers they give to the previous mentions of Israel doing evil and Israel's oppressors.

    Israel did evil:
    Judges 2:11-13; 3:7, 12; 4:1; 6:1; 8:33-35; 10:6

    Oppressors the Lord sold Israel to:
3:8	Mesopotamia	8 years
3:14	Moab	18 years
3:31	Philistines	Unknown

© 2008 Precept Ministries International

UNIT SIX - TEACHER'S GUIDE

Judges

4:2	Canaanites	20 years
6:1	Midian	7 years
10:7	Philistines and Ammonites	18 years
13:1	Philistines	40 years

Discuss how Samson's parents learned they were going to have a child and how they responded.

    The angel of the Lord told Samson's parents they were going to have a child and that he would be a Nazirite from the womb.

    Manoah and his wife believed the Lord.

    Discuss what it meant for Samson to be a Nazirite.

    The Nazirite vow dedicated a person to the Lord. He was separated and holy to the Lord for the time of his separation.

    The word "Nazirite" means "separated" or "dedicated."[1]

    He was not to eat or drink anything produced by the grape vine.

    A razor was not to pass over his head.

    He was not to go near a dead person. If someone died in his presence, he was to go through a cleansing ritual for his dedicated head. Verses 9-12 of Numbers 6 detail the process of that cleansing.

    Numbers 6:13-21 relate what happened when the days of separation were fulfilled.

    The Lord designated Samson to be a Nazirite before he was born – from the womb until death. His mother was not to take anything from the grape vine while she was carrying him in her womb and she could not eat any unclean thing.

    Note: "The word Nazirite, not to be confused with Nazarene, means 'separated,' and in this context means specifically 'one who was separated unto the Lord.' It was probably similar to a vow that existed among the Hebrews prior to Mount Sinai, but in this passage, it is brought under the regulation of the law. By the terms of the vow, men or women could voluntarily separate themselves unto the Lord for a specific period of time, even for life. They did not, however,

---

[1] Spiros Zodhiates, *The Complete Word Study Dictionary : Old Testament*, electronic ed. (Chattanooga, TN: AMG Publishers, 2000, c1992, c1993). H5139.

Unit Six - Teacher's Guide

Judges

become hermits, separating themselves from society. Samson (Judges 13:5) and Samuel (1 Samuel 1:11, 28) are two of the Nazirites mentioned in the Bible. It is also thought that John the Baptist might have been a Nazirite (Luke 1:15) and that perhaps this is the vow associated with the Apostle Paul (Acts 21:23–26)."[1]

Ask your class what they learned from the last two verses of Judges 13.

> The Lord blessed Samson. The Spirit of the Lord began to stir him in Mahaneh-dan, between Zorah and Eshtaol. Relate this to Judges 2:16-18; 3:10; 6:34; and 11:29.

> Manoah was from Zorah. Locate these places on the map so your students can see how close they are to the locations of Judges 14-16 events.

Ask students to discuss what they learned about God from this chapter and how that information can change how they live.

---

[1] Spiros Zodhiates, *The Complete Word Study Dictionary : Old Testament*, electronic ed. (Chattanooga, TN: AMG Publishers, 2000, c1992, c1993).

Unit six - Teacher's Guide

Judges

UNIT SIX - TEACHER'S GUIDE

LESSON THREE:

 Judges 13 Observation Worksheets, Bible, The "Judges of Israel" chart in the Appendix

OBJECTIVES:

In this lesson, students will look at cross-references to comprehend the role of the angel of the Lord in Judges. They will also compare and contrast Samson's call to judge with the previous judges, and determine how principles learned from his life apply to their lives.

Lesson 3/Assignment 1 - Observation/Interpretation
Students will look up the following cross-references and record what they learn about the angel of the Lord:

a. Judges 2:1-4: the angel of the LORD came up from Gilgal to Bochim to punish the people for their disobedience. He describes himself as the one who brought Israel from Egypt, led them into the land, swore to their fathers, covenanted with them, was to be obeyed, and drove out their enemies.

b. Judges 5:23: the angel of the Lord curses Meroz for not helping the Lord against Sisera.

c. Judges 6:11-23: the angel of the Lord tells Gideon that the Lord will use him to deliver Israel from Midian.

d. Judges 13: the angel of the LORD tells Samson's mother she will have a son. He instructs her in the Nazirite vow and tells her Samson will deliver Israel.

Lesson 3/Assignment 2 - Observation/Interpretation
According to John 16:4-15, Jesus tells his disciples He is going away, but is sending a Helper – the Holy Spirit

---

LESSON THREE
U-6, Lesson 3, Chapter 13

A **barren** woman is told she's going to give birth to a son. Think of the times! Doctors and drugs were not around to help people become pregnant. What startling news Manoah's wife received! You have already seen several references to the one who brought this news throughout your study of Judges. Today you will look at the various places the angel of the Lord is mentioned in Judges and understand the roles he plays in this book.

Lesson 3/Assignment 1
1. Look up the following references to the angel of the Lord in Judges and record what you learn about him.

   a. Judges 2:1

   b. Judges 5:23

   c. Judges 6:11

   d. Judges 13

Lesson 3/Assignment 2
2. The "angel of the Lord" is also mentioned in several other books of the Bible. Why doesn't the "angel of the Lord" appear today? Read the following passage (Jesus is speaking) and write out your thoughts.

JOHN 16:4-15

© 2008 Precept Ministries International

Student Page 149

UNIT SIX - TEACHER'S GUIDE

Judges

who convicts the world concerning sin, righteousness, and judgment, and discloses the Father's will to believers.

Lesson 3/Assignment 3 - Interpretation
Students should see that the Holy Spirit Jesus promised does everything the angel of the Lord did in Judges. He convicts the world of sin (Judges 2:1-4 and 5:23) and He discloses the Father's will (Judges 6:1-23, Judges 13).

Lesson 3/Assignment 4 - Observation/Interpretation
Students will compare and contrast Samson with the other judges they have studied. They can use "The Judges of Israel" chart to help them complete this assignment.

a. Samson is the only judge God calls to be a deliverer prior to his birth. He is also the only judge required to live by the Nazirite vow.

b. Samson was set apart (dedicated to God) from birth with restrictions not required of other judges.

Lesson 3/Assignment 5 - Observation/Interpretation

In this listing assignment, help your students summarize main points concerning Samson's parents encounter with the angel of the Lord. Remind them not to write down every detail.

- *v. 2 - was barren*
- *v. 3 - told by angel of the Lord she will conceive a son*
- *v. 4 - Not to drink wine or strong drink or touch anything unclean.*
- *v. 5 - Will raise Samson as a Nazarite; he will deliver Israel*
- *v. 6 - Tells her husband angel's message*
- *v. 8 - Asks God to send the "man of God" again to teach them what to do when their son is born.*
- *v. 9 - Angel of God comes again*

Lesson 3/Assignment 3 *U-6, Lesson 3, Chapter 13*
3. Based on what you learned from John 16:4-15, does God do the things in believers' lives today that He used the "angel of the Lord" for? Explain your answer.

Lesson 3/Assignment 4
4. Now, compare and contrast what you learn about Samson with the other Judges you've seen.

   a. How does Samson's call compare or contrast with the calls of the other judges you have studied?

   b. What is different about Samson's relationship to God? List below what the text says:

Lesson 3/Assignment 5
5. Finally, what did you learn from this chapter about Samson's parents? List highlights.

Lesson 3/Assignment 6
6. What have you learned from Samson's story that you can apply to your life?

Hint: What examples can you follow? What choices or behaviors are you going to avoid?

Student Page 150
© 2008 Precept Ministries International

Unit six - Teacher's Guide

Judges

and repeats what he said the first time
- *v. 16. - When he comes again, both parents don't recognize him*
- *v. 19 - They prepare an offering*
- *v. 20-23 - When the angel of the Lord ascends in the flame from the altar Manoah fears for their lives, but his wife assures him*

Lesson 3/Assignment 6 - Application

Students will apply what they learned to their lives. If they need help, ask them to consider the following: How would they respond if God gave them the amazing news and instructions He gave Samson's parents? Do they believe God can make a barren woman conceive? How do they respond to the Holy Spirit? Do they recognize what an amazing gift the Holy Spirit is to believers?

UNIT SIX - TEACHER'S GUIDE

Judges

UNIT SIX - TEACHER'S GUIDE

Judges

DISCUSSION GUIDE LESSON THREE:

Discuss with your class what they learned about the angel of the Lord from Judges 13 and related cross-references.

> The angel of the Lord tells Samson's parents he will be born and a Nazirite from birth.
>
> The angel of the Lord is mentioned several times in Judges. Ask students to discuss what they learned.
>
> Judges 2:1-5, the angel of the Lord describes himself:
> brought Israel from Egypt
> led them into the land
> swore to their fathers
> covenanted with them
> must be obeyed
> drove out their enemies
>
> Judges 5:23: He curses Meroz.
>
> Judges 6:11-24:
> He sits under the oak in Ophrah.
> He appears to Gideon.
> As with Manoah and his wife, Gideon does not recognize Him immediately.
> He is called "Lord" in verses 14, 16, 22, and 23.
> He gives a sign to Gideon that He was the One Who spoke to him.
> Gideon builds an altar and names it "The Lord is Peace."
>
> When He appears the second time to Samson's parents, He says His name is "wonderful." He does wonders while Manoah and his wife look on. He is described as "very awesome."

Ask your students if they know the "wonderful" One.

Ask your students to discuss what they learned about how God instructs, convicts, and reveals His will to believers today.

Have them discuss how they can apply the truths of this lesson to their lives.

UNIT SIX - TEACHER'S GUIDE

Judges

UNIT SIX - TEACHER'S GUIDE

Judges

LESSON FOUR:

 Judges 14 Observation Worksheets, colored pencils, key word bookmark, "Samson's Women" chart found at the end of the lesson, Bible, "The Judges of Israel" chart and "At A Glance" chart from the Appendix

OBJECTIVES:

In this lesson, students will observe Judges 14 and identify the main theme. They will also recognize the characters of Samson's women and look at cross-references to learn more about Israel's history with the Philistines.

Lesson 4/Assignment 1 - Observation
Students will observe Judges 14 marking key words from their bookmarks including *love, hate, die, the woman from Timnah*, and references to Samson's eyes.

Lesson 4/Assignment 2 - Observation
Students will record information about the woman from Timnah on the "Samson's Women" chart at the end of the unit. See the chart key at the end of this unit.

 Remind students to write what the text says and put chapter and verse references next to the information.

Lesson 4/Assignment 3 - Interpretation
Students will briefly list what Samson's parents do in this chapter.

- *v.3 - when Samson asks his father and mother to get him the woman from Timnah they ask if there isn't someone of his own people rather than a Philistine*
- *v.4 - they do not know that this is from the Lord*
- *v.5 - they go down to Timnah with Samson*
- *v.6 - don't know Samson has killed a lion*

LESSON FOUR

U-6, Lesson 4, Chapter 14

In lessons 1-3 you saw that Samson's parents **dedicated** him to God before he was born. You saw God bless him and the Holy Spirit begin to stir within him. How does Samson go from this miraculous beginning to a tragic end? What choices does he make that lead to his downfall? As you look at these things, think about how you can avoid making the same mistakes Samson did.

Lesson 4/Assignment 1
1. Observe Judges 14, marking the words on your bookmark.

   a. Add the word *love* to your bookmark. You can mark this word with a red heart ♡. Mark *hate* with a heart with a slash through it.

   b. Also mark every reference to *die* and *kill* with a black tombstone. Add them to your bookmark.

   c. Continue to mark every geographical reference.

   d. Mark the locations mentioned in this chapter on the map at the end of this lesson. (Some places listed in the text may not be on the map because their locations are not known.)

   e. Mark main references to the *woman from Timnah* with a red T.

   f. Draw an eye like this over *saw* or references to *Samson's eyes*.

Lesson 4/Assignment 2
2. What do you learn about the Philistine woman from Timnah? List your insights on the "Samson's Women" chart located at the end of this unit.

Lesson 4/Assignment 3
3. Record below what Samson's parents do in Chapter 14.

   a. Were Samson's parents pleased with his choice of wife? How do you know?

   b. What do you learn from Judges 14:4?

Student Page 151

UNIT SIX - TEACHER'S GUIDE

Judges

- *v.9 - Samson gives them some of the honey from the lion carcass but does not tell them where it came from*
- *v.10 - Samson's father goes to the woman from Timnah*

a. Samson's parents are obviously not pleased with his choice. They suggest he find a wife from his own people.

b. According to Judges 14:4, this situation is "of the Lord"; He was seeking "an occasion against the Philistines."

c. Students should think about how God used Samson's sin to accomplish His will. They should see that their sins won't prevent God from accomplishing His purposes.

If your students don't recognize Samson's choice as a sin, they will in the next lesson's cross-reference assignments. You can let them answer this question after they complete Lesson 5, if they are unsure.

Lesson 4/Assignment 4 - Observation/Interpretation
Samson didn't tell his parents he killed a lion or took honey from a lion's carcass.

Lesson 4/Assignment 5 - Observation/Interpretation
Students will look up the following cross-references and record what they learn about the Philistines and the Philistine captivity during Samson's time. As you assign these cross-references, remind students of time frames in each.

Genesis 21:32-34: Abraham made a covenant with Abimelech from the land of the Philistines. Abraham sojourned in Philistine land for many days.

Genesis 26:1: Isaac went to Gerar to see Abimelech, king of the Philistines, because there was famine in the land.

U-6, Lesson 4, Chapter 14

a. What does this tell you about God? Can He use your mistakes to accomplish His will? How does that encourage you?

Lesson 4/Assignment 4
4. What does Samson neglect to tell his parents in this chapter?

Lesson 4/Assignment 5
5. You may recall that Goliath, young David's foe, was a Philistine. Who were the Philistines? How did they happen to be in the land? Was this Israel's first encounter with them? Do a little research to better appreciate Samson's day and age.

Look up the following scriptures and record pertinent information next to each. As you note geographical locations, consult the map at the end of this unit.

GENESIS 21:32-34 — This is the second mention of the Philistines in the Bible.

> Judges 13:1 tells us that the Lord gave Israel into the hands of the Philistines – a people established in five major cities, each having its own lord. The cities were Gaza, Ashkelon, Ashdod, Ekron, and Gath. Beth-shan and Gerar were also prominent Philistine towns.

GENESIS 26:1

From Abraham to the Exodus is approximately 700 years.

EXODUS 13:17-18

UNIT SIX - TEACHER'S GUIDE

Judges

Exodus 13:17: "When Pharaoh had let the people go, God did not lead them by the land of the Philistines, even though it was near; for God said, "The people might change their minds when they see war, and return to Egypt." God led the people around by the way of the wilderness to the Red Sea; and the sons of Israel went up in martial array from the land of Egypt."

Exodus 23:31, God said He would fix Israel's boundary from the Red Sea to the sea of the Philistines, and from the wilderness to the River Euphrates; "for I will deliver the inhabitants of the land into your hand, and you will drive them out before you."

Joshua 13:1-3: Joshua campaigned to take the Promised Land; the only land that remained unclaimed was "all the regions of the Philistines and all those of the Geshurites; from the Shihor which is east of Egypt, even as far as the border of Ekron to the north (it is counted as Canaanite); the five lords of the Philistines: the Gazite, the Ashdodite, the Ashkelonite, the Gittite, the Ekronite; and the Avvite."

Judges 3:1-4: God left these nations to test Israel, find out if they would obey the LORD's commandments, and teach them war. The nations were: the five lords of the Philistines and all the Canaanites and the Sidonians and the Hivites who lived in Mount Lebanon, from Mount Baal-hermon as far as Lebo-hamath.

Judges 3:31: "Shamgar struck down 600 Philistines with an oxgoad."

Judges 10:6-11: Israel served Philistine gods and the LORD's anger burned against them. He sold them into the hands of the Philistines and the sons of Ammon, and they afflicted and crushed the sons of Israel for 18 years. Israel cried out to God for deliverance.

Lesson 4/Assignment 6 - Observation
According to Judges 13:1, Israel did evil in the sight of the Lord, so the Lord gave them into the hands of the Philistines 40 years.

Lesson 4/Assignment 7 - Interpretation

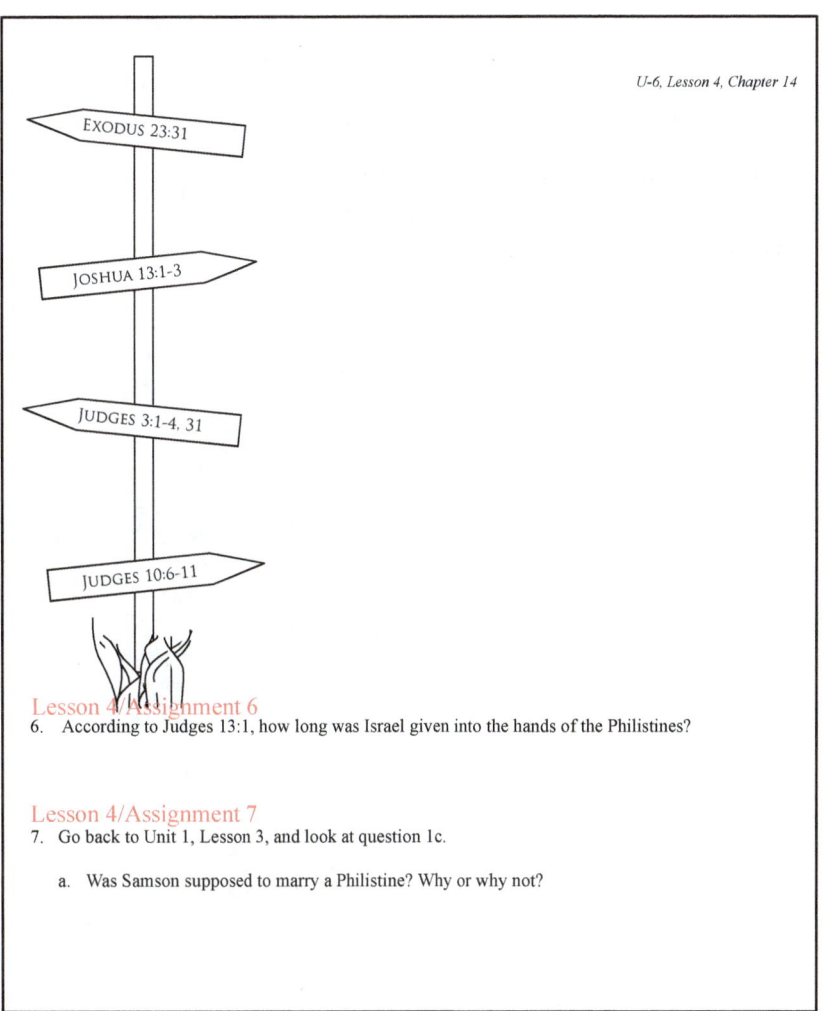

U-6, Lesson 4, Chapter 14

Lesson 4/Assignment 6
6. According to Judges 13:1, how long was Israel given into the hands of the Philistines?

Lesson 4/Assignment 7
7. Go back to Unit 1, Lesson 3, and look at question 1c.

   a. Was Samson supposed to marry a Philistine? Why or why not?

Student Page 153

UNIT SIX - TEACHER'S GUIDE

Judges

a. According to Joshua 23:1-13 the sons of Israel were forbidden to marry Gentiles in the land. If they did, they would become traps and snares to them (to serve idols), and whips in their sides and thorns in their eyes. Samson should <u>not</u> have married a Philistine.

b. Students should see that God used Samson's disobedience to bring an "occasion against the Philistines." After this, Samson kills 30 Philistines.

c. Help students realize that while Samson disobeyed God's commands, God fulfilled His purpose – to begin Israel's deliverance from the Philistines. As your students complete this assignment or during the following discussion, help them understand that their disobedience cannot stop God's plan; however, there are still consequences as they will see in Samson's life.

Lesson 4/Assignment 8 - Observation
Students will record relevant information about Samson on "The Judges of Israel" chart from the Appendix.

Lesson 4/Assignment 9 - Observation/Interpretation
Students will determine the theme of chapter 14 and a summary statement to help them remember this chapter. A possible summary statement is:

Judges 14 – Samson and the Woman from Timnah

U-6, Lesson 4, Chapter 14

a. What did God want to do through Samson's choice of a wife?

b. What does this teach you about God's character?

> Do you see any areas in your life where you may be like Samson?
>
> Guys, what are you attracted to in ladies? Do you only look at their outer appearance? Do you ignore or resent your parents' input or do you seek their counsel when thinking about dating someone?
>
> Ladies, how are you trying to attract guys? Are you consumed with your outer appearance or more concerned with the inner beauty of godliness? Do you go behind your parents back instead of listening to their advice?
>
> Samson managed to convince his parents to get him the girl he wanted. He satisfied his lust but where did it lead him? The same place lust will lead you if you let it consume you... destruction.

Lesson 4/Assignment 8

8. Fill in your "The Judges of Israel" chart and be sure to include the following:

   a. who the oppressors were

   b. how long Israel lived under their oppression before God delivered them through a judge

   c. how long the land had rest afterward

Lesson 4/Assignment 9

9. Add the chapter theme for Judges 14 to your "At A Glance" chart.

Student Page 154

266 © 2008 Precept Ministries International

UNIT SIX - TEACHER'S GUIDE

Judges

DISCUSSION GUIDE LESSON FOUR:

JUDGES 14
Ask students what they learned from their study of this chapter. Help them discuss main events and related cross-references.

> Samson saw a woman in Timnah who "looked good to him."
> The NASB footnote says this statement means "is right in my eyes." Relate this to the repeated phrase in Judges 17-21.

> He married this woman even though she was a Philistine. God told Israel not to marry the people of the land. Ask your students to think about whether they make decisions based only on what looks good to them.

> Some in your class may have a problem with the fact that Samson was:
> a judge the Lord raised up
> set apart from before birth to be a Nazirite (dedicated to the God)
> blessed by the Lord and
> stirred by the Spirit of the Lord
> **yet**
> married a Philistine woman just because she looked good to him.

> Help them understand that the Holy Spirit was not permanently indwelling people at this time. These are Old Covenant events. God's Spirit came upon specific men for specific purposes.

> Verses 6 and 19 state that the Spirit of the Lord came mightily upon Samson, but He did not lead Samson to sin. Those incidents are directly related to his strength and delivering Israel from the Philistines.

> The Lord did not stop Samson from marrying the Philistine woman, but He used it to deliver Israel from the Philistines.

Note: Some believe verses 5-9 evidence Samson breaking his vow. But Numbers 6 says Nazirites were defiled by dead people: animals are not mentioned. Be careful about being too dogmatic on this point.

Discuss with your students what they learned about the Philistines.

> They were around as early as Abraham. Isaac went to the land of the Philistines when there was a famine. Refer to the map.

> When the Lord brought Israel out of Egypt, He did not bring them up the coast, into the

UNIT SIX - TEACHER'S GUIDE

Judges

Philistines' land because of the threat of war.

The Philistines lived in the land the Lord gave Israel.
    They were one inhabitant Israel was to drive out.

    Philistine land was part of the land remaining to be possessed after Joshua conquered the major cities and nations. God left them to test Israel's obedience and to train future generations to fight.

    Five Philistine lords and cities are mentioned: Gaza, Ashdod, Ashkelon, Ekron, Gath.

    Shamgar was the first judge to deliver Israel from the Philistine oppression.

    The Philistines and Ammonites oppressed Israel when Jephthah was raised up as judge. Israel served Philistine gods. Judges 10:11 refers to a prior deliverance from the Philistines, possibly during Shamgar's time.

    This land is still a major site in Israel.

Verses 10-20
Ask your students about events in these verses.

    Samson's weakness and strength is clearly seen in these verses.
    Samson's 30 companions told his Philistine wife to get the answer to the riddle.

    She enticed him to tell her; when he did, she told the men.

    When he learned this, Samson went to Ashkelon and killed 30 Philistines.
    The Lord had said before he was born that he would deliver Israel from the Philistines.

    Samson's wife was given to his friend.

Ask your students to discuss the principles they learned that apply to their lives.

Unit Six - Teacher's Guide

Judges

LESSON FIVE:

 Judges 16 Observation Worksheets, colored pencils, key word bookmark, "A Summary of the Life of Samson" at the end of the unit, "The Judges of Israel" chart and "At A Glance" chart from the Appendix

OBJECTIVES:

In this lesson, students will complete their Judges 15 observations and determine the main theme. They will study the chapter's main events including Samson's interactions with the Philistines.

Lesson 5/Assignment 1 - Observation
Students will read Judges 16 and mark the key words on their bookmarks including references to *the woman from Timnah*.

a. Students will identify main events in this chapter and record them in the space provided or in the margins of their Observation Worksheets.

This assignment will help students remember what this chapter is about and ensure they did not miss important information.

b. Students will fill in the information requested in the appropriate column. The chart key is available at the end of this lesson.

Lesson 5/Assignment 2 - Interpretation
Encourage students to think through these questions and then discuss their answers together during the scheduled discussion for this lesson. This will help them learn to reason through Scripture by themselves.

a. Samson says his actions against the Philistines are blameless and he takes revenge for their murdering his wife

---

LESSON FIVE

U-6, Lesson 5, Chapter 15

Remember, that the Nazirite vowed to be separate, dedicated to God. In Judges 14 you saw some ways Samson did not keep the Nazirite vow. In this lesson, you'll discover the rest of his story.

Lesson 5/Assignment 1
1. Observe Judges 15. Mark repeated words from your bookmark and references to the *woman from Timnah* in this chapter as you did before.

   a. Record the events in order from this chapter, either in the margin of your Observation Worksheets or in the space provided below.

   > It's helpful to keep track of main events in the margins of your Observation Worksheets, particularly when studying historical books. Summarizing what takes place will help you remember what the text says.

   b. Record who does what to whom and why on the chart below.

Samson's Father-in-law to Samson	Samson to the Philistines	Philistines to Samson's Father-in-law & Wife	Men of Judah to Samson

Student Page 155

© 2008 Precept Ministries International

UNIT SIX - TEACHER'S GUIDE

Judges

and father-in-law. He says he is doing to them what they did to him.

b. The Spirit of the Lord comes upon Samson mightily so that he is able to take off the ropes that bind him and kill 1,000 Philistines with a donkey's jawbone. God gives him the ability to defeat the Philistines and He provided water to strengthen him after the battle.

Lesson 5/Assignment 3 - Observation/Interpretation

Students will use information from Judges 14 and 15 to continue filling in the chart "A Summary of the Life of Samson" at the end of this unit. The chart is not available in the Teacher's Guide.

Students will identify the main point of Judges 15. Have them fill out their chapter theme on the "At A Glance chart." A possible theme for this chapter is:

Judges 15 – Samson kills 1,000 Philistines

Lesson 5/Assignment 2
U-6, Lesson 5, Chapter 15

2. Now let's **evaluate** the events in chapter 15 by answering the following questions. Think about each individual event that took place. (It will be helpful to have "The Nazirite Vow" chart available.)

   a. What is Samson's attitude toward the Philistines?

   b. Examine the references to the *Spirit of the Lord* and *God*. What involvement does God have in the events of this chapter?

Lesson 5/Assignment 3

3. Don't forget to fill in the chart "A Summary of the Life of Samson" and the "Judges At A Glance" chart.

Unit Six - Teacher's Guide

Judges

Samson's Father-in-law to Samson	Samson to the Philistines	Philistines to Samson's Father-in-law & Wife	Men of Judah to Samson
v.1 - did not let Samson go into his wife	v.3 - said he will be blameless when he hurts the Philistines	v.6 - burned the woman of Timnah and her father with fire	v.11-12 - went to Samson to bind him and give him to the Philistines
v.2 - gave her to Samson's companion; offered her younger sister	v.4 - caught 300 foxes, tied torches between their tails		v.13 - swore not to kill him; bound him with two new ropes and brought him to the Philistines
	v.5 - set fire to the torches and sent the foxes into the standing grain of the Philistines; burned their grain, vineyards and groves		
	v.8 - struck them ruthlessly with a great slaughter after they burned his wife and father-in-law		
	v.14 - Spirit of the Lord came upon him; bonds dropped from his hands		
	v.15 - took a jawbone of a donkey and killed 1,000 men		

© 2008 Precept Ministries International

UNIT SIX - TEACHER'S GUIDE

Judges

UNIT SIX - TEACHER'S GUIDE

Judges

LESSON SIX:

 Judges 16 Observation Worksheets, "Samson's Women" chart at the end of the unit, "At A Glance Chart" from the Appendix

OBJECTIVES:

In this lesson, students will complete their Judges 16 observations and determine the main theme for this chapter. They will extract lessons for their lives after analyzing the consequences of Samson's choices of women.

Lesson 6/Assignment 1 - Observation
Students will complete their Judges 16 observations by marking the key words from their bookmarks including the word *Nazirite*.

Lesson 6/Assignment 2 - Observation
Students will identify main events in this chapter and record them in the space provided or in the margins of their Observation Worksheets.

Lesson 6/Assignment 3 - Observation
Students will briefly describe what happened to Samson in this chapter.

First, Samson went in to a harlot (you may need to explain that he had sexual intercourse with her) and then overcame the Gazites by taking their city gate up a mountain. Second, he fell in love with Delilah and she betrayed him to the Philistines. His head was shaved, he lost his strength, his eyes were gouged out, and he was put into prison. Finally, he killed 3,000 Philistines after God gave him back his strength one last time.

a. Students should see that neither woman in this chapter was his wife.

LESSON SIX

Lesson 6/Assignment 1
U-6, Lesson 6, Chapter 16
1. Observe Judges 16. Mark the words from your key word bookmark and *Nazirite* (again).

Lesson 6/Assignment 2
2. Record the main events of this chapter on your Observation Worksheets or in the space provided below.

Lesson 6/Assignment 3
3. What happens to Samson in this chapter?

    a. What is wrong with the two relationships Samson has in this chapter?

    b. List your insights on the "Samson's Women" chart located at the end of this lesson.

Lesson 6/Assignment 4
4. Do you see a similarity between what happens with Delilah in this chapter and what happens with the other women in Samson's life? Explain your answer.

Student Page 157

© 2008 Precept Ministries International

UNIT SIX - TEACHER'S GUIDE

Judges

b. Students will add the information about the harlot and Delilah to the "Samson's Women" chart at the end of this unit. See chart key at the end of this unit.

Lesson 6/Assignment 4 - Observation and Interpretation
Students should see that Samson always chose the wrong woman. His only wife was a Philistine – neither the harlot nor Delilah was his wife. Each woman Samson chose was a key player in Samson's interactions with the Philistines.

Lesson 6/Assignment 5 - Application
Students will examine their lives to determine what God is saying to them through Samson's life. These questions will help students examine Samson's life and recognize how they can learn from his sins. Students may not feel they relate to Samson, but help them realize his life can be a warning against making similar poor choices in the future.

a. Students will see that Samson did not choose women according to God's commands. He chose ungodly and immoral women.

b. Scripture records that he chose two women based on what he saw alone. Though Scripture does not say Samson chose Delilah based on her beauty alone, it's clear that she did not have good character.

c. Samson's wife betrayed him to her countrymen by telling them the answer to his riddle. Then, she was given to another man, which led to Samson's attack on the Philistine fields and ultimately the slaughter of 1,000 men after they burned her and her father. The Philistines set an ambush for Samson while he was with a harlot in Gaza. Delilah manipulated him and betrayed him for money, which led to his capture.

d. Students will consider Samson's choices and the consequences he experienced. They should note that Samson chose women based on their

---

Lesson 6/Assignment 5 *U-6, Lesson 6, Chapter 16*

5. Before you move to the next lesson, is God raising "caution flags" to you through Samson's life? How does Samson's story apply to you? Answer the following questions.

   a. What kind of women did Samson choose?

   b. How did he choose these women? (Look back at 14:1-3.)

   c. What resulted from his choices?

   d. From what you observed, is choosing a mate based on physical beauty alone wise? Why or why not?

   e. Did Samson know he was making poor choices when he initiated relationships with these three women? If so, how did he know?

Student Page 158

UNIT SIX - TEACHER'S GUIDE

Judges

looks and his feelings instead of God's commands. This resulted in pain, betrayal, and ultimately his destruction.

e. Samson's parents warned him to choose a woman from his own people. God's command was clear. Samson did not learn from his past experiences.

f. Samson's anger in Judges 14 made him leave his wife and go back home to his parents. After he left, she was given to another man. Samson's response to this resulted in her and her father's death.

g. Students will consider how they can keep from disobeying God the ways Samson did. They should recognize that godly parents, the Bible, pastors, teachers, etc. are all legitimate sources of wise counsel.

h. Students will evaluate their lives to determine if anger controls them and if so, what consequences they have experienced. According to James 1:19-20, "everyone must be quick to hear, slow to speak and slow to anger; for the anger of man does not achieve the righteousness of God."

U-6, Lesson 6, Chapter 16

a. What were the painful consequences of Samson's anger? (Look at Judges 14:19 and the resulting events that take place.)

b. How will you know if you are making wise choices concerning relationships?

　1) Who or what can give you counsel in this area?

　2) Do you listen to this counsel?

h. Do you allow anger to control you?

　1) If so, what has this resulted in?

　2) Look up the following verses and record what you learn concerning anger.

JAMES 1:19-20

Student Page 159

Unit Six - Teacher's Guide

Judges

Lesson 6/Assignment 6 - Interpretation
Students will learn that Samson's strength left him because the Lord departed from him.

Lesson 6/Assignment 7 - Interpretation
Students will identify the main point of Judges 16 and fill out their chapter theme on the "At A Glance" chart. A possible theme for this chapter is:
Judges 16 – Samson and Delilah

U-6, Lesson 6, Chapter 16

Lesson 6/Assignment 6
6. Many people think Delilah caused Samson's defeat by cutting his hair. What *was* the cause of Samson's downfall?

7. Don't forget to fill in the charts "A Summary of the Life of Samson" and "Judges At A Glance."

> Samson is a sad example of someone controlled by **passions**. He saw something he wanted and he got it. Isn't that the world's message today? If you see something you want, go for it! But like Samson, you may find that what you end up getting is heartache and painful consequences. You always have a choice to either give into your lusts or choose obedience to God. What leads you – your lusts or God's Word?

Student Page 160

Unit Six - Teacher's Guide

Judges

DISCUSSION GUIDE LESSONS FIVE AND SIX:

JUDGES 15
Discuss events in this chapter and relate them to Judges 13 and 14.

> When Samson went to visit his wife, he discovered that she had been given to another. So, he burned the Philistines' grain, vineyards, and groves.
>
> In return the Philistines burned his wife and her father, which incited Samson to slaughter the Philistines in revenge.
>
> When the Philistines came to Judah looking for him, Samson asked his fellow Israelites not to kill him, but just bind him. He freed himself later and killed 1,000 with a donkey's jawbone – another instance of the Spirit of the Lord coming on him mightily to deliver Israel from the Philistines.

Verses 18-19
Some of your group may have difficulty understanding these verses.

> Try to help your students not to impose interpretations on the text based on emotions. Just discuss what it says – it does not state Samson's attitude toward the Lord. It seems disrespectful but this shouldn't take a lot of discussion time.

Verse 20

> Samson judged Israel for 20 of the 40 years the Philistines oppressed Israel.
> He only began the deliverance of Israel from the Philistines; it was not completed until later.

JUDGES 16
Question your group about events in this chapter and about what they learned from Samson's life.

> Verses 1-3: Samson went to a harlot in Gaza, a city of the Philistines.
>
> While there, the Gazites surrounded the place because he was their enemy. But he left at midnight and took the doors of the city gate to the top of a mountain.
>
> Again his strength is shown but contrasted with his weakness in verses that follow.

Verses 4-20: his dealings with Delilah, a woman who lived in the valley of Sorek.
Compare his experiences with Delilah with Judges 14 (the account of his wife).

UNIT SIX - TEACHER'S GUIDE

Judges

    Men wanted to know something from Samson, so they went to his wife.
    She enticed and pressed him to tell her what the men wanted to know. The results were devastating both times.

    Samson did not display much sense with women.

    He wanted the woman who looked good to him to be his wife.

    He went to a harlot.

    He loved a woman who betrayed him.

Verses 21-30
Discuss the end of Samson's life.

    Samson was taken to Gaza with no hair and no eyes.

    The Lord departed from him when his head was shaved.
    His strength from the Lord was also gone.

    His hair grew while he was bound in prison.

    After he asked the Lord to give him strength to bring vengeance on the Philistines, the Lord answered and his strength returned.

    He killed more in his death than in his life – 3,000 on the roof and many more inside including all the lords of the Philistines.

Discuss with your students what they learned that they can apply to their lives.

UNIT SIX - TEACHER'S GUIDE

Judges

LESSON SEVEN:

 Proverbs 7 Observation Worksheets, colored pencils, "Summary of the Life of Samson" at the end of the unit, "At A Glance" chart from the Appendix, Bible

OBJECTIVES:

In this lesson, students will evaluate Proverbs 7 to identify traits of the adulterous woman and the naïve boy. They will comprehend their characteristics, and the negative consequences of adultery.

Lesson 7/Assignment 1 - Observation
Students will complete their observations of Proverbs 7 marking references to the *adulterous woman* and the *naïve boy*.

Lesson 7/Assignment 2 - Observation
a. The adulterous woman is a married woman, not a harlot. She dresses like a harlot, is cunning of heart, boisterous and rebellious. She does not stay home, but lurks in the streets, squares, and every corner. She brazenly kisses the naïve boy and entices him to her home.

b. The naïve boy is a young man lacking sense. He passes near the adulterous woman's corner, taking the way to her house in the evening, in the middle of the night, and in darkness. Students should see that he plan to go where she is. Lacking sense, he positions himself to be ensnared by her.

c. Following the adulterous woman leads to the discipline of a fool. It ultimately costs him his life. Her house is the way to Sheol, or death.

Students will compare the naïve boy to Samson and recognize that like the

---

LESSON SEVEN

U-6, Lesson 7, Chapters 13-16

In this lesson you will focus on Samson's weakness. What weakness brought one of the strongest men in the Bible, a man dedicated to God from birth, into captivity? Review your "Samson's Women" chart before you begin this lesson.

What was the problem with the women Samson was attracted to? You are going to look at Proverbs 7 today to see the dangers of the adulterous woman and the **naïve** boy.

Lesson 7/Assignment 1
1. Observe Proverbs 7:1-27 using the Observation Worksheet at the end of this lesson.

    a. Mark references to the *adulteress* including pronouns and synonyms with a big red A.

   b. Mark references to the *naïve boy* with a blue circle.

Lesson 7/Assignment 2
2. Now think about what you learned and answer the questions below.

   a. Is the adulterous woman a harlot? What makes her like one?

   b. How is the naïve boy described? How do these things make him more likely to be ensnared by the adulterous woman?

   c. Where does listening to the adulteress lead?

   1) How did it impact Samson's life?

   2) Where will it lead in your life?

Student Page 161

© 2008 Precept Ministries International

UNIT SIX - TEACHER'S GUIDE

Judges

naïve boy Samson's choices of women ultimately led to his death. Students should learn that if they make these choices they will die. Encourage them to think about and record ways death can come to them if they follow the naïve boy's ways by going after the adulterous woman.

d. In Proverbs 7:1-5 and 24-25, a father exhorts his son to keep his words, treasure his commandments within him, and live. He is to keep them as the apple of his eye, bind them on his fingers, and write them on his heart. If he will walk in wisdom and understanding, pay attention to his father's warnings and not let his heart turn aside to her ways, he will keep himself from the adulterous woman and not stray into her paths.

Lesson 7/Assignment 3 - Application
Students will consider all they learned from Samson and record principles they can apply to their lives.

Lesson 7/Assignment 4 - Interpretation
According to Hebrews 11:32-34, Samson is listed with other men who by faith "conquered kingdoms, performed acts of righteousness, obtained promises, shut the mouths of lions, quenched the power of fire, escaped the edge of the sword, from weakness were made strong, became mighty in war, put foreign armies to flight." In spite of his sins, Samson is recorded in Scripture as a man of faith.

a. Students should see that Hebrews' "from weakness were made strong" describes Samson's end.

U-6, Lesson 7, Chapters 13-16

d. You aren't without hope! Notice what the father says to his son in Proverbs 7. How do you avoid the adulteress?

Lesson 7/Assignment 3
3. What have you learned from Samson's life? How can you apply it?

Lesson 7/Assignment 4
4. Samson is mentioned nowhere else in the Bible except in Hebrews 11:32-34 in a list of men of faith. Look at this final word on Samson and record what you learn about him.

HEBREWS 11:32-34

a. What in verses 33 and 34 describe what happened to Samson at the end of his life?

Student Page 162
© 2008 Precept Ministries International

UNIT SIX - TEACHER'S GUIDE

Judges

b. Students will understand that faith in spite of weakness and failure is encouraging. Samson made poor choices, but in the end he trusted God and God restored his strength to crush the Philistines.

c. According to 2 Corinthians 12:9, Christ told Paul, "My grace is sufficient for you, for power is perfected in weakness." Paul boasted about his weaknesses so the power of Christ would shine through him. Believers have weaknesses, but when they humble themselves they discover power is perfected in weakness. They are able to obey His will when they trust and depend on Him <u>alone</u> rather than their abilities or strength.

d. According to Galatians 5:16-17, believers who walk by the Spirit do not carry out the desire of the flesh. The flesh sets its desire against the Spirit, and the Spirit against the flesh; they are in opposition to one another. If believers walk by the Spirit, they do not do things of the flesh. In other words, true believers are led by the Holy Spirit not by their own desires and feelings (flesh). They know the Word and obey it, even if it opposes the preferences of their flesh.

U-6, Lesson 7, Chapters 13-16

b. Is it encouraging to know that even with his weaknesses he was still ultimately described as a man of faith? Can you explain why he was considered faithful?

c. Do you have any weaknesses? Can you still be faithful? Look up this verse and write out your thoughts.

d. Read the following verses and write out how you will be able to walk in strength in spite of areas where you are weak.

Good job! There was a lot to learn from Samson, wasn't there? What will you do with what you learned? Will you repeat his mistakes or learn from them? How seriously will you take your commitment to God? Will you allow your lusts and desires to ensnare and trap you? Most importantly, will you walk in the strength and power God has given you through His Spirit to overcome your enemies?! You can be a mighty man or woman of God!

Well, you are done looking at the judges. Right after Judges 16, there is a change in the book – a new segment which you will study in the next unit.

Student Page 163

Unit Six - Teacher's Guide

UNIT SIX - TEACHER'S GUIDE

Judges

DISCUSSION GUIDE LESSON SEVEN:

Discuss with your students what they learned about the adulterous woman and naïve boy in Proverbs 7.

    The naïve boy lacks sense.
    He passes near the adulterous woman's corner.
    He takes the way to her house and goes there in the darkness. He seeks her out under the cover of darkness when he thinks no one will know. He lacks the sense to know that pursuing her leads to death.

    The adulterous woman comes to meet him, dressed as a harlot.
    She is cunning, boisterous, and rebellious.
    She does not stay at home – she lurks everywhere.
    She seizes the naïve boy and kisses him.
    She brazenly entices him.
    She tells him she has come looking for him and has prepared her home and bed for him.
    She unashamedly tells him her husband is gone and she wants him to stay the night with her.
    She entices and seduces him with flattery.

Ask your students what they learned from Samson's behavior and Proverbs 7.

    Samson lacked sense with respect to women.

    He went after women God said don't sleep with or marry.

    They enticed, seduced, deceived, and pressed him daily to get what they wanted.

Ask your students to discuss how a boy can keep from falling into an adulterous woman's trap, according to Proverbs 7.

    The father in this chapter exhorts his son to:
    Keep his words.
    Treasure his commandments within him and he will live.
    Keep them as the apple of his eye, bind them on his fingers, and write them on the tablet of his heart so that wisdom and understanding will keep him from the adulterous woman.
    Pay attention to his father's words and not let his heart turn aside to an adulteress.

Ask your students to discuss what they learned and can apply to their lives from Proverbs 7.

    Young men need wisdom and must understanding how adulterous women seduce. They should avoid women (girls) who flatter and lurk about to entice with "charms." They should realize that her path leads to death and destruction.

UNIT SIX - TEACHER'S GUIDE

Judges

> Young women need to look at the description of the adulterous woman and determine if they are acting like her. Do they flatter young men? Are they enticing and seducing men rather than pursuing a holy relationship with God?

Ask your students if they can say to wisdom "you are my sister" and to understanding "you are my intimate friend."

Ask your students what they learned about Samson from Hebrews 11.

> Hebrews 11 says he was a man of faith.
>
> Help them remember that he was not a New Covenant believer who had the Holy Spirit permanently indwelling.

Ask your students to discuss what they learned about God from these chapters and how they can apply what they learned about Samson to their lives.

Unit Six - Teacher's Guide

Judges
U-6, Chapters 13-16

Samson's Women

Woman from Timnah	Harlot from Gaza	Delilah
14:1 - one of the daughters of the Philistines	*16:1 - Samson saw her in Gaza and went in to her.*	*16:4 - lived in the valley of Sorek; Samson loved her.*
14:3 - looked good to Samson		*16:5-6 - each lord of the Philistines offered her 1,100 pieces of silver to entice Samson to tell her the secret of his strength so they could overpower him. She agreed.*
14:16 - wept before Samson and said: "You only hate me, and you do not love me; you have propounded a riddle to the sons of my people, and have not told it to me."		*16:9-14 - asks him his secret three times and he deceives her each time*
14:17 - wept before him seven days while their feast lasted; because she pressed him so hard, Samson told her his riddle and she told it to her people.		*16:15 - asks Samson how he can love her when his heart is not with her*
14:20 - given to his companion who had been his friend		*16:16 - presses him daily with her words so much that his soul was "annoyed to death"*
		16:18 - he tells her the truth and she tells the Philistines
		16:19 - makes him sleep on her knees, shaves his hair, afflicts him; his strength leaves him.
		16:20 - told Samson "The Philistines are upon you;" they overpower him.

© 2008 Precept Ministries International

Unit Six - Teacher's Guide

UNIT SIX - TEACHER'S GUIDE

Judges
U-6, Chapters 13-16

ENRICHMENT WORDS

Barren – incapable of producing offspring.

Dedicated – given over to a particular purpose.

Evaluate – to determine the significance, worth, or condition of usually by careful appraisal and study.

Naïve – simple or lacking wisdom or informed judgment.

Nazirite – consecrated, dedicated, or devoted one.

Passions – intense, driving, or overmastering feeling.

Progressive Revelation – the gradual revealing or making known of God and His ways in Scripture.[1]

---

[1] Enns, P. P. 1997, c1989. *The Moody Handbook of Theology*. Moody Press: Chicago, Ill.

UNIT SIX - TEACHER'S GUIDE

Judges

Unit Six - Teacher's Guide

Judges
Unit Six Quiz

Name: _____ Date: _____

Unit Six - Quiz Key

Multiple Choice - Circle one.

1. Which of the following is a possible chapter theme for Judges 13?
    a. Samson and the Philistines
    b. Samson and Delilah
    c. Samson and the woman from Timnah
    d. *The angel of the Lord appears to Samson's parents*

2. Which of the following is a possible chapter theme for Judges 14?
    a. Samson and the Philistines
    b. Samson and Delilah
    c. *Samson and the woman from Timnah*
    d. The angel of the Lord appears to Samson's parents

3. All of the following are restrictions on Nazirites from Numbers 6 EXCEPT:
    a. Touch a dead person
    b. Cut hair
    c. Drink strong drink
    d. *Eat honey*

4. The purpose of the Nazirite vow according to Numbers 6 is to:
    a. *Dedicate one's self to the Lord*
    b. Show others how Christ would act
    c. Earn forgiveness for sin
    d. Remember Jephthah's vow

5. How was Samson's Nazirite vow different from that described in Numbers 6?
    a. *He was to be a Nazirite from birth until death.*
    b. He was allowed to cut his hair.
    c. He was a Nazirite for the first 12 years of his life.
    d. He was allowed to go near dead people.

Short Answer

6. What was Samson's criterion for choosing the woman from Timnah as a wife?

She looked good to him.

© 2008 Precept Ministries International

Judges
Unit Six Quiz

7. Why does the angel of the Lord appear to Samson's parents?

To announce Samson's birth and tell them Samson will be a Nazirite from birth to death. He also gives Samson's mother restrictions during her pregnancy.

8. What does Samson do on his way to Timnah with his mother and father?

A young lion comes roaring toward him. The Spirit of the Lord comes on him mightily and he tears him although he had nothing in his hand.

9. Where did Samson get the honey that he gave to his parents?

From the carcass of the lion he killed on the way to Timnah.

10. How do Samson's companions solve his riddle?

They tell Samson's wife they will burn her father's house if she doesn't tell them the answer. She presses Samson until he tells her.

Unit Six - Teacher's Guide

Judges
Unit Six Test

Name: _____   Date: _____

Unit Six - TEST KEY

MATCHING - Choose one and write the letter in the blank.

    c   1. Simple or lacking wisdom or informed judgment

    b   2. Given over to a particular purpose

    a   3. Incapable of producing offspring

    e   4. The gradual revealing or making known of God and His ways in Scripture

    d   5. Consecrated or devoted one

a. Barren
b. Dedicated
c. Naive
d. Nazirite
e. Progressive revelation

MULTIPLE CHOICE - Circle one.

6. Which of the following is a possible chapter theme for Judges 13?
   a. Samson and the Philistines
   b. Samson and Delilah
   c. Samson and the woman from Timnah
   d. The angel of the Lord appears to Samson's parents

7. Which of the following is a possible chapter theme for Judges 14?
   a. Samson and the Philistines
   b. Samson and Delilah
   c. Samson and the woman from Timnah
   d. The angel of the Lord appears to Samson's parents

8. Which of the following is a possible chapter theme for Judges 15?
   a. Samson and the Philistines
   b. Samson and Delilah
   c. Samson and the woman from Timnah
   d. The angel of the Lord appears to Samson's parents

9. Which of the following is a possible chapter theme for Judges 16?
   a. Samson and the Philistines
   b. Samson and Delilah
   c. Samson and the woman from Timnah
   d. The angel of the Lord appears to Samson's parents

UNIT SIX - TEACHER'S GUIDE

Judges
Unit Six Test

10. All of the following are restrictions on Nazirites from Numbers 6 EXCEPT:
    a. Touch a dead person
    b. Cut hair
    c. Drink strong drink
    d. *Eat honey*

11. The purpose of the Nazirite vow according to Numbers 6 is to:
    a. *Dedicate one's self to the Lord.*
    b. Show others how Christ would act.
    c. Earn forgiveness for sin.
    d. Remember Jephthah's vow.

12. How was Samson's Nazirite vow different from that described in Numbers 6?
    a. *He was to be a Nazirite from birth until death.*
    b. He was allowed to cut his hair.
    c. He was a Nazirite for the first 12 years of his life.
    d. He was allowed to go near dead people.

13. Samson judged Israel for _____ of the 40-year Philistine oppression.
    a. 10 years
    b. *20 years*
    c. 30 years
    d. 40 years

14. The angel of the Lord did all of the following according to the book of Judges EXCEPT:
    a. Led Israel into the land
    b. Cursed Meroz
    c. Appeared to Gideon
    d. *Helped Jephthah*

15. All of the following are true about Samson EXCEPT:
    a. The Lord raised him up to judge.
    b. The Lord blessed him and the Spirit of the Lord stirred within him.
    c. Samson was married to a Philistine woman.
    d. *Samson raised an army and slaughtered the Philistines.*

16. Which of the following is NOT true about the Philistines?
    a. They were around during the time of Abraham and Isaac.
    b. The Lord did not lead the Israelites through their land on the way to the Promised Land.
    c. They were some of the inhabitants left in the land after Joshua's time.
    d. *They were as numerous as the locusts, destroying the produce and the animals.*

UNIT SIX - TEACHER'S GUIDE

Judges
Unit Six Test

17. Which of the following women pressed Samson for an answer to his riddle three times and then was burned by the Philistines?
    a. The Adulteress
    b. Delilah
    c. The harlot from Gaza
    d. *The woman from Timnah*

18. Which of the following women pressed Samson for days for an answer to his riddle and received a reward for her betrayal?
    a. The Adulteress
    b. *Delilah*
    c. The harlot from Gaza
    d. The woman from Timnah

19. Which of the following women flatters the naïve boy with her words and leads him to Sheol if he follows?
    a. *The Adulteress*
    b. Delilah
    c. The harlot from Gaza
    d. The woman from Timnah

20. Samson did all of the following EXCEPT:
    a. Carried the gate of a city to the top of a mountain
    b. Killed 1,000 Philistines with a donkey's jawbone
    c. Ate honey out of a dead lion's carcass
    d. *Killed his 70 brothers*

TRUE OR FALSE

_T_ 21. Samson killed more Philistines in his death than he did in his life.

_F_ 22. Samson kept the Nazirite vow throughout his entire life.

_T_ 23. According to Numbers 6, women can take the Nazirite vow.

_F_ 24. Samson's strength came from his hair.

_T_ 25. God warned the Israelites not to marry the inhabitants of the land; Samson's parents tried to persuade him not to marry the woman from Timnah.

UNIT SIX - TEACHER'S GUIDE

Judges
Unit Six Test

SHORT ANSWER

26. Briefly describe the naïve boy in Proverbs 7.

The naïve boy is a young man lacking sense. He passes near the adulterous woman's corner taking the way to her house in the middle of the night.

27. Briefly describe the adulterous woman from Proverbs 7.

The adulterous woman is a married woman. She is dresses like a harlot, is cunning of heart, boisterous and rebellious. She does not stay home, but lurks in streets, squares, and corners. She brazenly kisses the naïve boy to entice him to her house.

28. Briefly describe the end of Samson's life.

Delilah betrays Samson and the Philistines capture him. His eyes are gouged out and he is bound and made a grinder in a prison. When the Philistines assemble to worship their god, they bring out Samson for entertainment. Samson's hair has grown back in prison and he asks God to strengthen him one last time. Samson leans on the pillars of the house and bends with all his might; the house falls on the lords of the Philistines and all the people and kills them.

29. Briefly describe Delilah's betrayal.

The lords of the Philistines each offer her 1,100 pieces of silver to entice Samson to tell her the secret of his strength so they can overpower him. She asks him his secret three times and he deceives her each time. She asks Samson how he can love her when his heart is not with her and presses him daily until he tells her the truth. She has his hair cut while he is sleeping, awakens him, and then the Philistines overpower him.

30. Explain Hebrews 11:32-34's description of Samson.

According to Hebrews 11:32-34, Samson is listed with other men of faith, who by faith, "conquered kingdoms, performed acts of righteousness, obtained promises, shut the mouths of lions, quenched the power of fire, escaped the edge of the sword, from weakness were made strong, became mighty in war, put foreign armies to flight." In spite of Samson's sins, Scripture records him as a man of faith.

Unit Six - Teacher's Guide

Judges
Unit Six Test

ESSAY

Choose one of the following topics; briefly summarize it and discuss how it applies to your life:

    a. How a young man can keep from being ensnared by an adulterous woman
    b. What you learned about God in Judges 13-16
    c. Principles from Samson's life

Students will identify the main points for each of these topics and then discuss how the truths they learned apply to their lives.

UNIT SIX - TEACHER'S GUIDE

Judges

UNIT SEVEN - TEACHER'S GUIDE

Judges

CHAOS AND CORRUPTION

UNIT OBJECTIVES:

In this unit, students will review and discuss the key phrase *every man did what was right in his own eyes* in chapters 17-21. They will observe Judges 17 and 18 and then look at cross-references in the Old Testament to understand the Levitical priesthood. Insight into the priesthood will help them interpret events in chapters 17 and 18.

Students will observe Judges 19-21 to identify main events and recognize how "every man was doing what was right in his own eyes." Students will analyze how these last chapters fit chronologically with the first two segments of Judges.

Introduction/Prayer

Encourage your students to write a prayer asking God to help them remember the lessons they learn from these chapters. This unit will reveal how far into sin the nation of Israel went when they forgot God and went after other gods.

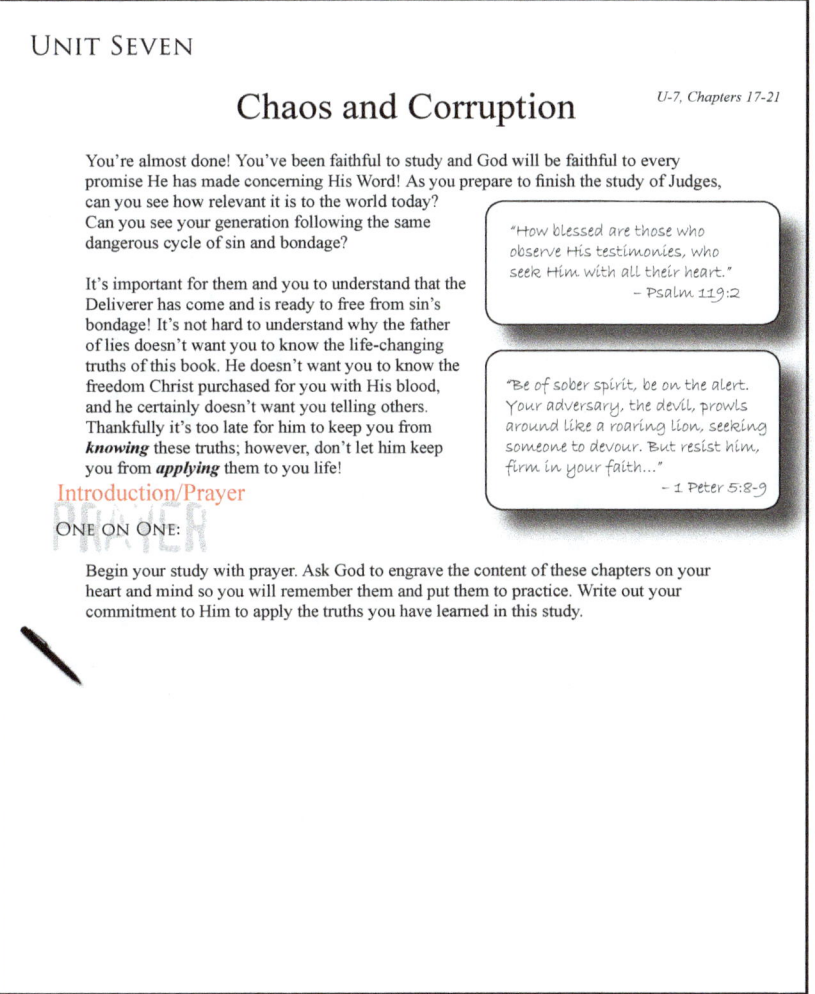

© 2008 Precept Ministries International

UNIT SEVEN - TEACHER'S GUIDE

UNIT SEVEN - TEACHER'S GUIDE

LESSON ONE:

 Judges 17 Observation Worksheets, key word bookmark, colored pencils

OBJECTIVES:

In this lesson, students will observe Judges 17 marking the key words from their bookmarks and recognize the importance of the Judges key phrase in this last segment.

Lesson 1/Assignment 1 - Observation
Students will observe chapter 17 marking the key words from their bookmarks including *graven* and/or *molten image*, *ephod*, *the Levite*, and *Micah*. These words do not have to be added to their key word bookmarks because they are key only to Judges 17 and 18.

Lesson 1/Assignment 2 - Interpretation
a. Students should recognize that the key phrase follows the story of Micah and his mother. Micah had stolen from his mother, confessed, and returned the money. She praised God for her son, took the money and dedicated it to the Lord. The problem is the money was used to make a graven image (something strictly forbidden by God). Then Micah consecrated one of his sons to be a priest in his household over his shrine and idols (Micah and his family were not Levites). These blatant offenses to God's law are examples of the sons of Israel doing right in their own eyes but against God's law.

b. "Did what was right in their own eyes" summarizes the events conveyed in the preceding verses.

LESSON ONE

U-7, Lesson 1, Chapter 17

You have come to the third and final **segment** of Judges! Today you'll observe these final chapters closely to understand their content and live in the light of their instruction.

Lesson 1/Assignment 1
1. Observe Judges 17. Mark the key words on your bookmark and include the following (also add them to your bookmark):

 a.   *graven* and/or *molten image*.

 b.   *ephod*.

 c.   the *Levite*.

 d.   *Micah*.

 e.   geographical locations (mark them on the map at the end of the unit).

Lesson 1/Assignment 2
2. In Judges 17:6 you encounter the first occurrence of a key phrase used only in this final segment of Judges. You already marked this phrase in a Unit 1, Lesson 6 assignment.

 a. How does it relate to the verses preceding and following it?

> **Context** - When you're looking at verses before and after another verse, you are examining the context for understanding. Remember, context rules in interpretation!

 b. Why did the author of Judges place this phrase here?

Student Page 177

UNIT SEVEN - TEACHER'S GUIDE

UNIT SEVEN - TEACHER'S GUIDE

PRECEPT UPON PRECEPT®
Judges

LESSON TWO:

 Bible

OBJECTIVES:

In this lesson, students will look at scriptures concerning Levites and the priesthood to accurately interpret Judges 17.

Note: This lesson is lengthy when done individually. If you assign it to a group, you should have time to do Lessons 2 and 3 in one class.

Lesson 2/Assignment 1 - Interpretation
Remind your students to gather basic facts about the Levites. To complete this lesson in groups, divide the class and assign some cross-references to each group. Then ask each group to share what they discovered while the other groups record the information in their workbooks.

Exodus 28:1-2 – Aaron and his sons separated from Israel to serve God as priests. They wore holy clothes made for them.

Numbers 3:6 – Tribe of Levi presented to Aaron as priests to help him.

Numbers 8:14-19 – Levites set apart from other Israelites; they belong to God; they serve in the tent of meeting.

Exodus 32:14-29 – When Moses returned from receiving the Ten Commandments and saw that Israel had made the golden calf, he called for people to stand with him. The family of Levi gathered around him. They served the Lord by killing 3,000 Israelites and so God blessed them.

Deuteronomy 10:8-9 – The Lord chose the tribe of Levi to carry the Ark of the

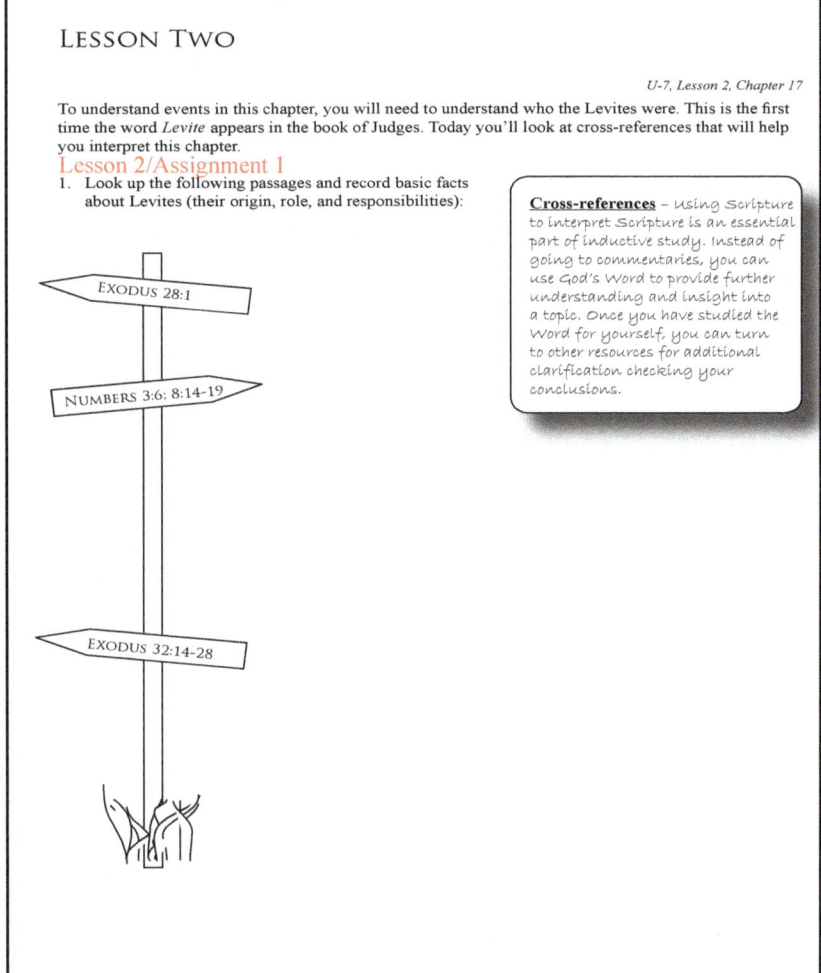

LESSON TWO

U-7, Lesson 2, Chapter 17

To understand events in this chapter, you will need to understand who the Levites were. This is the first time the word *Levite* appears in the book of Judges. Today you'll look at cross-references that will help you interpret this chapter.

Lesson 2/Assignment 1
1. Look up the following passages and record basic facts about Levites (their origin, role, and responsibilities):

EXODUS 28:1

NUMBERS 3:6; 8:14-19

EXODUS 32:14-28

Cross-references – Using Scripture to interpret Scripture is an essential part of inductive study. Instead of going to commentaries, you can use God's Word to provide further understanding and insight into a topic. Once you have studied the Word for yourself, you can turn to other resources for additional clarification checking your conclusions.

Student Page 179

UNIT SEVEN - TEACHER'S GUIDE

Covenant. They were to serve the Lord and bless the people in His name. They did not receive land; the Lord Himself was their inheritance.

Deuteronomy 18:1-8 – They did not receive land. They ate offerings made to the Lord by fire. They inherited the Lord Himself, as He promised them. Everyone had to share their offering with the priests, give them the first of their grain, new wine, oil, and first wool. God chose the priests and their descendants to serve Him always. Levites could live in a town God chose.

Deuteronomy 33:1-5, 8-11 – The Urim and Thummim belonged to Levi, whom God loved. He didn't treat family as favorites before the Law. He taught God's laws to the people. He burned incense and made burnt offerings to God.

Joshua 14:1-5 – The tribe of Levi was not given land. It received towns to live in and pastures for its

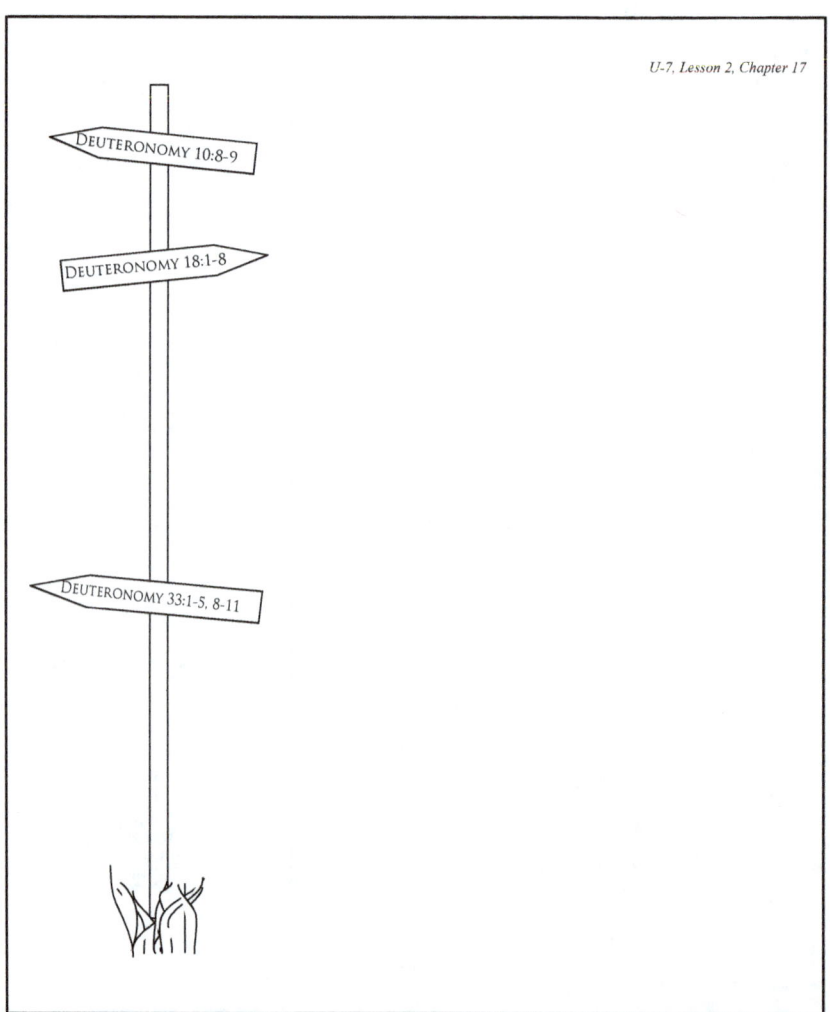

UNIT SEVEN - TEACHER'S GUIDE

animals. The Lord told Moses how to divide the land to the tribes of Israel.

Joshua 21:41 – Levites given 48 towns and pastures in Israel.

Numbers 35:1-8 – Israelites were to give cities and pasture lands to the Levites, also six cities of refuge for accidental killers. They gave 48 cities.

Numbers 25:1-13 – Phinehas son of Eleazar, the son of Aaron, killed an Israelite man and Midianite woman. The terrible sickness among the Israelites stopped. The Lord told Moses that Phinehas had saved the Israelites from His anger. God said Phinehas hated sin as much as He did and he had tried to save God's honor so God promised that he and his descendants will always be priests.

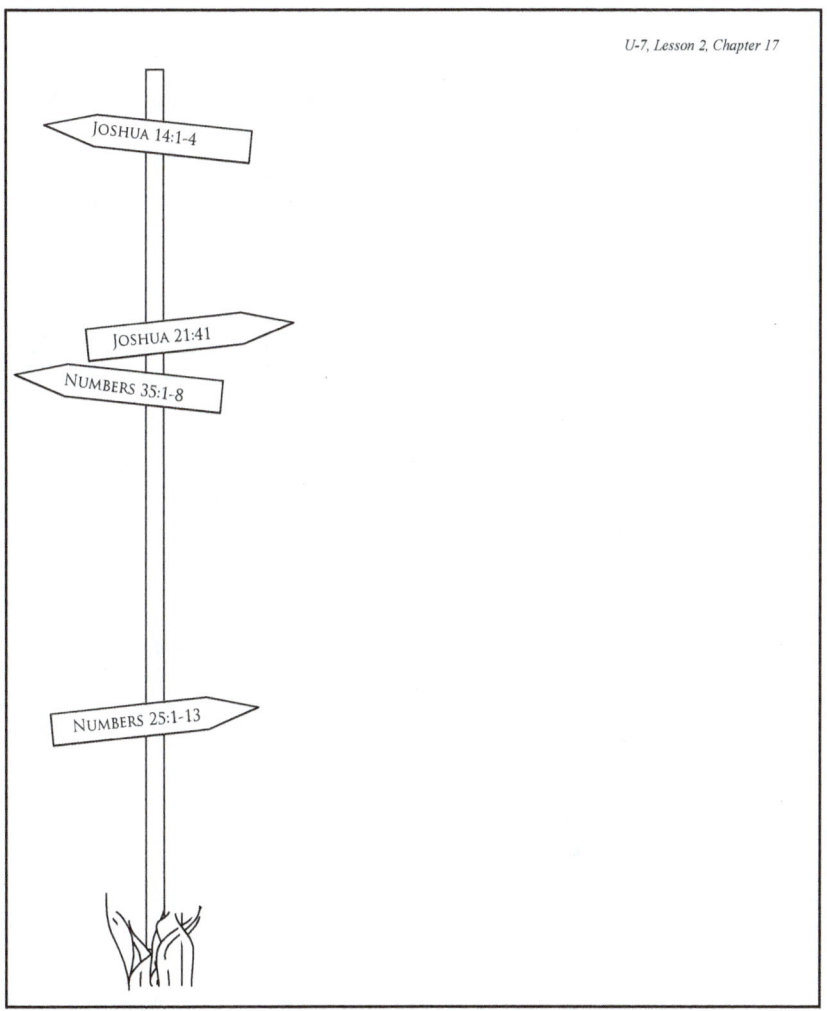

UNIT SEVEN - TEACHER'S GUIDE

Judges

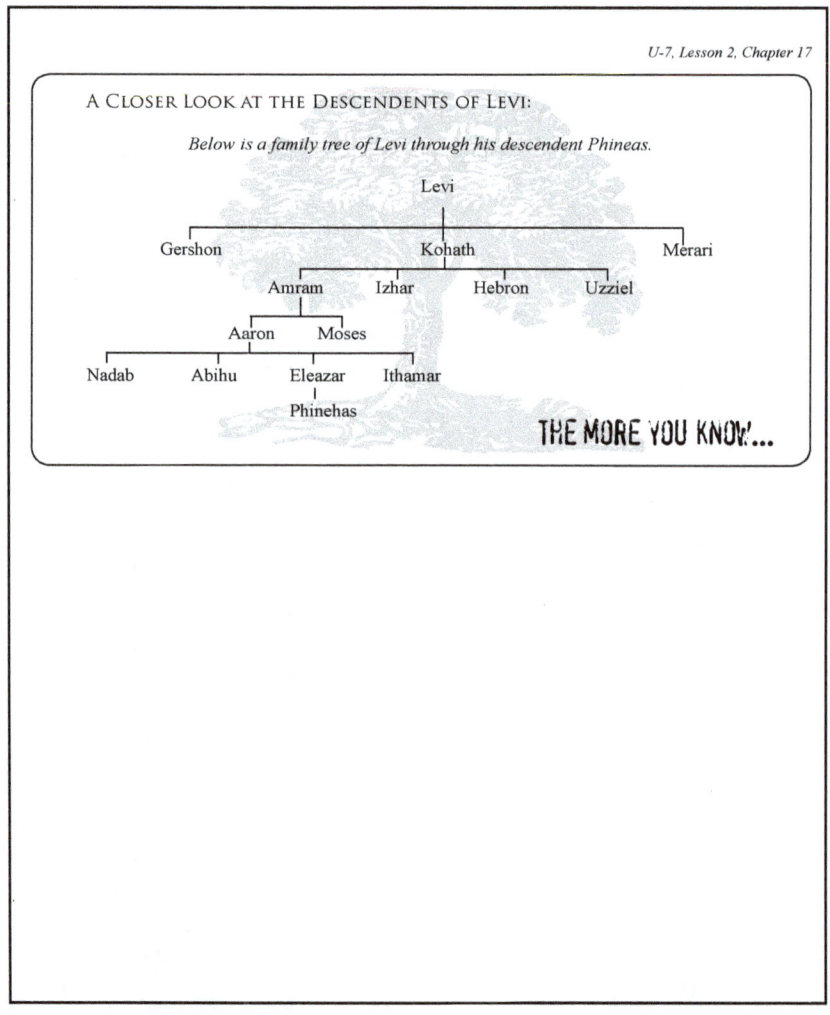

UNIT SEVEN - TEACHER'S GUIDE

Judges

LESSON THREE:

 Judges 17 Observation Worksheets, "Judges At A Glance" chart

OBJECTIVES:

In this lesson, students will interpret Judges 17 in light of information they gleaned from Lesson 2. They will also work to find life applications from this chapter.

Lesson 3/Assignment 1 - Observation/Interpretation
Micah
- v. 1 - lived in the mountains of Ephraim
- v. 2 - confessed to his mother he took her silver
- v. 3 - gave silver to his mother; his mother gave some of the money to him to make a graven image
- v. 4 - put the idol in his house
- v. 5 - had a special holy place; made a holy vest and some household idols; chose one of his sons to be his priest
- v. 9 - asked a passing Levite where he was from
- v. 10 - offered the Levite silver, clothes and food to be his priest
- v. 11 - thought God would be good to him because a Levite was his priest

Levite
- v. 7 - young man from the city of Bethlehem
- v. 8 - left Bethlehem to look for another place to live; came to Micah's house
- v. 11 - agreed to be Micah's priest

a. Students should see that both men knew God's commands but not enough to follow them closely. From cross-references they completed in Lesson 2, they should recognize that neither Micah nor the Levite followed God instructions.

LESSON THREE
U-7, Lesson 3, Chapter 17

Now that you understand who the Levites were, go back to Judges 17 and use the information to help you understand the **gravity** of this situation.

Lesson 3/Assignment 1
1. List below what you learn from marking *Micah* and the *Levite* in this chapter.

   a. What do the actions of these two men tell you about them?

   b. Does this narrative tell you anything about the times in Israel, or do you think this is a unique incident? Explain your answer.

Lesson 3/Assignment 2
2. In what ways do you see people today making the same choices Micah and the Levite made? Answer the questions below to help you reason through this question.

   a. What was wrong with Micah consecrating one of his sons to be the priest for his household? (Remember what you learned in the last lesson.)

   b. Do people today decide for themselves how they will worship God? How?

Student Page 183

© 2008 Precept Ministries International

UNIT SEVEN - TEACHER'S GUIDE

Judges

b. Students should recognize that this incident is a good example of how "every man did what was right in his own eyes."

Lesson 3/Assignment 2 - Interpretation/Application
a. The cross-references from Lesson 2 clearly state that only Levites can serve the Lord as priests. By consecrating his son, Micah worshipped God on his terms, not God's.

b. Students will evaluate their culture to determine if like Micah it disregards God's commands and worships Him on its own terms.

c. Students will examine their lives to determine if like Micah they have ignored God's commands. Help them think about this by offering suggestions.

d. The cross-references from Lesson 2 clearly indicate that Levites could move to towns God chose. In this case, there is no indication that God chose a place for this Levite, who decided to stay with Micah after Micah's offer. He received payment for his services and a portion of sacrifices in lieu of land.

e. When evaluating their culture, students may conclude that some "ministers" today openly water down God's commands to keep people participating in and giving to their organization. They may know examples.

f. Students should examine their lives to determine if they have ever served God for something other than His glory.

Lesson 3/Assignment 3 - Interpretation
Help your students determine the main point of chapter 17 and a summary statement to help them remember the chapter. A possible summary statement for this chapter is:

Judges 17 – Micah and the Levite

Student Page 184

© 2008 Precept Ministries International

UNIT SEVEN - TEACHER'S GUIDE

Judges

DISCUSSION GUIDE LESSONS ONE, TWO AND THREE:

In this discussion, help your students summarize the whole book of Judges. Be sure they understand what times are like when every man does what is right in his own eyes. There are records in Judges of people doing what they *thought* the Lord wanted, but they weren't complying with His Word. They were doing evil in the sight of the Lord.

This is much like current times: "Christians" do what they think is right but not according to the Word of God. Use this discussion to encourage your students to continue their study of the Word so that they will know what the Lord says and obey it.

Judges 17 through 21 are sad chapters in the Bible. Israel was called to be a holy nation, set apart from others to reflect God's holiness. In these chapters Israel degrades itself.

JUDGES 17

Ask students what they learned from events in this chapter. Encourage them to relate the events to cross-references given in the lesson.

> Every man did what was right in his own eyes, but it was evil in the sight of the Lord. Examples:
>
> Micah took silver from his mother, and she rejoiced when he confessed.
> She dedicated the silver to the Lord for Micah to make an image.
> Right to them was: make an image to the Lord.
> Right to the Lord was: make no image.
>
> Micah consecrated one of his sons as a priest and made an ephod.
>
> Micah was from the tribe of Ephraim but God ordained priests only from the tribe of Levi and Aaron's line within that tribe. Also, the high priest was the only one who could consecrate a new priest.

Encourage your students to keep studying the Word of God to learn what is right in His sight, not just theirs.

Note: You may want to consult Numbers 3:10.

The discussion of *the Levite* in Judges 17 should prove interesting as your group shares what they learned about Levites.

Verse 7 says the man was a Levite from Judah, but only Aaron's descendents could be priests.

UNIT SEVEN - TEACHER'S GUIDE

Judges

Note: Judges 18:30 states that Jonathan, the priest, was a son of Gershom, the son of Manasseh. The NIV Bible Expositor's Commentary says, "Gershom was a son of Moses (Exodus 2:21-22), but the Masoretes inserted the letter 'nun' in his name so that 'Manasseh' was read instead . . . In the consonantal text the difference between Moses—mosheh (mosheh)—and 'Manasseh'—menasheh (menashsheh)—is only the one letter. The nun (n) was raised above the line to show that it was a later editorial insertion."[1] Since the lineage of the "Levite priest" is debatable, don't be dogmatic about it. Either way, he was not from Aaron's line and so didn't qualify to be a priest.

> God chose the Levites to gather to Him in Exodus 32. He set them apart to carry the ark and stand before Him (Deuteronomy 10).
>
> They were also to perform the service at the tent of meeting (Numbers 8). Phinehas was a priest, the grandson of Aaron.
>
> The Levites were also to teach the Law of the Lord to Israel. Since they were to live in 48 cities throughout the land, all Israel would hear the law of the Lord.
>
> They had no land but were given those cities to live in and minister to the people.
>
> Micah again consecrated a priest for his own household, thinking the Lord would prosper him for it.

Ask your students what people do today assuming the Lord will bless them.

Also discuss the application questions at the end of Lesson 3.

---

[1] Frank E. Gaebelein, General Ed. *Expositor's Bible Commentary, Old Testament* (electronic edition) (Grand Rapids, MI: Zondervan Publishing House, 1976-1992).

UNIT SEVEN - TEACHER'S GUIDE

Judges

LESSON FOUR:

Judges 17-18 Observation Worksheets, key word bookmark, colored pencils, the "Locations in Judges 17-21" map at the end of the unit

OBJECTIVES:

In this lesson, students will learn how Judges 17 and 18 fit chronologically within Judges and complete their observations of Judges 18. They will also comprehend why the ephod was significant to the Danites.

Lesson 4/Assignment 1 - Observation
It's important for students to see that events in chapter 18 are concurrent with events at the end of 17. They were happening "At that time…"

Lesson 4/Assignment 2 - Observation
Students will observe this chapter marking key words from their bookmarks including *the Levite, Micah, the five men,* and *Shiloh.* Instructions on how to mark them are given in the Student Guide. These words do not have to be added to key word bookmarks because they are key only to Judges 18.

Lesson 4/Assignment 3 - Observation/Interpretation
Students should be able to clearly identify and mark main events either in the space provided or margins of their Observation Worksheets.

Lesson 4/Assignment 4 - Interpretation
Refer to Unit 4, Lesson 8, Assignment 5 to help students understand why the Danites wanted Micah's ephod. The ephod was part of the priest's clothing and carried the Urim and Thummim, which helped the priest determine God's judgments.

LESSON FOUR

Lesson 4/Assignment 1
U-7, Lesson 4, Chapter 18

1. Before you begin Judges 18, notice once again: you find a portion of the key phrase in this final segment of Judges. When the Bible was written, there were no chapter or verse divisions. Read Judges 17:13 and 18:1 as if there were no chapter break. Then write below how 17:13 and the beginning of 18:1 fit together.

Lesson 4/Assignment 2
2. Observe Judges 18. As you read, mark:

    a. the *five men* including pronouns so that you can easily distinguish them by circling them brown.

   b. *Micah* and the *Levite.*

   c. *Shiloh* with a green double underline, and note in the margin of your Observation Worksheet what was there.

    d. geographical references. Locate and highlight them on the map at the end of this lesson..

Lesson 4/Assignment 3
3. List main events covered in this chapter below or in the margin of your Observation Worksheet.

Lesson 4/Assignment 4
4. If needed, review what you learned about the ephod in Unit 4, Lesson 8, number 5. Does the information give you insight into why these men wanted an ephod?

Student Page 185

UNIT SEVEN - TEACHER'S GUIDE

UNIT SEVEN - TEACHER'S GUIDE

Judges

LESSON FIVE:

 Judges 18 Observation Worksheets, colored pencils, Bible, "At A Glance" chart

OBJECTIVES:

In this lesson, students will continue to observe Judges 18 marking references to *Dan*. Students will identify the tribe of Dan and its history using cross-references.

Lesson 5/Assignment 1 - Observation/Interpretation

Students should list most of these details in the space provided.

The tribe of Dan
- *v. 1 - was still looking for land to live in; had not yet been given their own land among the tribes of Israel*
- *v. 2 - chose five soldiers from their tribe who spent the night at Micah's house*
- *v. 3 - These men recognized the voice of the young Levite; asked who he was and why he was there*
- *v. 5 - asked him to ask God for their journey to be successful*
- *v. 6-7 - saw how good the land of Laish was*
- *v. 8-10 - returned and told Danites to attack the land they believed God gave them*
- *v. 11 - six hundred Danites left Zorah and Eshtaol ready for war*
- *v. 14 - as they traveled, men told them Micah's house had a holy vest, household gods, an idol, and a statue*
- *v. 17 - five spies went into the house and took the idol, the holy vest, the household idols, and the statue*
- *v. 19 - told the priest to go with them and be their priest*
- *v. 25 - they threatened Micah*
- *v. 27-29 - took Laish, killed the people and burned the city*
- *v. 30 - worshipped idols*

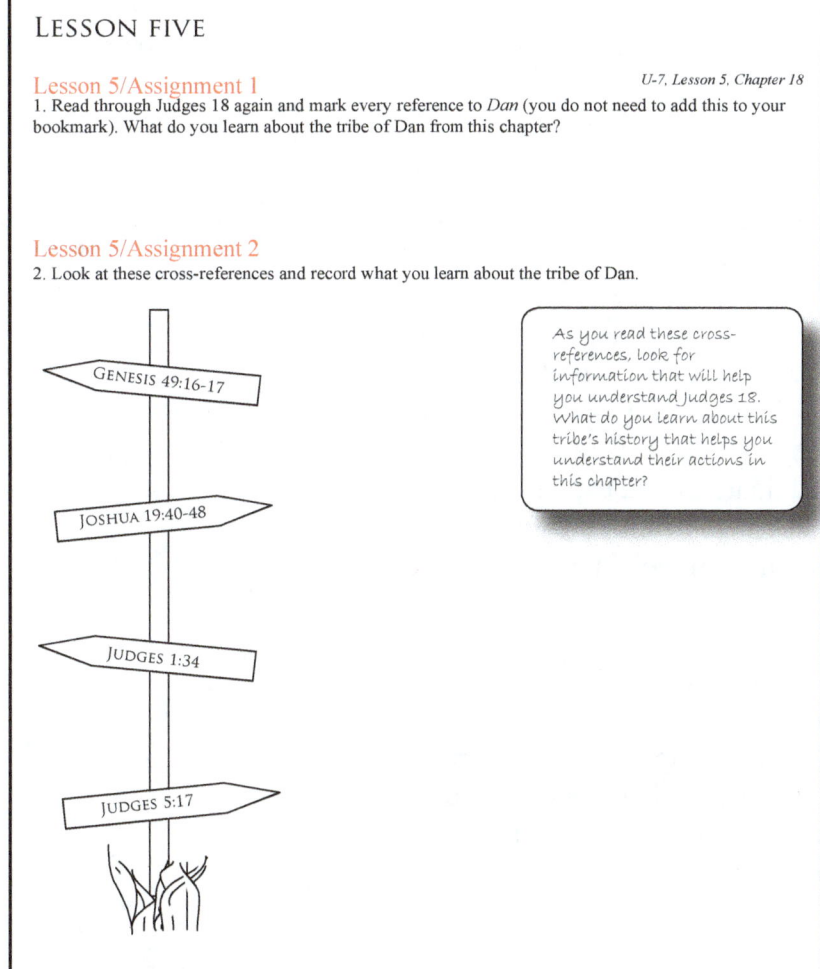

Student Page 187

UNIT SEVEN - TEACHER'S GUIDE

Lesson 5/Assignment 2 - Observation/Interpretation
Students should record some of the following from the cross-references:

Genesis 49:16-17 – Dan will rule his people; will be like a dangerous snake by the side of the road, near the path.

Joshua 19:40-48 – Joshua gave Dan a portion of the land (Note: You may need to explain that this occurred before the times of the judges). The Danites had trouble taking their land. They fought against Leshem, defeated it, and killed the people who lived there. They moved into this town and changed its name to Dan, the father of their tribe.

Judges 1:34 – Amorites force Danites into the mountains (Note: You may need to explain that this event happens after Joshua 19).

Judges 5:17 – (Note: remind your students that this is part of Deborah's song). Dan was one of the tribes that didn't go to war with Deborah and Barak; they stayed by their ships.

Lesson 5/Assignment 3 - Interpretation
The Danites "did what was right in their own eyes" when they killed the inhabitants of Laish and took it for themselves. They also took Micah's priest, ephod and idols by force.

Lesson 5/Assignment 4 - Application
Students should evaluate the Danites' actions to determine how they can learn from their sins.

Lesson 5/Assignment 5 - Interpretation
Help students determine the main point of chapter 18 and a summary statement to help them remember this chapter. A possible summary statement for this chapter is:
Judges 18 – The Danites and Micah's Levite

UNIT SEVEN - TEACHER'S GUIDE

Judges

DISCUSSION GUIDE LESSONS FOUR AND FIVE:

JUDGES 18
Discuss the main points of this chapter and related cross-references to Dan. Refer your class to a map during this part of your discussion.

> The tribe of Dan was seeking land because they did not take land from the Amorites that had been given to them as their inheritance (Judges 1:34-35).
>
> Zorah and Eshtaol are mentioned as origins of Dan. Relate this to Judges 13:2, 25. Samson was a Danite from Zorah.
>
> Most of the Danites went north toward the hill country of Ephraim. Five spies went first; then 600 warriors went to take land.
>
> Relate the prophecy of Genesis 49 to the actions of the tribe of Dan in Judges 18.
> They took what they wanted: Micah's priest, idols, ephod, etc.
> They took land from a quiet and secure people and burned their city.
> They did not come to help Deborah and Barak in the battle against the Canaanites (Judges 5).
>
> They did what was right in their own eyes.

An ephod is mentioned in this chapter and in the account of Gideon. You may ask your students what they remember about the purpose of the ephod.

> The priest wore the ephod when he went before the Lord.
> Micah and the Danites thought this was one way of inquiring of the Lord.
> The "priest" in Judges 18–19 took advantage of the situation (18:5-6).

Verses 27-31

> After taking Laish (sometimes called Leshem; Joshua 19:47), the Danites rebuilt it and named it Dan. They set up a graven image there, and all the time the house of God was at Shiloh, the idol was at Dan, the same image Micah made from the silver he had stolen from his mother. She had dedicated it to the Lord for an image.
>
> They all did what was right in their own eyes, and it was all abomination to a holy God.
>
> Ask your students if the same kinds of things happen now and how.

UNIT SEVEN - TEACHER'S GUIDE

UNIT SEVEN - TEACHER'S GUIDE

Judges

LESSON SIX:

 Judges 19 Observation Worksheets, key word bookmark, colored pencils, "At A Glance" chart

OBJECTIVES:

In this lesson, students will complete their observations of Judges 19. They will also identify sins committed and determine how events in this chapter apply to their lives.

Lesson 6/Assignment 1 - Observation
Students will observe this chapter marking the key words from their bookmark including *concubine*. Instruction on how to mark this word is given in the Student Guide. It does not have to be added to their key word bookmarks because its key only to Judges 19.

Lesson 6/Assignment 2 - Observation/Interpretation
Students should identify main events in this chapter and record them in the space provided or in the margins of their Judges 19 Observation Worksheets.

Lesson 6/Assignment 3 - Observation/Interpretation
Students should be able to identify the following sins:
- *v. 2- The concubine playing the harlot against the Levite*
- *v. 22 - Homosexuality (men from the city asked to have relations with the Levite)*
- *v. 24 - Owner of the home offers his virgin daughter and the concubine*
- *v. 25-26 - Rape, abuse, and murder (The men of the city take the concubine, rape and abuse her all night.)*

Students should recognize these actions as sins according to God's Word. If they do not, you may need to

---

LESSON SIX

Lesson 6/Assignment 1 *U-7, Lesson 6, Chapter 19*
1. Observe Judges 19, noticing how the author introduces events.
   a. Underline in red references to the Levite's *concubine*. Note once again: we have a Levite!!!
   b. Don't forget to mark geographical locations; find and highlight them on your map.

Lesson 6/Assignment 2
2. List main events covered in this chapter in the space below or in the margin of your Observation Worksheet.

Lesson 6/Assignment 3
3. What sins are committed? How do you *know* they're sins?

Lesson 6/Assignment 4
4. Record a theme for Judges 19 on your "At A Glance" chart.
Lesson 6/Assignment 5
5. Record what you learned from this chapter that you can apply to your life.

Apathy! Anarchy! Apostasy! Can you see where the lack of regard for God's Word led these people? Can you see how the slow but steady growth of apathy toward the truth of God's Word is affecting your society, generation, and peers? Aren't you absolutely awed at the way the Word of God speaks to every generation? The question is: are you listening? And how will it impact your life?

Student Page 189

UNIT SEVEN - TEACHER'S GUIDE

show them scriptures.

Lesson 6/Assignment 4- Interpretation
Help students determine the main point of chapter 19 and a summary statement to help them remember this chapter. A possible summary statement for this chapter is:

Judges 19 – The Levite's concubine

Lesson 6/Assignment 5 - Application
Students should evaluate any principles from this chapter they can be apply to their lives.

UNIT SEVEN - TEACHER'S GUIDE

Judges

LESSON SEVEN:

 Judges 20 Observation Worksheets, key word bookmark, colored pencils

OBJECTIVES:

In this lesson, students will complete their observations of Judges 20 as they identify and mark the key words from their bookmarks. They will interpret the chapter by closely examining main events.

Lesson 7/Assignment 1 - Observation
Students will observe this chapter marking the key words from their key word bookmark.

Lesson 7/Assignment 2 - Observation/Interpretation
These deaths occurred when the sons of Israel gathered to fight Benjamin for the crimes they committed against the Levite's concubine.

- *v. 21 - Benjamin killed 22,000 men of Israel*
- *v. 25 - Benjamin killed 18,000 men of Israel*
- *v. 31 - Benjamin killed about 30 men of Israel*
- *v. 35 - the sons of Israel destroyed 25,100 men of Benjamin*
- *v. 39 - Benjamin killed about 30 men of Israel*
- *v. 44-46 - Israel killed about 25,000 men of Benjamin*
- *v. 47 - only 600 men escaped*
- *v. 48 - The men of Israel struck Benjamin "with the edge of the sword, both the entire city with the cattle and all that they found."*

Lesson 7/Assignment 3 - Observation/Interpretation
a. Students should note that Benjamin chose to war with their own brothers to giving up the men who raped, abused, and ultimately killed the Levite's concubine.

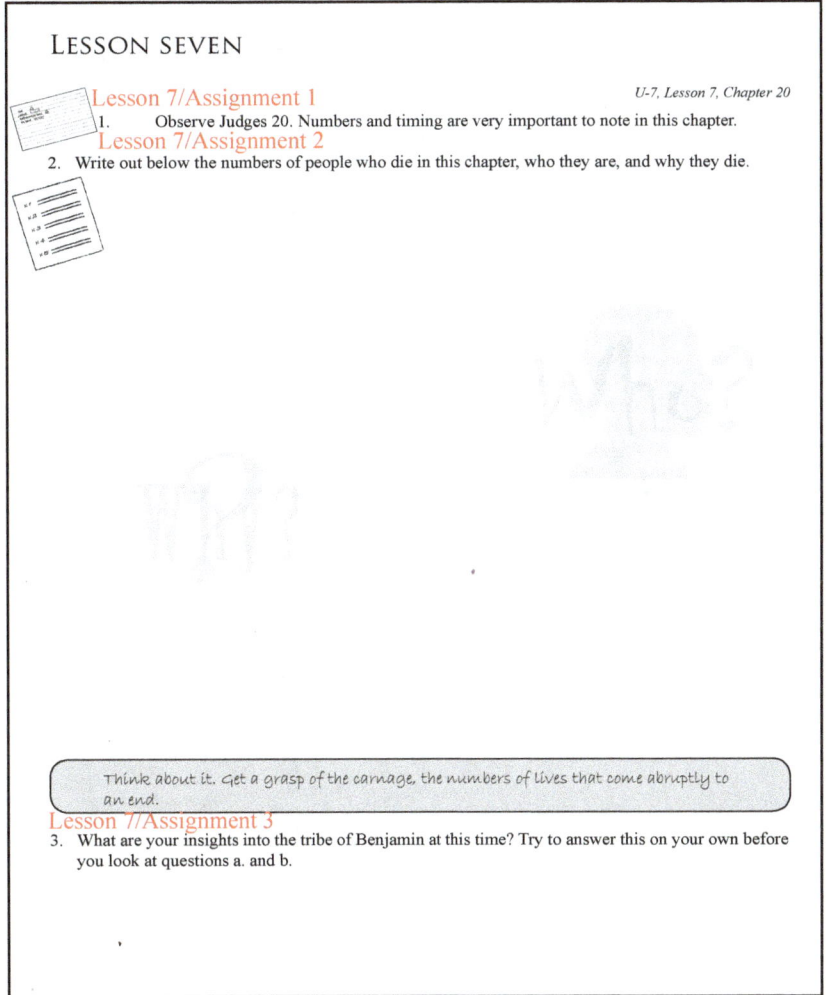

© 2008 Precept Ministries International

UNIT SEVEN - TEACHER'S GUIDE

Judges

b. They were also arrogant to believe they would defeat the sons of Israel.

Lesson 7/Assignment 4 - Interpretation
Students will think about why the sons of Israel did not immediately conquer Benjamin. Encourage them to think about what they ask from God and how they ask each time. The following questions will help them reason through these verses.

Lesson 7/Assignment 5 - Observation/Interpretation
a. In verse 18, the sons of Israel go to Bethel and ask God who should go first to fight Benjamin. The Lord says Judah. In verse 23, "the sons of Israel went up and wept before the Lord until evening," and asked again if they should fight Benjamin. The Lord says, "Go up against him." Then according to verses 26-28, the sons of Israel and all the people go to Bethel and weep; they fast all day and offer burnt offerings and peace offerings to the Lord – they ask Him if they should fight Benjamin or quit. The Lord says, "Go up, for tomorrow I will deliver them into your hand."

b. God promises victory after they ask him at Bethel where the ark and the priests are.

U-7, Lesson 7, Chapter 20

a. What did they do when asked to deliver up the worthless men of Gibeah?

b. What do you learn about them from verses 31-34?

Lesson 7/Assignment Prayer4
4. Do you know why the 11 tribes weren't immediately victorious?

Lesson 7/Assignment 5
5. Now, look again at Judges 20:17-28.

   a. Record what the sons of Israel do each time they inquire of God.

   b. When did God finally promise them victory?

Student Page 192
318
© 2008 Precept Ministries International

UNIT SEVEN - TEACHER'S GUIDE

Judges

Lesson 7/Assignment 6 - Application
Students should record their reactions to events in this chapter.

Lesson 7/Assignment 6   U-7, Lesson 6, Chapter 20
6. How do you feel after studying this chapter? What are your thoughts?

Good job! There is a lot of information in these last chapters. Do you feel like you are getting a better understanding of the times of the judges? If you had to describe these times to someone else, what would you say? As you look at the description of the people and the things they were doing, would you say they deserved the judgment God brought on them? What does that make you think about the time you are living in? Would God be justified in judging your country?

Student Page 193

UNIT SEVEN - TEACHER'S GUIDE

Judges

DISCUSSION GUIDE LESSONS SIX AND SEVEN:

JUDGES 20
Ask your students to discuss the main points in this chapter.

> Israel gathered as one man to the Lord at Mizpah to decide what to do about the men of Gibeah's sin.

Note: This Mizpah is not the one mentioned in Judges 10 and 11 near Gilead on the <u>east</u> of the Jordan River and where Jacob and Laban made their covenant in Genesis 31. This Mizpah (Judges 20) was on the <u>west</u> side of the Jordan. "Mizpah" means lookout or watchtower – several places in the Old Testament were given that name.

Verse 18 says that Israel went to Bethel to ask God who should go first into battle. Bethel is also mentioned in verse 26 and 21:2 as the place to inquire of God.

Note: The KJV and NKJV correctly translate Bethel "house of God." This could be confusing to some in your class if they have read this translation. Although the tabernacle was at Shiloh (not Bethel), the ark was sometimes taken into battle – for example to Jericho while the tabernacle remained at Gilgal. The ark may have been at Bethel (Judges 20:27) without the tabernacle.

> At this time the Lord was counseling Israel through Phinehas, the high priest, who ministered before the ark. He was the rightful high priest after his father Eleazar, Aaron's son.
>
> Phinehas was zealous for righteousness according to Numbers 25 and he turned the Lord's wrath away from Israel. Because of this, the Lord said priests will come from his line.
>
> In Judges 20, he gave the Lord's counsel when Israel asked for it.
>
> Twice Israel suffered loss when they fought the tribe of Benjamin (about 40,000 total). Ask your students why they think this happened.
>
> Israel killed all but 600 men of the tribe of Benjamin (25,100) and lost 30 men of their own. These civil wars, brought on by sin, killed more than 65,000 of God's people.
>
> Israel degenerated during the time of the judges.
> Ask your students to discuss their thoughts on the state of Israel at this time.

UNIT SEVEN - TEACHER'S GUIDE

UNIT SEVEN - TEACHER'S GUIDE

LESSON EIGHT:

 Judges 17-21 Observation Worksheets, key word bookmark, colored pencils, "At A Glance" chart, Bible

OBJECTIVES:

In this lesson, students will observe Judges 21 marking the key words from their bookmarks and including the *inhabitants of Jabesh-gilead*. Students will interpret the text as they examine main events and look at cross-references to determine how the final segment fits chronologically in the book.

Lesson 8/Assignment 1 - Observation
Students will observe this chapter marking the key words from their key word bookmarks and including the *inhabitants of Jabesh-gilead*.

Lesson 8/Assignment 2 - Observation/Interpretation
Help students identify main events in this chapter and then tell them to record them in the space provided or in the margins of their Judges 21 Observation Worksheets.

Lesson 8/Assignment 3 - Observation/Interpretation
The problem in Judges 21 is that the sons of Israel swore to marry none of their daughters to Benjamites. The people were grieved because without wives the tribe of Benjamin would ultimately disappear. So Israel decided to go fight Jabesh-gilead because they did not come up to the assembly of the Lord. They killed everyone except the virgins and gave them to the men of Benjamin. There were not enough for every man so they told the men of Benjamin to kidnap wives from the daughters of Shiloh when they came out to dance.

LESSON EIGHT

Lesson 8/Assignment 1 *U-7, Lesson 8, Chapter 21*
1. Observe Judges 21, your final chapter, today! Underline in blue the *inhabitants of Jabesh-gilead*.

Lesson 8/Assignment 2
2. Once again summarize the events of this chapter. List them below or in the margin of your Observation Worksheet.

Lesson 8/Assignment 3
3. What is the problem with the "solution" to the dilemma facing the tribe of Benjamin?

Lesson 8/Assignment 4
4. Was there a better solution? Could someone have straightened out this mess?

Lesson 8/Assignment 5
5. Record a theme for Judges 21 on the "At A Glance" chart.

Lesson 8/Assignment 6
6. Now, let's take a look at Judges 17–21 and see how this segment fits with the rest of the book.

   a. How does this segment of Judges differ from the other segments you studied (e.g., events, key words, etc.)?

UNIT SEVEN - TEACHER'S GUIDE

PRECEPT UPON PRECEPT®
Judges

Lesson 8/Assignment 4 - Interpretation
Asking God for a solution would have been the best course of action.

Lesson 8/Assignment 5 - Interpretation
Help students determine the main points of chapters 20 and 21 and a summary statement to help them remember these chapters. Possible summary statements for these chapters are:
Judges 20 – The sons of Israel vs. Benjamin
Judges 21 – Wives for Benjamin

Lesson 8/Assignment 6 - Observation/Interpretation
a. Students will see that these last chapters in the book of Judges are specific stories that convey how every man was doing what was right in his own eyes. They will need to remember that the first segment of Judges overviews the <u>times</u> of the judges; and the second chronicles their <u>lives</u>.

b. Students will determine how the last segment fits chronologically within the book of Judges. They should conclude the following:

1) Judges 17 and 18 contain the story of Micah and the Danites; Judges 19-21 the story of the Levite's concubine and the tribe of Benjamin.

2) According to Joshua 19:47-51, the Danites took Laish (Leshem) – the end of Joshua and Judges 18 give more information. So, these events occurred at the very beginning of the times of the judges.

3) According to passages in Numbers, Exodus, and Joshua, the high priest Phinehas was ministering prior to Israel conquering Canaan (Numbers 25) and during the time Joshua divided the land. Therefore if the times of the judges cover a span of 340-360 years, the events of Judges 20 occurred at

---

U-7, Lesson 8, Chapter 21

a. Where does this segment of Judges fit in **chronologically** with the rest of Judges? Although it comes at the end of the book, is it the end of the approximate 340-year period? See if the following questions help you determine the answer.

1) What chapters in Judges 17–21 are linked together event-wise?

2) Review what you learned about the tribe of Dan and their acquiring their inheritance by conquering Laish. Look again at Joshua 19:47-48. Leshem is another name for Laish. Does the timing of all this seem to be near the beginning of the days of the judges or toward the end of the 340–360 years?

3) Look at Judges 20:27-28. This passage mentions Phinehas, the son of Eleazar, Aaron's son. Compare this with what you observed in Numbers 25 in Lesson 2. What does it tell you about when this event happened? Also look at Exodus 6:25; Joshua 22:13,30-32; 24:33.

4) Now when did Judges 17-21 occurs within the period of the judges, and why?

Student Page 196
© 2008 Precept Ministries International

UNIT SEVEN - TEACHER'S GUIDE

Judges

the beginning of this span. Phinehas would not be alive at the middle of the times of the judges.

4) *By carefully examining the answers to 1-3, students will determine the events chronicled in Judges 17-21 occurred toward the beginning of the times of the judges.*

5) Students will explain why they think the author of Judges placed the segment of Judges containing the description of the times at the end of the book.

U-7, Lesson 8, Chapter 21

3) Why do you think the author would include this segment where he does?

> Does your stomach turn a little to think about how bad things had gotten in Israel? Remember, these were God's people – the people He had set apart to be holy unto Himself! Their behavior began with a generation that did not know the Lord or remember the work He had done for them (Judges 2:10). Look where they ended up!
>
> Where are you headed? Do you know the Lord? Will you remember the things He has done for you? Studying this book has helped you know the Lord – will you remember? Will you apply what you learned to your life?

Student Page 197

UNIT SEVEN - TEACHER'S GUIDE

Judges

DISCUSSION GUIDE LESSON EIGHT:

JUDGES 21
Begin your discussion by asking your class how Israel decided to restore the tribe of Benjamin.

> Since Israel had sworn an oath at Mizpah not to marry their daughters to the men of Benjamin, a solution was needed to save the tribe.
>
> Relate the seriousness of this oath to what your students learned from studying vows in connection with Jephthah.
>
> Israel came up with a couple of solutions to their problem. This chapter does not tell us whether or not they inquired of the Lord as before (we just don't know).
>
> They destroyed all the inhabitants of Jabesh-gilead except 400 virgins, since no one from Jabesh-gilead had been at Mizpah and made the oath – they still needed 200 wives for the 600 men of Benjamin.
>
> Letting virgins be taken from the feast of the Lord at Shiloh was the next course of action by Israel. Were they doing what was right in their own eyes?

TIME FRAME OF JUDGES 17–21
Ask students what they learned in these chapters that evidences timing in relation to the rest of Judges.

> Judges 17-18 related Dan's taking of Laish. According to Joshua 19:47-51, the Danites took Laish (Leshem) at the end of Joshua. Judges 18 gives more details. So these events occurred at the very beginning of the times of the judges.
>
> Phinehas was high priest during the events of Judges 19-21. He was Aaron's grandson, Moses' nephew, and he was born before Israel left Egypt (Exodus 6:25). This puts his priesthood at the beginning of the 300+ years of the judges. After his father Eleazar the priest died, then he became the next high priest. Eleazar's death, recorded at the end of Joshua, parallels Judges 2:8-10.
>
> On the chart "Dates of the Judges," these events are recorded as during the time of Othniel, the first judge of Israel. Othniel was a contemporary of Phinehas; both are mentioned in Joshua and Judges. Othniel was Caleb's nephew and son-in-law, and Phinehas was Aaron's grandson, Eleazar's son. Caleb, Aaron, and Eleazar, all came out of Egypt in the Exodus.
>
> So the events in Judges 17-21 take place during the times of the beginning chapters of Judges. The repeated fact *everyone did what was right in his own eyes* spans the whole time of the

UNIT SEVEN - TEACHER'S GUIDE

Judges

judges. The times after Joshua and his generation died were dark (Judges 2:8-13).

The generations after them did not know the Lord or the work that He had done for them: bringing them out of Egypt, sustaining them in the wilderness, and giving them Canaan to possess. From taking the land of Sihon and Og east of the Jordan to Jephthah was 300 years (Judges 11:26). Israel abandoned the Lord for a long time and the sin cycle of Judges 2:11-19 continued through all the judges.

These last five chapters are grouped by tribe:
        Judges 17–18 are about Dan.
        Judges 19–20 relate to Benjamin.
                Both tell the story of a Levite.

These events occur at the beginning of the time of the judges in spite of their placement in the book.

They sum up the times of the judges – when there was no king and relativism prevailed.

Note: On the chart, Jensen (author) puts Shamgar's judging during Ehud's time. But Judges 3:31–4:4; 5:6-7 says that after Ehud, Shamgar "saved" (delivered) Israel. It seems that Shamgar fought the Philistines during Deborah's, not Ehud's time.

UNIT SEVEN - TEACHER'S GUIDE

LESSON NINE:

 Bible, "The Dates of the Judges" chart

OBJECTIVES:

In this lesson, students will look at cross-references to see how the books of Ruth and 1 Samuel fit chronologically with the book of Judges. Students will also discuss how events during the times of the judges apply to their lives.

Lesson 9/Assignment 1 - Observation/Interpretation

a. Samuel judged Israel. His sons were judges too, but they were corrupt so the people asked Samuel to appoint a king and he was the last judge.

b. Events in Ruth take place during the times of the judges.

c. Samuel lived toward the end of the times of the judges and the beginning of King Saul's reign.

Lesson 9/Assignment 2 - Application

Students will evaluate each of these questions to determine how the book of Judges applies to their lives and culture.

LESSON NINE

Lesson 9/Assignment 1 *U-7, Lesson 9, Chapters 17-21*

1. You have finished the book of Judges, but is it the end of the judges? Look at the following cross-references to answer this question.

   a. What do you learn from these verses?

   b. How does it relate to the period of the judges?

   c. Look at your chart "The Dates of the Judges" at the end of this lesson. See where Samuel fits in relationship to the other judges.

Lesson 9/Assignment 2

2. Your last assignment in this unit is to think through Judges 17-21 and compare it to today's culture.

   a. What is the **philosophy** of your day? What principles guide people to live and make decisions? Do you see any parallels to principles in the book of Judges?

UNIT SEVEN - TEACHER'S GUIDE

U-7, Lesson 9, Chapters 17-21

b. What is your responsibility to your the culture and to the kingdom of God? In other words, what part do you play in speaking God's commands, warning unbelievers about His them of God's judgments, encouraging fellow believers?

c. How has God spoken to you through this course? What will you change? Never forget that you are not merely to know the precepts of God, you are to live by them.

Judges of Israel Chart

Judges

Name:	*Othniel* (Judges 3:7-11)	*Ehud* (Judges 3:12-30)	*Shamgar* (Judges 3:31)
Heritage (Tribe):	Tribe of Judah (Joshua 15)	Benjamite, Son of Gera	Son of Anath
Physical Traits:		Left handed	
Occupation & Weapons:	Warrior	Tribute carrier Sword	Oxgoad
Years Judged:	40 Years	80 years	
God's Dealings:	Spirit of the Lord came upon him	God raised him up, gave king a message through him, gave the Moabites into the hands of the Israelites	
Reactions & Behaviors:	Answered Caleb's call to fight for his inheritance Won Caleb's daughter	Strategic – put sword on right thigh, killed King Eglon	Killed 600 men with ox goad Saved Israel (Judges 3:31)
Enemies:	Mesopotamia, Cushan-rishathaim	Moabites, Eglon	Philistines
Length of Oppression:	Before-8 years After-18 years	18 years	

Judges of Israel Chart

Judges

Name:	**Deborah** (Judges 4-5)	**Gideon** (Jerubbaal) (Judges 6-8)	**Tola** (Judges 10:1-5)
Heritage (Tribe):	Wife of Lappidoth	Manasseh, son of Joash the Abiezrite	Son of Puah, Son of Dodo, Tribe of Issachar
Physical Traits:	Woman		
Occupation & Weapons:	Prophetess, judged sons of Israel in Ephraim	Pots, torch, and trumpets	
Years Judged:	40 Years	40 years	23 years
God's Dealings:	God gave battle strategy to her; she relayed it to Barak. Predicted that glory would go to a woman (Jael)	Angel of the Lord appeared to him, gave multiple signs, "The Lord is Peace," Spirit of the Lord upon him, spoke through enemy's dream	
Reactions & Behaviors:	Awoke Barak to fight	Fearful Obedient Tore down family's altars	
Enemies:	Canaanites, King Jabin, Commander Sisera	Midianites	
Length of Oppression:	7 years	Not mentioned	

Judges of Israel Chart

Judges

Name:	**Jair** (Judges 10:3-5)	**Jepthah** (Judges 10:17-12:7)	**Izban** (Judges 12:8-15)
Heritage (Tribe):	*Gileadite*	*Gileadite* *Son of a harlot*	*From Bethlehem*
Physical Traits:			
Occupation & Weapons:		*Valiant Warrior*	
Years Judged:	*22 years*		*7 Years*
God's Dealings:		*Spirit of the Lord came upon him* *Made a vow to the Lord for victory over Ammon*	
Reactions & Behaviors:		*Knew some of Israel's history with Ammon* *Partial knowledge of God's word*	
Enemies:		*Ammonites*	
Length of Oppression:			

© 2008 Precept Ministries International

Judges of Israel Chart

Judges

Name:	**Elon** (Judges 12:8-15)	**Abdon** (Judges 12:8-15)	**Samson** (Judges 13-16)
Heritage (Tribe):	Tribe of Zebulun	Son of Hillel the Pirathonite	Tribe of Dan, son of Manoah
Physical Traits:			Strength, Long hair (Nazirite)
Occupation & Weapons:			Jaw bone of a donkey, foxes set on fire, bare hands
Years Judged:	10 Years	8 years	20 Years
God's Dealings:			Dedicated as a Nazarite from birth, Sovereign plan for Samson's marriage, Spirit of the Lord came upon him mightily several times
Reactions & Behaviors:			Lust, Anger, Didn't learn from previous mistakes
Enemies:			Philistines
Length of Oppression:			40 years

UNIT SEVEN - TEACHER'S GUIDE

Judges
U-7, Chapters 17-21

ENRICHMENT WORDS

Appetites – instinctive desires or an inherent cravings.

Chaos – a state of utter confusion.

Chronologically – of, relating to, or arranged in or according to the order of time.

Forfeit – to lose or lose the right to by some error, offense, or crime.

Gravity – importance, significance, seriousness; a serious situation or problem.

Philosophy – the most general beliefs, concepts, and attitudes of an individual or group.[1]

Prestige – standing or estimation in the eyes of people.

Segment – in inductive Bible study, a major division in a book such as a group of verses or chapters that deal with the same subject, doctrine, person, place, or event.[2]

---

[1] Merriam-Webster, I. 1996, c1993. *Merriam-Webster's Collegiate Dictionary.* Includes index. (10th ed.). Merriam-Webster: Springfield, Mass., U.S.A.
[2] Arthur, Kay, *How to Study Your Bible*, Precept Ministries International, Harvest House, Eugene, Oregon, 1994.

UNIT SEVEN - TEACHER'S GUIDE

PRECEPT UPON PRECEPT®
Judges

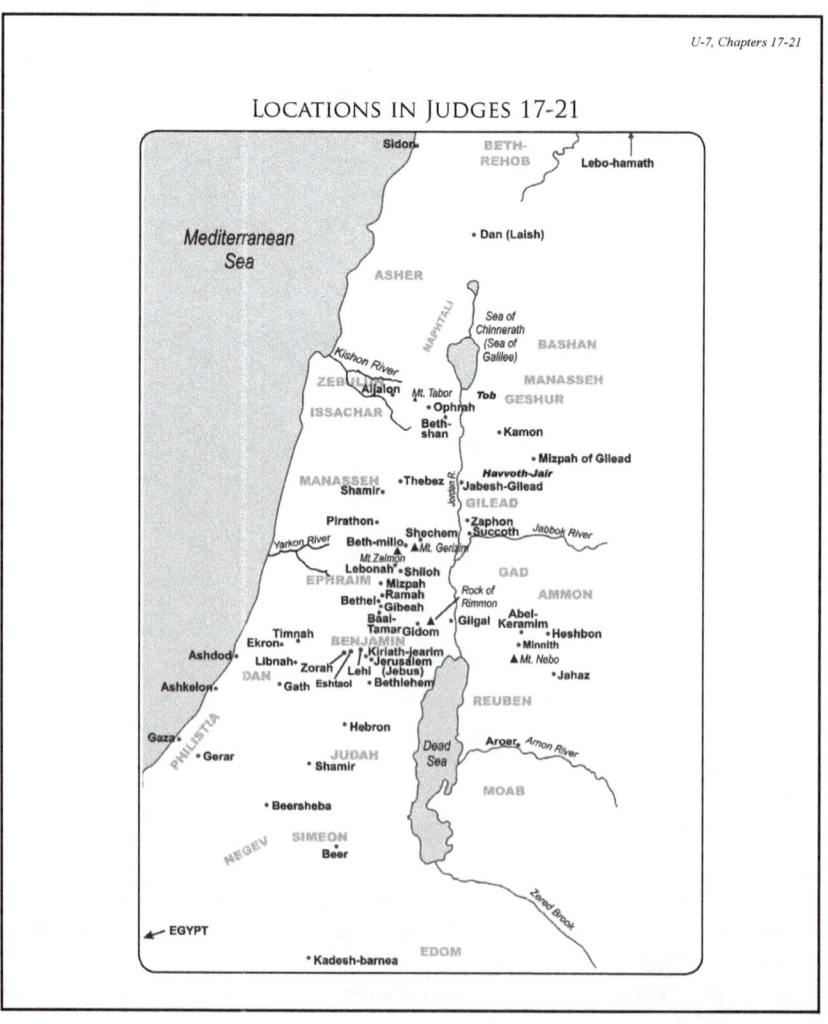

U-7, Chapters 17-21

LOCATIONS IN JUDGES 17-21

UNIT SEVEN - TEACHER'S GUIDE

Judges
Unit Seven Quiz

Name: _____ Date: _____

UNIT SEVEN - QUIZ KEY

MULTIPLE CHOICE - Circle one

1. Which of the following is a possible chapter theme for Judges 17?
    a. The Levite and the concubine
    b. Civil War: Israel vs. Benjamin
    c. The Danites and Micah
    d. *Micah and the Levite*

2. Which of the following is a possible chapter theme for Judges 18?
    a. The Levite and the concubine
    b. Civil War: Israel vs. Benjamin
    c. *The Danites and Micah*
    d. Micah and the Levite

TRUE OR FALSE

____*F*____ 3. A key repeated phrase in Judges 17-21 is, "Neither I, nor my sons shall rule over you, but God shall rule over you!"

____*T*____ 4. Micah's mother dedicated the money he stole to the Lord and gave it to him to make an idol.

____*F*____ 5. The Danites refused to disobey God's commands concerning Levites the way Micah did.

____*F*____ 6. The Danites searched for land because God didn't allot any to them.

SHORT ANSWER

7. Give an example of how the key repeated phrase in Judges 17-21 describes the events of Judges 17.

Students can use any portion of the following: This statement is made after the story of Micah stealing money from his mother then confessing and returning it. She then praises God for her son, takes the returned money, and dedicates it to the Lord. The problem: the dedicated money is used to make a graven image (something strictly forbidden by God). Then Micah consecrates one of his sons to be a priest in his household over his shrine and idols (They're not Levites). These blatant offenses to God's law are examples of how the sons of Israel did what was right in their own eyes instead of adhering to God's Law.

© 2008 Precept Ministries International

UNIT SEVEN - TEACHER'S GUIDE

Judges
Unit Seven Quiz

8. Give an example of how the key repeated phrase in Judges 17-21 describes events in Judges 18.

Students can use any portion of the following: This statement is made at the beginning of the chapter. The tribe of Dan was still looking for land they could live in (had not yet been given land among the tribes of Israel). They also asked the Levite to ask God for their journey to be successful. The spies saw Lashish; it looked good to them, so they called 600 Danites to war. As they traveled men told them Micah's house had a holy vest, household gods, an idol, and a statue. Five spies went in the house and took the idol, the holy vest, the household idols, and the statue and told the priest to go with them and be their priest. The men threatened Micah. They took Laish, killed the people, burned the city, and celebrated by worshipping idols.

UNIT SEVEN - TEACHER'S GUIDE

Judges
Unit Seven Test

Name: _____ Date: _____

UNIT SEVEN - TEST KEY

MATCHING - Choose one and write the letter in the blank.

___d___ 1. Importance, significance, seriousness; a serious situation or problem

___b___ 2. To lose or lose the right to by some error, offense, or crime

___c___ 3. The most general beliefs, concepts, and attitudes of an individual group

___e___ 4. Standing or estimation in the eyes of people

___a___ 5. Of, relating to, or arranged in or according to the order of time

a. Chronologically
b. Forfeit
c. Philosophy
d. Gravity
e. Prestige

MULTIPLE CHOICE - Circle one.

6. Which of the following is a possible chapter theme for Judges 17?
    a. The Levite and the concubine
    b. Civil War: Israel vs. Benjamin
    c. The Danites and Micah
    d. *Micah and the Levite*

7. Which of the following is a possible chapter theme for Judges 18?
    a. The Levite and the concubine
    b. Civil War: Israel vs. Benjamin
    c. *The Danites and Micah*
    d. Micah and the Levite

8. Which of the following is a possible chapter theme for Judges 19?
    a. *The Levite and the concubine*
    b. Civil War: Israel vs. Benjamin
    c. The Danites and Micah
    d. Micah and the Levite

© 2008 Precept Ministries International

UNIT SEVEN - TEACHER'S GUIDE

Judges
Unit Seven Test

9. Which of the following is a possible chapter theme for Judges 20?
    a. The Levite and the concubine
    b. *Civil War: Israel vs. Benjamin*
    c. The Danites and Micah
    d. Wives for Benjamin

10. Which of the following is a possible chapter theme for Judges 21?
    a. The Levite and the concubine
    b. Civil War: Israel vs. Benjamin
    c. The Danites and Micah
    d. *Wives for Benjamin*

11. When do the events in Judges 17-21 occur?
    a. After Samson is judge in Israel
    b. *During Othniel's time since Phinehas was still alive at this time*
    c. At the same time as Deborah and Barak
    d. When the Levites killed the sons of Israel for worshipping Baal

12. When doing inductive Bible study, what RULES interpretation?
    a. Observation
    b. *Context*
    c. Time phrases
    d. Historical setting

13. What is the goal of inductive Bible study?
    a. Interpret correctly
    b. Know about God
    c. Know how to study the Bible for myself
    d. *Know God resulting in a transformed life*

14. Establishing the _____ will give clues to the philosophical, social, political and religious conditions of the times.
    a. Observation
    b. Context
    c. Time phrases
    d. *Historical setting*

15. What helps "unlock" the meaning of the text?
    a. Application words
    b. Context words
    c. *Key words*
    d. Important words

UNIT SEVEN - TEACHER'S GUIDE

Judges
Unit Seven Test

SHORT ANSWER

16. What is the key repeated phrase in Judges 17-21?

There was no king in Israel and every man did what was right in his own eyes

17. Give an example of how the key repeated phrase in Judges 17-21 describes events in Judges 17.

Students can use any portion of the following: This statement is made after the story of Micah stealing money from his mother then confessing and returning it. She then praises God for her son, takes the returned money, and dedicates it to the Lord. The problem: the dedicated money is used to make a graven image (something strictly forbidden by God). Then Micah consecrates one of his sons to be a priest in his household over his shrine and idols (They're not Levites). These blatant offenses to God's law are examples of how the sons of Israel did what was right in their own eyes instead of adhering to God's Law.

18. Give an example of how the key repeated phrase in Judges 17-21 describes events in Judges 18.

Students can use any portion of the following: This statement is made at the beginning of the chapter. The tribe of Dan was still looking for land they could live in (had not yet been given land among the tribes of Israel). They also asked the Levite to ask God for their journey to be successful. The spies saw Lashish; it looked good to them, so they called 600 Danites to war. As they traveled men told them Micah's house had a holy vest, household gods, an idol, and a statue. Five spies went in the house and took the idol, the holy vest, the household idols, and the statue and told the priest to go with them and be their priest. The men threatened Micah. They took Laish, killed the people, burned the city, and celebrated by worshipping idols.

19. Give an example of how the key repeated phrase in Judges 17-21 describes the events of Judges 19.

Students can use any portion of the following: The concubine played the harlot against the Levite. Men in the city requested to have relations with the Levite (homosexuality). The owner of the home offered his virgin daughter and the concubine instead. The men of the city raped and abused the concubine all night and left her dead on the doorstep.

© 2008 Precept Ministries International

UNIT SEVEN - TEACHER'S GUIDE

Judges
Unit Seven Test

20. Give an example of how the key repeated phrase in Judges 17-21 describes the events of Judges 21.

Students can use any portion of the following: The problem in Judges 21 is that the sons of Israel swore to marry none of their daughters to Benjamites. The people were grieved because without wives the tribe of Benjamin would ultimately disappear. So Israel decided to go fight Jabesh-gilead because they did not come up to the assembly of the Lord. They killed everyone except the virgins and gave them to the men of Benjamin. There were not enough for every man so they told the men of Benjamin to kidnap wives from the daughters of Shiloh when they came out to dance.

ESSAY 1

Choose one of the following topics, briefly summarize it, and then discuss how it applies to your life:

  a. Principles from Judges 17-21 and how they apply to your generation
  b. Principles from the book of Judges
  c. What you have learned about God in Judges 17-21

Students will identify the main points of each of these topics and then discuss how truths they learned apply to their lives.

UNIT SEVEN - TEACHER'S GUIDE

Judges
Unit Seven Test

ESSAY 2 THIS SECTION IS OPTIONAL FOR TEACHERS WHO DECIDE TO TEST STUDENTS ON THEIR UNDERSTANDING OF INDUCTIVE STUDY PRINCIPLES.

1. Observe 1 John 4. Read the passage and identify and mark at least three key repeated words. On the back of this page choose one of the words you marked and make a list.

1 JOHN 4

1 Beloved, do not believe every spirit, but test the spirits to see whether they are from God, because many false prophets have gone out into the world.
2 By this you know the Spirit of God: every spirit that confesses that Jesus Christ has come in the flesh is from God;
3 and every spirit that does not confess Jesus is not from God; this is the spirit of the antichrist, of which you have heard that it is coming, and now it is already in the world.
4 You are from God, little children, and have overcome them; because greater is He who is in you than he who is in the world.
5 They are from the world; therefore they speak as from the world, and the world listens to them.
6 We are from God; he who knows God listens to us; he who is not from God does not listen to us. By this we know the spirit of truth and the spirit of error.
7 Beloved, let us love one another, for love is from God; and everyone who loves is born of God and knows God.
8 The one who does not love does not know God, for God is love.
9 By this the love of God was manifested in us, that God has sent His only begotten Son into the world so that we might live through Him.
10 In this is love, not that we loved God, but that He loved us and sent His Son to be the propitiation for our sins.
11 Beloved, if God so loved us, we also ought to love one another.
12 No one has seen God at any time; if we love one another, God abides in us, and His love is perfected in us.
13 By this we know that we abide in Him and He in us, because He has given us of His Spirit.
14 We have seen and testify that the Father has sent the Son to be the Savior of the world.
15 Whoever confesses that Jesus is the Son of God, God abides in him, and he in God.
16 We have come to know and have believed the love which God has for us. God is love, and the one who abides in love abides in God, and God abides in him.
17 By this, love is perfected with us, so that we may have confidence in the day of judgment; because as He is, so also are we in this world.
18 There is no fear in love; but perfect love casts out fear, because fear involves punishment, and the one who fears is not perfected in love.
19 We love, because He first loved us.
20 If someone says, "I love God," and hates his brother, he is a liar; for the one who does not love his brother whom he has seen, cannot love God whom he has not seen.
21 And this commandment we have from Him, that the one who loves God should love his brother also.

© 2008 Precept Ministries International

UNIT SEVEN - TEACHER'S GUIDE

Judges
Unit Seven Test

Examples of key words are:
1. Love
2. Abide
3. God
4. Jesus
5. Holy Spirit

There are others less obvious but if they are repeated or key to the passage they are acceptable.

The list should include the information from chapter 4 pertaining to the topic.

2. Write below a possible chapter theme for 1 John 4.

1 John 4 - Love your brother

3. What and how can you apply 1 John 4 to your life?

Answers will vary.

A Deliverer Arises
the book of Judges

Do you fall into the same sin with little hope of breaking free?

Do you feel too ordinary to be used by God?

Is your culture so depraved, so far from God,
that it seems pointless to stand for truth?

In *Judges: A Deliverer Arises*, you will discover the chilling similarities between the ancient nation of Israel and your world today. Discover what happens to a culture when everyone does what is right in their own eyes. For Israel, this lack of absolutes led to moral anarchy and a downward spiral of sin resulting in defeat, bondage, and judgment. The book of Judges not only details these devastating consequences as a warning to those who would follow in their footsteps... but it also reveals hope for those caught in this deadly trap – a hope for victory, restoration, and peace through God the Deliverer.

Additionally, you will explore the characters of ordinary men and women called by God to save His people from bondage. Despite fear, status, weakness, and feelings of inadequacy, God enabled them to lead this rebellious nation to victory.

These truths about God and His plans for deliverance will challenge you to reject complacency and apathy toward sin and embrace God's Word as a holy and relevant text book for your life. You too can be freed from sin's bondage and strengthened to stand boldly for truth. You too can be a deliverer to a culture in moral crisis.

Judges: A Deliverer Arises is based on Precept Upon Precept: Judges and follows *Joshua: The Battle Begins*. Additional studies in this curriculum series for students, grades 6-12, will include: Abraham, Joseph, Exodus, John, Acts, Romans, James, 1 John and Revelation.

Precept Ministries International
P.O. Box 182218
Chattanooga, TN 37422
Telephone (800)763-8280/(423)892-6814
Fax (423)894-2449
www.precept.org
Email: info@precept.org

www.ingramcontent.com/pod-product-compliance
Lightning Source LLC
Chambersburg PA
CBHW081149290426
44108CB00018B/2488